Copy Editing

Need	Symbol	How to Use the Symbol
PARAGRAPH		HOUMA (AP)—Two children were
INSERT LETTER		thse officers don't have any idea
DELETE LETTER		muusic program was answered by
INSERT WORD/S	the word	treated at St. Patricks hospital (at Haynes)
DELETE WORD/S	word	in this this awful play, nothing is quite
DELETION CONNECTION		was unusual. "I can't see that she has
		a prayer," Eades said. No member is a
MASS DELETION, CONNECTION		Remick denied suing. When he was
		on the board, he had 80% absenteeism.
		By law, a suit must be filed by July 30.
TRANSPOSITION/S		taht man identified was Albert Jake
UPPER CASE		j. Reid McClanahan said that he could
LOWER CASE		any Mother knows that poisons need
ABBREVIATE		Lieutenant Martin T. Knutson was
SPELL OUT		7 out of eighty on Maple St. were said
SEPARATE		ifshe didn't know him, why did she then
ADD PERIOD		was finished Ethan Allen was marked
ADD OTHER PUNCTUATION		was gone, she said. A 10 story bubble
		of Martins design a ghastly error in a
ITALICS		movie Shine was nominated for 18 best
BOLD FACE		White Sox 8 Cleveland 0

THE COPY-EDITING

AND

HEADLINE HANDBOOK

THE COPY-EDITING
A N D
HEADLINE HANDBOOK

◆ ◆ ◆

BARBARA G. ELLIS, PH.D.

PERSEUS PUBLISHING
Cambridge, Massachusetts

Cataloging-in-Publication Data is available from the Library of Congress.
ISBN 0-7382-0459-5

Perseus Publishing is a member of the Perseus Books Group.

Perseus Books are available at special discounts for bulk purchases in the U.S. by corporations, institutions, and other organizations. For more information, please contact the Special Markets Department at HarperCollins Publishers, 10 East 53rd Street, New York, NY 10022, or call 1-212-207-7528.

Visit us on the World Wide Web at www.perseusbooks.com

Text design by Jeff Williams
Set in 11-pt. Granjon by Perseus Publishing Services

First printing, May 2001
1 2 3 4 5 6 7 8 9 10—03 02 01 00

CONTENTS

ACKNOWLEDGMENTS

This book is dedicated to all the thousands of copy editors who have toiled quietly through the nearly three hundred years of American journalism. They are the unsung "brain trusts," the mainstays behind any newspaper's success. Their encyclopedic and eclectic minds, their sharp eyes, and their quick hands process the daily events of human life from the historic and the humdrum to the humorous and the horrible. And all with careful attention to accuracy, style, organization, libel, grammar, mechanics, spelling, count—and on deadline.

From quill pens to computers, the women and men of the "desk" have caught millions of errors ranging from the monumental to the minuscule. Never expecting (or getting) public plaudits or private appreciation from either cubs or newsroom stars, they nevertheless have stood behind Pulitzer Prize winners as well as ordinary reporters. Their headlines—word magic in 12-point or 144—have netted publishers billions in profits over the decades because heads are the principal selling tool at newsstands and on subscriber doorsteps.

The book is also dedicated to the "slots" who provided my education on a half-dozen copydesks around the nation: Ellis Lucia, Hans Knight, Saul Frelich, Jim Wood, Al Ryan, Seth Wilson, Barbara Taylor, and Frank Murray. Grateful tribute also goes to the rigorous training that I received at Time, Inc., when I was a LIFE magazine reporter—and from its exacting staffers like Marian

MacPhail, Muriel Hall, Joe Kastner, Grayce Horan, and the terrifying and punctilious Copy Editing and Letters Departments, who always kept us on our mark.

Special thanks also go to the two longtime copy editors who were the consultants for this book and provided immense assistance:

Trudi Hahn of the Minneapolis *Star Tribune* and
Ed Alderman, formerly of the Lake Charles (La.) *American Press*, who is now production editor at Mosby, Inc., St. Louis, Mo.

Tribute also goes to my copy-editing students at McNeese State University, who were the first to use the material in this book and who provided suggestions on its presentation and emphasis.

Above all, I dedicate this book to Dr. Robert Smith, Bill Wilson, and April Wasson.

Dr. Barbara G. Ellis
McNeese State University
Lake Charles, LA

PART I

HEADLINES

1 | Headlines: The Prime Seller of Newspapers and the Copy Editors Who Write Them

Headlines not only sell newspapers—and move readers straight through the contents and advertising—but also may subliminally convince thousands of "headline readers." Headlines rivet our attention, especially the ones above the "fold" on the newsstands, because street sales still play a large role in a newspaper's survival. When critics cry that publishers are "just out to sell papers," they're absolutely correct. This has been the reality of the business since the first gazette, *Acta Diurna*, was hawked around the Roman Empire from 59 B.C. to A.D. 222.[1] Who is not riveted by the Page-1 banner "head" that screams:

272 die in plane crash

Or enraged when the sports page ridicules the home team's valiant, but vain, efforts:

Wildcats defanged 48–3

Many perceive that head writing must be fun when they see this famous "winner" crafted by a master for an otherwise ho-hum story about two New York detectives named Jack who raided what then was called a "sporting palace":

Pair of Jacks take full house

Or some may appreciate the whimsical spin over a hard-news item about disgruntled homeowners winning an injunction against an architect building a cubist-type house in their Georgian-styled neighborhood:

Squares win angle on cube

What Kind of People Work on the "Desk"?

Admittedly, copy editors take an elitist's pride in the ancient craft of fixing and polishing writing, in being the guardians of language and facts. They are the descendants of the medieval world's powerful scribes and "Renaissance-world" types. These men and women usually constitute the brightest, wisest, wittiest watchdogs in a newsroom. Those who are "called" tend to be the older members of a staff because all the knowledge that is packed into their heads—trivia to major events—takes years to amass. The resulting headlines empty out newsstands and keep circulation clerks busy enrolling subscribers, which, in turn, attracts advertisers. In other words, headline writers have played a major role in keeping other newspaper employees out of the breadlines for nearly 200 years.

You are about to learn the basics of a copy editor's skills. If you like this side of newspaper life, you're eligible for copydesks on the nation's major dailies or fast-growing weeklies, where you'll sit with a newspaper's "brain trust." Their global knowledge will stagger you, as will their common sense and incisive news judgment on deadline. You'll also learn why computers have yet to replace them.

Many copy editors come from the ranks of English teachers and professors. Yet few of the thousands in the classroom have ever had a greater mission vis-à-vis preserving the magnificence of the English language than these "green-eyeshade" sentinels.[2] Nor have teachers faced the high-speed, practical application of preserving rules about grammar, spelling, and mechanics. Most have never felt the hourly lash of the presses or endured the daily duty to accuracy and the threat of million-dollar libel suits. Nor have they or the self-appointed language specialists ever been forced to ensure that the quarterly profits continue.

Such is copy editors' passionate love affair with words that some do crossword puzzles (and in ink) between editions. Most would draw the line at playing Scrabble, once a tradition for LIFE magazine's lively collection of world-class copy editors. That would require play, a pastime almost nonexistent among those with daily deadlines of two or three editions. Crosswords are permissible, however.

A copy editor does not have to climb the reportorial ladder before graduating to the desk. Barbara Taylor, the late deputy managing editor of news at the *Washington Times*, a veteran copy editor, once reminded university students that her only reportorial stint was a summer spent on a small paper.[3] Nor does a candidate have to be just out of college, because many copy editors are thirty-something or older. But so exacting are the demands of knowing the language and newspapering that job candidates rarely wander in off the street to argue that they can learn on the job. Previous desk experience used to result in an instant hiring for a shorthanded desk. One woman with previous experience recalls being hired immediately on a major eastern daily just by telephoning the copy chief to ask if they needed an extra hand on the "rim."[4] Today, however, even veteran copy editors seeking employment may be confronted with a fierce copy-editing test at papers like *The New York Times*.

Time was when copy editors also served as "rewrite" staffers, instantly crafting superb stories from data phoned in by harassed reporters ("leg men") covering some major disaster or exposé.

"Gimme rewrite!!" was the command bellowed over the telephone from those out covering beats or unmasking sleaze at city hall. New York's terrible Triangle Waist fire (146 died) was covered that way by reporters who, like the United Press's William Gunn Shepherd, tied up telephones across the street from that 10-story building to call in the story despite the gruesome sight of over 50 workers, hair and clothes afire, jumping to their deaths from its top three floors.⁵ Copy editors on the other end of the call pulled the facts into a story, tossing each "take" (one page) to a copyboy who rushed it down to the compositors for an "Extra." Reporters might have resented sharing bylines with these laconic writing partners, but grudgingly accepted the axiom that without their efforts, scoops would be nonexistent.

Pulitzer Prizes have never been given for copy editing, but those who do win them usually recognize that the desk had a hand in attaining that or other distinguished reporting awards. At the Washington (D.C.) *Evening Star*, which had five Pulitzer holders in residence, a winner like Miriam Ottenberg was beloved by copy editors because she usually stopped to thank the staff for its "fixes and polish" on her daily output—and even for the headlines.

Copy editors not only catch errors in fact as well as those involving grammar, spelling, and mechanics, but they also reshape poor writing and reorganize stories. In the last two decades, papers that can afford it have hired "writing coaches" like a Jim Stasiowski or a Pulitzer winner like Jon Franklin to teach the deficient how to sharpen copy or to seek other careers, thus alleviating the time, effort, and frustrations of copy editors processing their marginal work. But most papers don't have that luxury. It is the copy editor who still serves as the unpaid curmudgeonly coach.

Copy editing is no career for those craving bylines, Pulitzers, or the seemingly adventurous life of a foreign correspondent. Copy editors are unsung, seemingly invisible, and usually unappreciated despite their day-to-day cosmeticizing and "catches" on the mistakes of even the most distinguished syndicated columnists and respected local reporters. The awesome Winston Churchill, Britain's famed wartime prime minister and a renowned writer, was taken aback when one of his "facts" was challenged by a LIFE magazine staffer. But he was humble enough to fix the error—and to thank the surprised, sharp-eyed woman on the other end of a transatlantic call.

That kind of stellar "catch" and response *is* thrilling, but so is preventing a potential libel suit. The daily reward for generations of copy editors has been knowing that their headlines, not the stories underpinning them, have heralded the nation's monumental events. Their headlines may be depicted in journalism history books or may decorate the walls of countless journalism classrooms. It's entirely possible that one day a headline of yours, dashed off on a tight deadline, might join the multidecked[6] classics of the last century such as the following:

OUR GREAT LOSS

———

Death of President Lincoln.

———

The Songs of Victory Drowned in Sorrow.

———

CLOSING SCENES OF A NOBLE LIFE.

———

The Great Sorrow of an Afflicted Nation.

———

Party Differences Forgotten in Public Grief.

———

Vice-President Johnson Inaugurated as Chief Executive.

———

MR. SEWARD WILL RECOVER.

———

John Wilkes Booth Believed to Be the Assassin.

———

Manifestations of the People Throughout the Country.
(*The New York Times,* April 16, 1865)

Today's newspapers undoubtedly would have emblazoned stories about the *Titanic* sinking in two-inch bold letters. But in 1912, *The New York Times* was as opposed to sensationalism as it is today, despite raucous rivals like Joseph Pulitzer's *New York World* and

William Randolph Hearst's *New York Journal,* which dwarfed the *Times*'s circulation. Carl Van Anda, a cold-eyed genius of a managing editor, commanded a copydesk crew well trained in his incisive and encyclopedic approach to handling epic news on deadline for extras. Catastrophes on the doorstep were the June 15, 1904, sinking of the *General Slocum* with a loss of 1,030 lives right on the East River[7] or the Triangle Waist fire of March 26, 1911, just a few blocks away. The copy editor assigned to write the Page-1 head for the *Titanic* story struggled with the same kind of distinctive head order that confronted his counterpart 50 years later when President John F. Kennedy was assassinated in Dallas.

Faced with presses ready to roll on what was to become one of the stories of the century, the unflappable deskman coolly took the order of a seven-column, three-line headline. Van Anda also wanted a complete sentence in each line. Further, the "count" was "eaten up" by italics, all-caps, and each line had to be successively indented (a stepline)[8] on both left and right ends by an "en."

It was a staggering assignment for a copy editor of *any* era. But in an edition still considered to be Van Anda's—and the *Times*'s— greatest achievement, the deskman composed a masterpiece yet to be surpassed:

> *TITANIC SINKS FOUR HOURS AFTER HITTING ICEBERG;*
> *866 RESCUED BY CARPATHIA, PROBABLY 1250 PERISH;*
> *ISMAY SAFE, MRS. ASTOR MAYBE, NOTED NAMES MISSING*
>
> (*The New York Times*, April 12, 1912)

His successors continue to work at achieving that impact for every earthshaking event.

What copy editor, even today, wouldn't have loved crafting headlines for these two historic stories?

'The Eagle Has Landed'—
Two Men Walk on the Moon[9]

(*The Washington Post*, July 21, 1969)

Impeached

Lake Charles, La., *American Press*

San Jose Mercury News   *Albuquerque Journal*
The Arizona Republic   *The San Diego Union-Tribune*
The Plain Dealer   *The Sunday Oregonian*

(*The Detroit News and Free Press,* December 20, 1998)

A Career That Lasts
Beyond Retirement

Hunched before computers or hard copy, copy editors constitute a kind of closed society in the newsroom, one able to applaud their colleagues on the rim, a rarity in the competitive and jealous writing business. Few lose their touch, even beyond age 80. Once you are accepted into that fraternity, the spirit of the desk, unlike reporting, is so strong that it endures through serious ailments and often past retirement.

Slots might humble rim regulars or interns, but they usually turn marshmallow-hearted when alumni beg to "take a sit" for free just to handle "fillers."[10] One vile-tempered slot for an Oregon daily always made room on one end of the rim for a razor-sharp octogenarian and, on the other end, for an ailing, once famous journalist who was willingly "carried" by the staff. He had paid his dues to the profession. To some rookies, such deeds may look like wasteful charity, but most note the unforgettable and heartening lesson that the day may come when the desk will look after them too.

The computer age and recent demands that copy editors take on the extra full-time job of page design have tightened those collegial bonds. Makeup used to be part of a managing editor's many responsibilities, yet on many newspapers copy editors are now asked to handle editing's overwhelming demands and then take on the equally heavy tasks of page design and pagination (pouring stories and headlines into the newsholes). The revolt of copy editors on major dailies has been apparent to even casual readers: unintelligible headlines, increasing numbers of typographical and factual errors, as well as near-libelous mistakes, and repeating stories in the same section. Another sign is captions being lifted verbatim from text.

A strong indication that the revolt has been effective is the trend of hiring full-time, highly paid paginators—designers or "creative directors"—positions that were nonexistent a decade ago.[11] You still would be well advised to master a page-design program such as QuarkXPress, especially if you're going to join a weekly or community newspaper.

So copy editing never will be a vanishing career. Aside from the high salaries,[12] the lure of the desk lies in producing one of the best-edited papers in the nation, in readers emptying newsstands within a few minutes, in basking in the sunlight of words, and in being privy to news before anyone else in town. Unlike reporters, copy editors don't have to brave the elements of rain, blizzards, or 100-degree weather. They're warm in winter, air-conditioned in summer, and close to the coffeepot. A few copy editors are honest enough to blurt out, however, that one of the main attractions has always been the fun of writing heads. After you do a few, you probably will feel the same way.

Another advantage of this career is genuine praise about headlines from rim mates.

Copy editors are great, if taciturn, cheerleaders of colleague genius under deadline. They are also the first to shudder empathetically when a peer's error slips into the paper. Their accolades for "a good one"—even from a rival across town, in another city, or across the nation—usually are manifested in sharing it around the desk. Sometimes they'll get an e-mail or a call from present and former copy editors. "Good ones" also get sent to newspaper monthlies or magazines like *Quill* or columns like "Winners & Sinners" to be savored around the nation by the fraternity. Many "good ones" are carefully filed away, to turn up as classics in copy-editing textbooks.

As for the authors, their proudest moments come at newspaper conventions when their work is adjudged "Headline of the Year" and is flashed on a big screen to admiring gasps if the "good one" is serious or to whoops of laughter if it is clever. The long round of applause is perhaps the only genuine response ever given them by the newspaper profession. But they learned long ago to applaud themselves, so their audience never really goes away.

Few copy editors ever forget their "personal best" headlines and are able to quote them verbatim, including the line breaks, decades later. The highest compliment of all is inclusion in a textbook like the "Pair of Jacks" headline quoted at the start of this chapter. That's as close to the only immortality possible in the newspaper business. Top contenders keep coming, like this recent one concerning the British stamp series commemorating Henry VIII's six wives, failures all at producing heirs for him:

After 500 years, Tudors produce mail issue

(Lake Charles, La., *American Press*)

2 | Headlines: The Door to Copy-Editing Mastery

Many copy editors and writing coaches have recognized that headline writing might well be the fastest, most easily retained, and most effective method of teaching copy-editing skills: grammar, mechanics, spelling, libel, the newspaper's taboos, and special ways of presenting news ("style") suited to a town. Headline writing, in other words, is seen as a shortcut to learning how to edit copy. You may have tuned out well-meaning language-arts instructors from the first grade to the twelfth when they were teaching parsing and punctuation. But if you ever have to apply those precepts to a newspaper at a mind-boggling clip, you could become even more expert than they are about composition.

Your copydesk trainer will not be Miss Kindly whose positive corrections indicated you had a future in writing. It is more likely to be someone who has inherited the fearsome Carr Van Anda "death ray"[1] and is implacably tied to the belief that the fastest, most effective way to train you is with the negative approach.

For instance, after a few days' grace period, you may receive a mild reproach on the privacy of your computer screen. This may escalate to a humiliating public inventory of your shortcomings if you appear unteachable and unreachable. Few interns have forgotten stinging rebukes like: "Don't they teach active voice at your college?" Or "12 percent of the city budget does *not* come to $12 million!" Or, if you let sentences slip past you like: "Born in Hoboken, he became president of Lancaster Electric Co.," you may get an unforgettable lesson about non sequiturs from a bellowing "teacher" like the following one: "Born in Savannah, the slot killed a green-horn who passed a non sequitur!!"[2]

Lessons in libel might come with the chilling comment: "The last time 'alleged' was used in a head, it cost the paper $500,000." Snide re-marks or savage scoldings are hard on the ego until you realize that if the slot hasn't recommended transferring you to other departments, you are viewed as a promising lifetime candidate for the "desk."

It's Your Turn to Write a Headline

Let's practice writing a headline involving a humorous wire service story. The only rules applied at this early stage are that your head must (1) match the story's mood and (2) contain two lines with a *maximum* of 20 characters (letters, numbers, spaces, punctuation) and a *minimum* of 15.

The only other guideline—the bedrock of masterly head writing—is that you write a short sentence summing up the story and then delete the extra words—like a telegram. These words are rarely used in hard-news headlines. Grammarians call them articles (the, a, an) and conjunctions (and, or, nor, yet, but, for, etc.). Here's the story:

> BATON ROUGE (AP)—Two Baton Rouge area men accused of stealing a car with no forward gears were nabbed after backing past a police station on the way to a service station, police said.
>
> "I've seen it portrayed on TV and in the movies before, but this is the first true-to-life backward driv-ing experience I've come across," said Cpl. Keith Cavell, a spokesperson for Baton Rouge police.
>
> Officer Larry Lewis said he'd just pulled into the Fourth District parking lot when he saw Daniel Smith, 27, of Zachary, and Louis Reed, 27, of Baton Rouge, backing by.
>
> "I saw this big green Impala backing southbound at about 30 miles per hour," Lewis said. "It attracted my attention—I mean, everybody was looking at it."

The 29-year-old car had no forward gears and had been reported stolen, said Cavell.

"We don't know how many miles they had traveled in their backward ploy, but we felt confident that, should they have continued, they would have been caught," Cavell said.

"He was just aimed back looking over his shoulder, and I mean he was getting it," he said. "And his passenger was just sitting there like it was an everyday thing for him."

Though proficient at driving in reverse, Smith was booked with improper backing, driving with a suspended driver's license, and possessing a stolen vehicle. Records also showed a bench warrant issued by Family Court.

The headline you just wrote is for a feature story. Most of the time, the stories are of the hard-news variety like the two examples below from the "cop" beat:

**Cops arrest 3 men
in Halsey shooting**

**8 Vancouver fires
set off FBI Probe
on serial arsonist**

Now it's your turn to try writing a headline for a hard-news story, this one shown below. Just stick to what happened. Not the implications about state laws or what the woman told police (she may change her story or it may turn out to be a murder plot). Because many libel suits stem from items off the police report, copy editors handle both stories and headlines with caution. Be vigilant. Be especially careful not to "try a case in the newspaper" with your headline when you sum up this story of what happened at the mall. So don't label the dead as a "car jacker" or assume what she said was true. The facts are that a man was shot dead in a mall lot and no charges have been filed yet.

The "head order" is two lines, each with a *maximum* count of *15* characters and a *minimum* of *13*. For this headline, set yourself a

20-minute deadline and turn on the radio or television to experience the pace and the distractive atmosphere of a noisy newsroom:

> A local man became the first shooting fatality under Louisiana's new law permitting victims to shoot to kill anyone attempting a car jacking.
>
> Police reported that Louis B. Thibodeaux, 23, of the 1800 block of Giovanni St., died instantly Thursday morning in the Section B parking lot of Prien Lake mall from shots fired by Valerie A. Broussard, 34, of New Orleans. She told police Thibodeaux demanded her keys at knife point when she attempted to step from her car. She admitted opening her purse, extracting a pistol and shooting him four times at close range. Charges are still expected to be filed, according to Police Chief Myron Sonnier and District Attorney Duval Robichoux.

A Gallery of Classic Headline Gaffes

After finishing the two headlines, you may have a sense of whether the copydesk is a career for you. Headline writing is addictive and enjoyable. Some fall under the spell of the "desk" because of the hilarity of headline bloopers. Embarrassing gaffes once were confined to a local readership or unveiled at state newspaper conferences or in a column called "Winners and Sinners." But today's bloopers travel at the speed of light along the Internet to convulse talk-show audiences on national television.

Gaffes *are* humbling. In the days when backshop "makeup men" locked metal type into chases at a breakneck clip, copy editors truly *were* innocent of committing the countless errors that triggered sniggers around town. An Oregon weekly, for example, once combined an obituary's banner head with a deck destined for the food page, a juxtapositional gem still memorable to area copy editors:

Salem man dies in East
Nuts, cream added for flavor

Because you too could err one day, an attitude you'd be wise to cultivate is extending charitable thoughts to all the red-faced copy editors responsible for the famed bloopers that follow.

Most have been grateful for the desk's protective cloak of anonymity; time has mercifully obliterated the erring newspapers' identities:

Iraqi head seeks arms

Council schedules March 12 meeting on incinerator

Oklahoman hit by auto riding on motorcycle

Stolen painting found by tree

Gov. Mondale hits Hart with Chrysler

Enraged cow injures farmer with axe

Dealers will hear car talk at noon

New state school plan gets pubic examination

Cemetery gets praise from former resident

Family gathers for mother's shower

Some headlines are inane because they state what is patently obvious:

Strike, if not settled quickly, may last awhile

Teenage girls often have babies fathered by men

Low wages said key to poverty

Scientists see quakes in L.A. future

Plane too close to ground, crash investigators told

Alcohol ads scored for pushing drinking

Rotary speaker: 'Boys and girls of today are the men and women of tomorrow'

Serious Stories = Serious Headlines

Be alert to the potential land mines awaiting the careless or fatigued that bring on a libel suit. Begin to practice the copydesk's safety slogan: When in Doubt, Leave It Out. A full treatment of words that may trigger legal action is found in Chapter 22 on libel suits and accuracy, especially those that might slip by you—usually one-paragraph items off the police blotter. Would you pass slanderous or libelous letters to the editor, for example? Would you approve a story containing remarks picked off a cordless telephone—not technically a wiretap—uttered by public officials (a current question in a case being appealed by two newspapers, a television station, and a failed candidate for a judgeship)?[3] The Associated Press Stylebook and Briefing on Media Law also includes a basic section defining libel, slander, and invasion of privacy and landmark case rulings of the U.S. Supreme Court.

On stories involving death and destruction, the number of dead and injured should get primary focus in the story's lead paragraph *and in the head.* That rule is paired with another stipulation on any well-run copydesk: be specific, but never call anyone aged 13 or older a "girl" or "boy" in a headline ("teen" will suffice). This age group despises the use of "teen" or "teenager" in text, preferring "youth" or "high school student." But they do understand a headline's space limits in using *teen.*[4]

Now write the headline for the story below. The head order is for a one-liner of *44* characters similar to this one:

8 die, 21 hurt in I-6 pileup near Cornelius

Use a count of 1/2 for space between words and punctuation. Once again, read the story carefully. Then write a brief one-sentence summary, starting with the "actor" who constitutes the fatality. Follow it by deleting unnecessary words (articles and conjunctions) that interfere with what the story is about. Here is the text:

> BOERNE, Texas (AP)—A 16-year-old student driver was killed after another vehicle struck her car while trying to pass.
>
> Another student passenger, the driving instructor and the driver of the other car also were injured in the Monday accident, the Department of Public Safety reported.
>
> Authorities said Jeannette Vidal was driving north and trying to turn left onto another road. A vehicle behind Vidal tried to pass her on the left and struck the driver's side of her car, authorities said.
>
> The second driver, a 21-year-old woman, was treated and released.

> Vidal's instructor, 25-year-old Courtland Brown, was in critical condition Tuesday afternoon at University Hospital in San Antonio, a hospital spokesperson said. A passenger, Joshua Delano, 17, was in stable condition with a broken leg.

Aside from being sensitive to words that may result in a lawsuit, don't forget good taste or get so hardened about all the bad news you process that you get cynical about people and the world around you. A heartless headline could mislead or be inappropriate or inaccurate. One intern got chuckles from younger copy editors for his "kicker" headline over a story about botulism death from canned soup, a kicker that fortunately never appeared lest it involve ridicule and contempt ("MMMMM, yuck"). But no such restraint was shown for a lifestyle head written by some insensitive young thing: "To be fat is bad, but to be old and fat is really sad." The subsequent outrage expressed by telephone and mail raised sensitivities around the entire newsroom.

Tragedy is such a large part of copydesk life, however, that old-timers believe comic relief is vital to retain sanity—in desk chitchat, not in headlines. That being the case, it may be better to take a coffee break than to write a headline intensifying heartbreak. Because you will be confronted with a heavy diet of serious stories on any copydesk and might find yourself toying with the idea of getting a laugh at someone's expense, it might be helpful at such times to think of the impact were the events in any story to involve those you love.

3 | "Counting" the Headline

Historically, most American newspapers between 1690 and 1765 that used headlines to call attention to stories—and many did not—confined them to one column of boldface type not much larger than the text you are now reading on this page.[1] The copy editor or publisher still had to calculate how many letters would fit across the top of the story. But when the improved presses of the 1840s permitted publishers to spread displays of their advertisers' goods and services over two columns or more, the era of small label headlines on news ended and the age of the multicolumn monsters began.

Calculating the letters by their width evolved into the "count" system for copy editors, who suddenly were pushed not just to make the headline fit where the publisher or chief editor wanted to place it, but to create what amounted to a major tool for street sales. Newsboys depended on those headlines to hawk their wares. Heads sold papers even then.

For the legendary "yellow-journalism" publisher William Randolph Hearst in 1898, that meant beating ferocious competitors like Joseph Pulitzer's *World* on the sidewalks of New York with a gigantic headline about the start of the Spanish-American War:

MANILA OURS!
DEWEY's GUNS
SHELL THE CITY[2]

That head order in Hearst's *New York Journal*, if issued today, probably would look something like this:

7/144/1/ ro5/120/2

The translation of that numerical code told the copy editor that Hearst wanted a seven-column head. The type had to be 144 points high (72 points = 1 inch) on one line. The "ro" stands for a "read-out deck," a subordinate headline that added details and eased the reader gently into the text. That five-column deck was set in two lines of 120-point type. Notice in the finished head that the copy editor also left a space at the end of the deck's first line so that it did not "butt" into a secondary story that was boxed in the neighboring two columns. The *Journal* style was to indent the second lines by one space ("step-line" heads).

Hearst's newsboys may not have outsold Pulitzer's, but he made thousands of dollars on that extra because of the talents of an unflinching headline writer, who, like every generation of copy editors, had to be at his best in a crisis. He, just like you, started out with a first headline, but not in the protective environment of a classroom or probation period on a copydesk.

The Copydesk Routine

The two most common errors of beginning headline writing are (1) assuming a maximum count is the total sum of all the lines and (2) failing to read a head order correctly. If the kind of headline ordered has a maximum count of, say, 14, *each* line has that same maximum whether the head has one, two, or three or more lines. Considering the fast pace on the desk, it's easy to get rattled and misread a "head order." But the habit of at least tapping a pen above *each* part of that order will save you from a reprimand and a reputation for inability to follow directions. You also won't have to spend time redrafting your work.

Let's practice. Select a story from today's paper and assume the slot has assigned a head order of 2/24/2. Translated, that means a head that covers two columns of text; it is 24 points high and requires two lines.

After you complete the exercise above, you'll understand that headline writing is not as simple as you and the general public may think it is. Not only must a head sum up the story's thrust, but it has to fit in a designated space. Other rules involve grammar and the newspaper's style, skills that will be dealt with in later chapters. For now, fit is the element to be mastered. That fit can be done either by computer or by the "count" system, but the latter is still the quickest and most efficacious (and satisfying) head-writing method.

In the decades since the computer entered newsrooms, its proponents have constantly declared that copy editors would be freed from "hand-counting" headlines. Software was expected to do it all. If the "fit" was a tad tight, somehow the magic of electronics would squeeze the head into the space allotted for it.

Most copy editing books announce the computer's assassination of hand-counting while hedging the obituary with instructions on hand-counting a headline anyway. The authors know that the system is far from dead and want to ensure that future copy editors will be the speediest on any desk. That feat involves a century-old technique rather than this computerized routine:

> . . . after the headline coding has been typed onto the video screen, the editor asks the computer how many characters a head of that size and measure allows per line. The computer may respond by telling the number of characters allowed, or it might respond with a line under the headline coding showing the length of the head. After the editor writes the headline, he asks the computer to measure it, and the computer responds with a message such as "2 characters short," "4 characters too long," or "it fits!" Some computer systems simply break the headline where it is too long. The number of characters on the next line indicates how much too long the head is. To find out how short a head is, the editor types additional letters after the headline and sees how many of those letters break to the next line when he measures the head.[3]

One copy editor in what he calls the first "no-count" generation reported that at a national copy editors' conference in Dallas, he was the only one unacquainted with the "count" system. Even those relying on the computer discovered that the count system enabled them to write heads in a fraction of the time that it took them on the computer.[4]

Computer counts also have weakened the looks of many papers. They have permitted copy editors to ignore space limits and write as they please and *then* select a headline size and weight. If that effort doesn't cram a head atop a story, of course, they can pull the letters together ("tracking"). That's accomplished by highlighting the prospective headline and reaching into the format menu for the character file either to condense or expand the line to fit. The tracking feature was intended for text, principally to fill gaping spaces ("rivers") that appeared when type was set in columns of justified lines.

None of that technological tinkering is necessary if copy editors are capable of "counting" a headline ordered by the makeup specialists. That means doing the same kind of job as the copy editor who wrote the *Titanic* headline and those in successive decades. Aside from a hand-count's speed, no cold, mechanical intermediary stands between the headline and its creator's mind. Michelangelo's heirs in sculpture still use a chisel and probably for the same hands-on reason. Once you've finished the count, all you have to do is keyboard it into the computer.

You've already had a rudimentary introduction to counting a headline. In the next pages you will learn how to hand-count. Get out the scratch paper.

Two Systems for Doing the Count

The last page of this book contains the "count." Scan that chart carefully. The font is Helvetica, which is popular with newspapers because it permits more space in a headline than those with wide strokes like old Roman faces such as Bookman or Garamond—or new Roman faces like Americana used in the chapter headings of this book. Nobody expects you to clutter your mind by memorizing counts for 40 different combinations of two or more fonts, so use the head chart in the back of this book as a ready reference.

The side row contains the column widths. Find the section for 2 columns. Then move across the top of the chart to the number 24. As you know from the Manila headline, the number 24 refers to the point size. Thus the count for a two-column, 24-point Helvetica head is 22.5 in regular type ("R"). If the slot had specified bold ("B"), the count would have been 21 because the wider stroke occupies more space. Italics, because they lean to the right, take up even more space in a newshole (nonadvertising space).

Use the count for R because unless a head is slotted for bold or italics, regular is the predominant weight used on most copydesks. "Regular" is just like a computer's default.

In just looking at the daily headlines, you *had* to have noticed that W and M were the fattest characters in the alphabet. They get a count of 2 in capital letters (uppercase), but 1 1/2 in small letters (lowercase).[5] The skinniest letters are f, i, j, l, and, in some fonts, the t. These letters get a count of 1 in caps and 1/2 in small letters. All other letters get a count of 1 1/2 in caps and 1 in small letters. Boldface heads have shorter counts because they have wider strokes.

On most papers today, the count for spaces is 1/2. Notice on the chart that punctuation (commas, colons, semicolons, apostrophes, quotes, etc.) also gets a count of 1/2.

Most copy editors devise counting systems to suit their comfort level while complying with the desk's overall operational command of all deliberate speed to complete a headline. One tempting trap some beginners fall into is writing the count values (1, 1/2, 1 1/2, etc.) *above* the characters. They then have to backtrack and count up the 1s, and backtrack again to pick up the 1/2s. But all this notation eats up inordinate chunks of time the desk cannot afford when high-paid pressmen are standing by. You must get up to speed by the end of your first week—and certainly will with experience. Fast and accurate counts are achieved mentally, so you might as well start with systems that breed good habits.

If you're inclined to "lose count," particularly on a long line, just put a slash after the last character or space you've done and write the count. That intermission mark should be your only exception to count notations.

Two methods in the hand-count system are guaranteed to make you a fast headline writer. Both require shedding inhibitions about counting aloud. For those who are inhibited about counting aloud, fearing it will annoy rim mates, be aware that most beginners quickly graduate to silent counts. Let's start with a head that constitutes real news:

Man bites dog

System 1: Counting in Numerical Sequence

Counting characters and spaces aloud in numerical sequence makes the system easy, even fun. When used in class or in a workshop session, a wonderful sense of kindred spirits emerged in the unison chant of:

(LOOK)	(COUNT ALOUD)
(M)	Two
(a)	three
(n)	four
(space)	four-and-a-half
(b)	five-and-a-half
(i)	six
(t)	six-and-a-half
(e)	seven-and-a-half
(s)	eight-and-a-half
(space)	nine
(d)	ten
(o)	eleven
(g)	twelve.

System 2: Counting by Character Widths

This lightning-fast system focuses on all characters with counts of 1 and 2, all the while matching "odd" counts of 1/2s (two constitute a count of 1) and 1 1/2s (two constitute a count of 3); pairing 1/2 with a 1 1/2 constitutes a count of 2. This system requires only a minimum of memory work and is more than twice as fast as System 1.[6] Thus the count for "Man bites dog" goes like this:

(LOOK)	(COUNT ALOUD)
(M)	Two
(a)	three
(n)	four
(b)	five
(space and i)	six
(e)	seven
(s)	eight
(t) and space	nine
(d)	ten
(o)	eleven
(g)	twelve.

You've now learned the two methods of the hand-count system. To determine which one you want to use, count the next headline using both counting methods on it and time yourself:

**Lenmark acquitted
on $1.4 million theft,
conspiracy charges**[7]

Into Action

Whether you use the computer or the hand-count system, you're now ready to begin the basics of headline writing. Your first task will be to read the story through. Take careful notes from top to bottom. You'll then know what the piece is about and can begin to edit it, skills taught in the second part of this textbook. You cannot write a headline unless you know what the story is about, and sometimes it will require reorganizing entire paragraphs or moving sentences around. You are being trained, after all, to edit copy.

The overall point—what the story is about—should be in the lead. However, sometimes in the heat of writing a deadline piece like a city council meeting, reporters might "bury the lead" because of many items on an agenda. They fail to see the most important one and place it at midpoint or near the end. Equally, in this era of "new journalism" and interpretative writing, many reporters tend to put a feature spin to hard-news stories in first paragraphs to grab the readers' attention. The story's point may be contained in the second paragraph—called a "nut graf" by papers tolerating this practice, presumably because it contains the meat in a "nutshell."

In taking notes as they read the story, experienced copy editors also jot down the names of the principal people or organizations as they first appear in the story. Reporters usually are scrupulous about spelling names correctly when they *first* use them, but may get careless as they progress beyond the opening paragraphs. *The New Yorker* magazine used to kid them and other writers for years about this lapse in filler items titled "Our Forgetful Authors."

Once you're clear on the story's main thrust and your notations spell out the names of principals and organizations, edit the story. Only when that is done are you ready to write the headline. As explained in the previous chapter, the shortest route to a good head is to jot down a brief one-sentence summation of the story and then strip out the articles (the, an, a) and conjunctions (and, or, nor, yet, but, for), as well as other nonessential words.

Deciphering the Head Order

The next step entails deciphering the head order. Some editors, designers, and slots write orders coded with a single number. For example, "No. 5" or "No. 12," and so on, might specify a 2/24/2—a two-column, 24-point head with two lines. A computer-coded head order might be "L362," specifying a Lucida font in a 36-point, two-line head.

Most newspapers utilize more than one font to provide "color" or contrast to the six columns of text that make the paper look gray. One font might be large and black, the other extremely thin. The mix might include a font like Lucida or Century Schoolbook that has ornamental trimmings called "serifs" and those plain and simple "sans serif" fonts like Helvetica. The editors may specify various "weights" contained in each font like bold, italic, condensed, and extended. Where, say, Helvetica is the most-used font at a newspaper, the slot doesn't need to specify it to copy editors. But the use of an additional font needs such specification. That second font may be wider and ornamented like Century Schoolbook to provide greater variety to a page. Wider fonts mean shorter and more difficult counts, of course, just as a boldface treatment of Helvetica is wider than its plain face.

A copy editor's greatest challenge (or headache) is a count of 8.5–9, most often found in an order of 1/36/3. For years, one guideline in page makeup was that headlines longer than three lines looked terrible and also were difficult to read. Today, "three-liners" (a three-line head) have evolved into four- and five-liners that make "headline skimmers" work hard and indicate the paucity of concise headline-writing skills. The solution would be to call for a larger point size with a maximum of three lines to fit the space that is obviously available. That was the rule of yore when slots choked off whines about "8 counts" by noting that copy editors who couldn't telescope a story's gist in three lines didn't belong on the desk.

Below are a pair of one-column heads of three lines with a maximum count of 14. A copy editor has expertly crafted one that is almost an exact fit with a 14 count on the first and third lines; the middle line is 13, creating a configuration called a "bow." A bow is designed for high readability because the middle line forces the head to curve inward. A bow also can involve the reverse, shown below at right. There the middle line has a perfect fit of 14 and curves outward with the shorter first and third lines at 1 count less:

> Wesleyan group
> sets convention
> in Dallas May 3

> Wesleyan club
> plans Dallas trip
> for convention

Headlines should not be too short. The minimum count traditionally permitted is 2 *less* than the maximum because "shorts" spoil the looks of handsome makeup. They also reveal a desk that is full of either beginners or bankrupt wordsmiths. "Shorts" look like this:

> Open House
> slated
> by Potter's Shed

> Mayor Smith
> to run
> for state senate

Learning Attitude Adjustments

To have a slot "bounce" a headline back to a copy editor for recrafting because it's too long or too short or has other flaws *is* humiliating, but it's also an opportunity to write a "winner" even on a third bounce. Most desk veterans have their share of bounces. Some days no head seems to work. After the third bounce, wise copy editors confess to the slot that they're "dry." Unless this is a frequent occurrence, feel no shame in having the slot toss the story to another colleague for a fresh look. Everyone has inherited someone else's dry hole. Most shrug off "going blank" and just keep going. If you find the slot bouncing your heads a time or two, try to avoid going into a perfectionist's tailspin and quitting when you're just getting started as a headline writer.

Last, remember that a good fit is only the start of learning how to write headlines. You'll soon write those that have grammatical agreement between subject and verb and appropriate verb tense. You'll also learn how to write heads that are specific and not something vague like this mystifying one-liner placed over an eight-inch sports story and data box: "Deal could be struck soon." Considering how many deals are struck in a day in the sports world, what reader would suspect this story involved a player-lockout by the National Basketball Association? Never assume your reader has your background and information.

4 | Specialty Headlines

Specialty headlines were conceived to lend variety to a page full of flush-left, straightforward headlines set in regular, bold, condensed, or extended weights. Their purpose was—and is—to play up a feature story, some major event, scoop, or series of articles (e.g., "Part 1 of a Series on State Taxes"). On inside pages, a specialty head called a "sidesaddle" rides alongside a one- or two-inch story placed atop an advertisement occupying nearly a full page.

To copy editors writing hard-news heads for an entire shift, a specialty head assignment is a welcome break. Nevertheless, they also are such a challenge that a copy editor usually is given more time and devotes more thought to them than a spate of four hard-news heads. Because they receive such focus, specialty heads often constitute a copy editor's personal best.

All the specialty heads included in this chapter except the sidesaddle are variations of the kicker, the first type, which was designed to "kick" the reader into the main headline and thus the story. A kicker and its companion main line look like this:

RUST IN PEACE
Car collector buried with 1964 Corvair

You'll recognize specialty heads because additional instructions appear on the head order. You already have learned that an order for, say, a 7/72/1/ ro2/36/2 requires a seven-column, 72-point, one-line head with a read-out deck of two columns, 36-point type set in two lines. There, the copy editor is asked to craft not only a banner, but a deck that is half its size.

Sometimes such paired heads contain a "top line" that might be nearly three times the size as the "main" line to attract reader attention. Again, that's the function of specialty heads and why they tend to be used on both the main story on Page-1 and on feature articles. They are like this "hammerhead" sample paired with a main line:

An IRS Oops!
He's Michael G. Fox, folks, *not* Michael J.

The typographic pairing distinguishes the main headline from a secondary one by point size, font, and weight. Usually, the eye-catching line is set in bold, italics, extended, or condensed styles of one font while the main line has a regular style in another typeface. The main thing to remember when you get a head order for specialty headlines like a kicker is that the main line must summarize the story. The kicker line is the "frosting." It either teases the reader into the main line and story or, like a deck, adds vital information to that main line.

The wise copy editor writes the main headline first and then adds the specialty trimming that lures readers into the page and into the story. So even if a kicker line absolutely begs to be written first, just make a note of the brainstorm. Set it aside until you've written the main headline so you can focus on that effort.

Kickers

As shown on the previous page, a kicker head is also paired. Its top line is set in caps and italicized, is often underlined, and generally is half the size of the main head and in a different font. The head order will look like 3/30/1-K, meaning that the main line will be in 30-point type with its piggyback rider set probably in 14-point.

More mistakes and "bouncers" are made on kicker heads by beginners as well as seasoned copy editors than perhaps any other headline because it has so many components to remember. One way to avert errors on kickers is to keep a model like the example of the buried car at hand while you're learning to write them so you'll recall its several components.

The first component is that the count on the main head is two less units than the maximum count on the head chart. It's indented under the kicker line by that amount of space.

The second is that the kicker line usually is at least half the size of the main headline, yet the head order will not provide instructions to that effect. It's assumed copy editors know this factor.

The third component is to set the kicker line in all caps and italics, another technique to distinguish it from the main line. Fourth, the kicker line should never be long. Keep it under one-fourth of the main headline lest it distract readers from that line. Brevity also allows for the width of italics, which, because they lean to the right, nearly double the count units of regular typefaces.

Last, many newspapers include an underline (a "rule") with this kind of head.

For practice, write heads for three stories from today's paper, each with a 2/24/2-K.

Hammerheads (a.k.a. Hammers) and Wickets

A "hammer" headline is the big, overgrown cousin of the kicker, as shown in the previous example of the mistaken identity. The hammer has the same "tease" into the main headline, but the teaser comes in giant size on many sports stories and in the tabloids.

A "wicket" comes from the same boisterous headline family of teases, but is a far more conservative and genteel cousin, as you'll note from the examples below. The head orders are included with them.

It's true!!   Paydirt?
Steelers in playoffs   **Vista couple finds gold buried in yard**

(A Hammer)   **(A Wicket)**
Head order: 3/24/1-H   **Head order: 4/24/1-W**

The typographical precept of "going by halves" on intermixed font styles and sizes is generally not applicable to hammers and wickets. What *is* in vogue is making the top line far larger than the main line, as shown. A main line might be in 36-point, but its hammer could be larger than a 72. Because of the wicket's less rowdy nature, the top line rarely exceeds 42-point. The main line could be 36-point.

Four things become apparent when the hammer is compared with the wicket above. Both attempt to entice readers into the main headline, just like a kicker. Neither has a rule separating one line from its mate. Copy editors try hard to give the hammer and its partner an equal fit in the space assigned. By contrast, the wicket becomes little more than a sophisticated kicker without all the decorative italics and underline rule.

The differences in these pairings also involve fonts, weights, and styles.

The hammer's kicker line is set in bold and sans serif type, with the main line usually in a regular serif font. The wicket reverses that style. If the kicker line is in regular weight, the main line offsets it in boldface.

The hammers may look small in this chapter, but many sports editors enlarge them to 96-point size on a regular basis. If set in Helvetica type, the lowercase letters receive a count of about 1.25. Tabloid editors have used them in 120-point screamers on front pages every day for so many years that most readers are inured to what looks like sensationalism. The banners might just as well be 36-pointers in the Toonerville *Record*.

Editors of weekly and small daily newspapers do not use 72-point type, however, unless some local event is truly electrifying or death defying. Readers don't like to be jolted with hammers unless the local basketball team wins the state tournament or an 18-wheel tanker collides with a train and destroys two city blocks. Wickets are acceptable, perhaps because of their modest dress and usefulness for feature stories.

Experiment with two hammers and one wicket for stories from the sports or business pages. Try to cover the main head entirely with the hammer and ensure that both come close to abutting the right-column rule. As for the wicket, just keep it sedate.

The Slammer

It's unclear how the "slammer" headline got its nickname unless it involved the police beat or, more probably, because its first words "slam" readers straight into the main head's thrust. But its kicker origins show because the first two or three words—set in bold—tease the reader into the regular type of that main headline. "It's a kicker 'come down' from on high," as one desk staffer described its removal from above the main head. A slammer and its head order look like this:

Hillary the Prof? First Lady gets offer from Georgetown
(5/36/1-Slam)

You can see that both bold and regular type are the same point size. That treatment provides zip to one-liners amid text grayness. The boldface type on the left side of the headline moves readers into the main headline with greater force than kickers or hammers. Makeup editors like the slammer for features, especially if they're prone to "stack" two or more such stories on an inside page.

Slammers also are used for "jumps," directional heads designed to help readers locate the second part of a continued story. Obviously, a slammer does not take up the kind of space required for kickers, hammers, or wickets—another reason for their popularity with editors.

Many readers, art directors, and copy editors don't share that fondness. A slammer may solve makeup dilemmas, but one-line multicolumns under 48 or 60 points are difficult to read and are downright unsightly to many newspaper designers. Copy editors regard the slammer as a royal pain because they must factor in the counts for both bold and regular type of the same point size. You may agree with them after you've struggled through writing your first slammer.

Although the head chart is clear on, say, a 5-column 42-pointer having a maximum count of 34 in regular, in bold the count is 32. Experienced copy editors count "short" with such a mix. They might set their sights on 32 and pray for a miracle on fit.

Kicker veterans usually have little trouble with the two or three bold words that slam readers into the rest of the head, but those with short-term memory problems have long-count difficulties.

A slammer with a head order of 6/42, for example, has a maximum count of 51.5. Even those with *no* memory problems may mark the intervals along that long journey, lest they miss a count.

Tripods

The tripod, so called because it has three lines, still has the earmarks of a kicker and some of the looks of a slammer. A look at the tripod below will show its challenges:

Watson here? Inventor asks for USC materials

(4/48/1-Tri)

Used mostly on features, tripods are also a popular choice for many sports pages, perhaps because they are such readable and inviting specialty heads. However, the tripod is the most difficult headline to write, chiefly because of the peculiar count of the main line and kicker. Notice that the main line is cut in two, and both of its lines are nearly the same length. Again, you are advised to first write the two-line main headline—trying for the same count with each line—before attempting this "side door" kicker. The main headline, set in regular type, is half the size of the bold kicker because the paired heads must be merged in the same space allotted the headline in the newshole. A tripod's many requirements make it an absolute bear to write, as most copy editors will attest.

The head order of, say, 4/48/1-Tri means that teaser must be in 48-point, but the entire headline will occupy *four* columns. Traditionally, the two-line main headline will be half of the head order's point size (24). If the "split" calls for a teaser line in 36-point, the main head should be two lines of 18-point type. Or the split could be a 60-point teaser with a 30-point main line.

But the nightmare gets worse. Once the point-size split is decided, the copy editor then faces the weight factor of type. How many columns should be allotted to the bold teaser and how many to the two-line main head set in regular type?

Slots usually leave column pairings up to the copy editor's judgment. To write a tripod like the Watson head initially required determining that the split would be three columns for the teaser, and one for the two-line main head. A five-column story could be split into two columns for the teaser and three columns for the main line. Or a three-column head might have two columns for the teaser and one for the main line—or vice versa.

Only the daring (or those balking at the constraints of columns) are likely to split a tripod in nontraditional ways because of the time-consuming complexity in calculating odd-sized columns.

After the splitting of columns, the copy editor determines the maximum counts for those columns for bold and regular type.

Suffice it to say, tripods require gifted headline writers with stamina, but those who master them increase their marketability for the nation's copydesks. So when your slot assigns a tripod, know that your grumbling is warranted, but producing this difficult head enhances your reputation.

Sidesaddles

After coping with a tripod, you should find the sidesaddle head one of the easiest to write. The sidesaddle is a multilined head that rides directly beside a story when an advertisement is not quite a full page and often leaves two inches of newshole space to fill—no room for a headline above the story.

A one- or two-inch, five-column story might have a five-line sidesaddle of 14-point type like this:

1st Fed defends
$45 million
paid last year
to six advisers
in investments

For makeup editors who cannot bear a story with no headline above it (a "raw wrap," "Dutch wrap"), this situation has been an ancient frustration that no amount of arguing with the advertising department is likely to solve. Ad representatives aren't about to pad out a nearly full-page ad, nor are they likely to agree to insert a "house" ad promoting the paper to fill that small newshole running atop a page. And for excellent reasons known for generations in the newspaper business. Both ad reps and their clients know that "selling up to an inch" is the strongest argument that it is news content that keeps readers from speeding past a full-page ad. Not for nothing did successful pre–Civil War publishers like John R. McClanahan of *The Memphis Daily Appeal* double and triple circulation with slogans like "Reading Matter on Every Page."[1]

The sidesaddle was born out of that newsroom frustration. The head is usually no larger than 18-point and might involve four or five lines. It is flushed alongside the story with as many lines as it takes to ride sidesaddle and still have equal amounts of white space above and below the lines for "air." White space *is* an important element in good design.

Readers generally have difficulty with text and captions being flushed to the right, but not heads shoved that way. The explanation appears to be that a head has a larger point size than text and captions and involves only two or three short words per line. Nor do readers assume they're reading a headless jump. As long as a head is close by, they see that it belongs to the story.

Sidesaddle treatment has spread to photo captions in some papers, with ten to 20 lines of text (plus the photographer's credit line) splayed down the side and at least an inch of space left at the bottom. Because copy editors usually write captions (or these days at least edit those written by photographers), you'll find that practice with sidesaddles will make this additional task easy.

5 | The Master Lists of Forbidden Words in Headlines

Before you can write heads and edit copy for a newspaper or for other publications, you need to be aware of worn-out words— clichés—and what our fiercest critics call "headline-ese" or, more recently, the pejorative "journal-sleaze." Other terms are fighting words that could cause a libel or slander suit against you and your paper. A pair of Washington, D.C., attorneys successfully sued one paper for half a million dollars some years ago for a headline that said they were "jailed," whereas they were actually only "held" by police. They proved that their practice was adversely affected by a word that had one more count than "held." To be safe, consult Chapter 22 on avoiding libel suits and for further information on dangers in heads, captions, and text.

Besides being hobbled by courts and counts, copy editors also have been nicked at the ankles by self-appointed Grand Inquisitors of English who for decades have charged them with being the principal perpetrators of "bastardizing" the language of Shakespeare and Milton with words and idiomatic expressions they have demoted to the status of clichés, bromides, jargon, and slang. Yet they also oppose the coinage of fresh additions to the language from publications like TIME magazine or a Louisiana governor calling his difficulties "woolly boogers."[1] They always have shuddered at the cryptic language of teenagers and minorities who seemingly "speak in tongues" to keep outsiders from decoding their messages.

But the purists do have a strong point in their favor: clarity. The real test is whether newspaper buyers comprehend the language in headlines and stories. Most understand verbs like "flay" and "nab," but not the compound adjective in this one:

House bill would pay ambulance services for their time during haz-mat situations[2]

Copy editors can't use alibis about an impossible count or blame readers for failing to keep up with our "living language." Yet they also know when it's time to relegate dead language to the graveyard, or we'd still be using Chaucer's "maken melodye" for heads in the arts and entertainment sections.

Unlike the use of "haz-mat" (hazardous materials) in the puzzler above, a copydesk's introduction of a new word has a well-worn path. In text it often warrants quotes, followed by a parenthesis explaining the term. It finally turns up unencumbered in the newshole five or ten years later.

Copy editors do have "rabbit ears," but as they struggle with a tight count about a conference, many will avoid the abhorred "confab" and may desist for a time in "flaying solon units." But few will ever part from "OK," a blessed three-count word with solid American credentials[3] despite it being on every critic's hit list.

Forbidden Words: Sports

If those Grand Inquisitors of English ever had a strong case about overblown vocabularies, it would have to center on both text and headlines pouring out of sports departments—especially the array of words for winning and losing.

No one has ever given these enthusiastic wordsmiths credit for utilizing almost every term describing winning and losing, hirings and firings, jailings and hailings. In the lore of those married to a thesaurus is a tale of warning from the English-language Beirut *Daily Star*. Its young sports editor was semifluent in English. Stuck for a synonym for "games," as in Olympic Games, he paged through *Roget's* and came up with "Rome Fiasco Opens Today." Are you any more certain of a word's *true* meaning than he?

Copy editors processing business stories have been just as guilty of using exaggerated, if colorful, verbs. Investors and those in business are as excitable as sports fans, if recent stock exchange scenes have been any indication. But there can be little doubt that sports stories and heads are the major offenders in huffing and puffing up a head. Jingoistic editorializing about the home team has long needed a checkrein. For example, when a score is 45–17 against the local lads or lasses, how honest are the verbs "edged" and "shaded"? Or if the home team wins in a 105–103 thriller, how accurate is a verb like "crushed" or "flattened"? Periodically, sardonic slots put sports types in their place by demanding photographs of a team "exploding" before that term can be used.

Sports, not unlike the battlefield, *does* involve great passions and deep disappointments, as some aficionados always remind detractors. But the *Titanic* went down and the Oklahoma City federal building went up with high death counts and even greater displays of human emotion, and yet copy editors didn't inflate the words. If you want to work in a sports department or an information office, it's time to cull exaggerated verbs and adjectives from your work.

Some of your favorite sports terms may be on the "forbidden list" below. Before using them, think: Is your headline diction stronger than it needs to be?

annihilates	bombs	cops
atomizes	booms	cracks
bashes	boots	crunches
batters	bumps	crushes
belts	chops	downs
bests	clips	drills
blanks	clobbers	drives
blasts	clouts	drops
bloops	conks	dumps

edges	paces	snares
ekes out	pastes	spanks
flattens	paydirt	spills
gallops over	pins	squeaks by
gangs up on	plasters	squeezes by
gets past	plunks	stampedes
gouges	pokes	stomps
gridder	pummels	stops
hacks	pumps	subdues
halts	punches	surges
hammers	pushes	swats
hardwoods	racks up	tags
hoopster	rallies	taps
humiliates	raps	tips
impales	rips	tops
knifes	rocks	trickles
knots	rolls over	triggers
laces	routs	trips
lashes	scores	trounces
lassoes	sets back	trumps
licks	shades	tumbles
lines	shaves	turns back
murders	sinks	vanquishes
orbits	slams	wallops
outplays	slaps	whips
outruns	slices	whomps
outscraps	slows	whoops
outslugs	slugs	wrecks
overcomes	smashes	zaps

Forbidden Words: Hard News

The hard-news head writers are not blameless in overdoing vivid short-count words like "flays" and "solons." Not long ago, a report

on American journalism from the august London *Times* attempted
to shame the "dull-witted and ill-read" perpetrators on the copydesk
into change.

Ignoring the "dull-witted and ill-read" copy editors in their midst
on the London tabloids, these British researchers "flogged"
American reporters and headline writers for oversimplifying and
distorting "political and diplomatic situations and developments . . .
in vivid, breathless, exciting prose so that the regular reader must
live with a perpetual state of crisis or develop a deliberate indiffer-
ence as a protection against it."[4]

But copy editors have been chided about their exaggerations of
news events since 1844, when famed British novelist Charles
Dickens visited the United States. They ignored his scathing review
about the state of American newspapers, and the headlines shouted
by newsies who sold them under his hotel window, with his heavy-
handed mockery:

> Here's this morning's New York Sewer! Here's this morning's New
> York Stabber! . . . Here's full particulars of the . . . last Alabama
> gouging case! And the interesting Arkansas dooel with Bowie
> knives! . . . Here's the papers![5]

The verdict of the London *Times* and Dickens about American
newspapers is one thing, but the proliferation of readers' surveys
continuing to doubt what's in most papers is quite another.
Defenders of exaggeration may cite the profits of Hearst and
Pulitzer and astutely point out that nobody ran surveys when these
two publishers dominated the business. Neither Hearst's *Journal* nor
Pulitzer's *World* are around today, but the supermarket tabloids certainly are. Tabloids like *The National Enquirer* and *The Star* attest
that the same kind of newspapering is still making the same high
profits off sensational headlines that exaggerate stories once the
reader is teased out of a half-dollar.

Supermarket tabs are not alone. Your local paper might also
permit the doings at city council or the courts to be blown out of

proportion by equally colorful reporting and heads. It bears repeating that no matter what our critics believe, copy editors do not establish a nation's language trends, but they do reflect them. Because most readers don't blow events out of proportion, especially in sports and public agencies, long-term survivors in the business like *The New York Times* don't engage in it. It is wise for you to follow their lead.

As a copy editor, you will play an active role by raising questions about vivid language. The risk may mean unpopularity in the coffee break room, but, as heavily emphasized in the first chapter, "people pleasing" ends when your stint on a desk begins.

Curb, too, the inclination to resuscitate a dull story with a stimulating headline. Nor is a tight count an excuse for a loose head. If the zoning board approves a hospital's move, what's wrong with writing, "Zoning board OKs hospital move"? Or instead of letting a headline shout that a convenience store holdup indicates a crime wave, why not write a toned-down and accurate head about "Xenwood Avenue store robbed"?

The long list of forbidden words below contains terms that were already stale generations ago when copy editors then struggled with short counts on hard-news stories and were well aware that these terms had lost their sparkle and should be retired.

Searching for new ways to say "flay," "solon," and "OK" instead of complaining about tough counts and the scarce supply of apt terms would be a good place to begin. At least keep this list of "forbidden" words within reach when you're tempted to go back to old geezers like these:

accord	Bluebeard	Demos
Adonis	board	dips
attacks	body/unit	Don Juan
balks	cites	ex
bares	confab	execs
bars	cops	eyes
bilks	cows	fell
blasts	curb	flap

flares	nails	slayer
flays	Oks	slays
foils	parley	smashes
G.I.	pit	soars
Good Samaritan	politicos	sparks
grills	post	stirs
guts	powwow	tell
halts	probe	tiff
hikes	raze	told
hops	Reds	try
hurls	rift	tryst
job	Romeo	unit
kids	row	ups
kill	rule	urges
kin	scan	veep
lambastes	score	vet
lashes	seen	voids
lop	sees	vow
love nest	seize	vs.
meet	set	yanks
Midas	shifts	Yanks
mum	sifts	
nabs	slate	

Alleged and Accused

At the top of today's list are the potentially libelous weasel words "accused" and "alleged." Those words have become so suggestive of guilt that judges and juries are expected to decide that publications using them have indeed harmed reputations and destroyed people's abilities to make a living. Or that such terms make a fair trial or an appeal impossible to achieve. Those behind bars have reason and the leisure to learn enough law to file a libel suit over "accused" and "alleged."

For years, the Associated Press stylebook has issued heavy warnings to all journalists, *including those on college publications,* about the litigatory dangers of using those two most tainted words:

> The word [allege] must be used with great care. . . . Avoid any suggestion that the writer is making an allegation.
> —Specify the source of an allegation. In a criminal case, it should be an arrest record, an indictment or the statement of a public official connected with the case.
> . . . [On *accused:*] To avoid any suggestion that an individual is being judged before a trial, do not use a phrase such as accused slayer John Jones, use John Jones, accused of the slaying.[6]

True, some headline writers continue to risk libel, gambling that the target is ignorant of the laws or that "everyone else is doing it," something that is just not true. One copy editor was faced with an 8.5 character count for the 60-point bold head on the front-page story about a 99-year sentence for armed robbery. But the suspect also had confessed to being a serial killer in another state, even though he had *not* been charged with that crime. The headline said:

Alleged killer gets 99 years

Conceivably, that suspect might sue that newspaper and win a sizable settlement, charging a future inability to get a fair trial or employment, because of that headline—particularly if the confession was coerced. Once again, When in Doubt, Leave It Out is a sound motto on the desk.

Sticking to safe words like "suspect" and "charge" and their forms should remove any suggestion that a case is being prejudiced by newspaper headlines. Heads can be written like the examples below and still indicate that criminal and civil cases are covered fully and fairly by the newspaper:

Suspect charged	**Police pick up**	**Twin-City MD**
with car theft	**Rockville woman**	**sued for failing**
in Bainbridge	**on fatality count**	**to return call**

6 | Setting Up a Work Regimen and Determining the First Word (the Subject)— and the Second (the Verb)

By now, you're well aware that headlines must summarize what's in a story, must be specific, and must instantly indicate whether the content is meant to inform (hard news) or edify or entertain (features, sports, etc.). Lesser functions for a head are to proclaim that fresh information has been added to yesterday's scoop and, by the head's size and page play, how that event ranks in importance.

Your next lessons will focus on how to remain calm through a 1-2-3 system of processing heads, how to develop the keenest sense for accuracy, and how to keep yourself from mistakes that set off libel suits and other unpleasantness.

Just as airline pilots run through a checklist of steps and safeguards before taking off with human cargo, you'll need to design a routine that will keep you from being rattled when you're about to write a headline. Distractions will be everywhere: ringing telephones, strident voices, messages handed to you, a television monitor carrying intriguing fare, and, above all, the copy that pours endlessly from a computer system's central storage "warehouse" or as hard copy (a printout).

A strong focus also will help you concentrate during the explosion of the "big story" that generates battle-station conditions, replete with barked commands and adrenaline rushes that overtake even the coolest hand on the desk. In the "old days," the cry "Stop the presses!" set off that rush.

One certainty about such emergencies, beyond the fact that most newspaper people love them, is that copy editors cannot fly by the seat of their pants in an emergency. A system saves them from going to pieces or freezing at the keyboard. And it can be as simple as what one copy editor called "just doing the next dumb thing" and processing each story and headline in 1-2-3 fashion.

Setting Up a System

The past assignments should have brought you five basic rules for a "shockproof" headline-writing system. They are the bedrock behavioral patterns of novelist Ernest Hemingway's famous characterization of the cool-headed hero: "Grace under pressure."

- Never proceed until you understand the head order—and its count.
- Never write a headline until you've read the story at least twice and have written a short sentence summing up its content.
- Never be afraid to clarify points with a reporter or the wire service.
- Never write vague, generic headlines. Readers want specifics on names, neighborhoods, numbers, places, dates, and so on.
- Never, never, NEVER put the count before accuracy.

Find Out "Whodunit" and the Headline's "First Word" Will Appear

The next lesson in fine-tuning your headline talents is to determine the headline's first word.

If you know what word is first, the head will almost always write itself. That short summary sentence of the content, the technique recommended for your first headline, should help because ideally headlines are structured like a sentence—or like a telegram.

In pruning that summary sentence so that it resembled a telegram or cable, you eliminated the articles (the, a, an) and the conjunctions (and, or, nor, yet, but, for, etc.).

Once you've reduced the sentence to that "telegram," find *who* or *what* is doing all the *action*. That "actor"—called the "subject"—could be a human or a committee or a nation or a disease. Study the three news briefs below and then determine *who* or *what* is the actor/subject. In short, *who* or *what* "dunit"? Don't be fooled if the actor/subject is buried at the bottom of the paragraph.

Story No. 1

    Complaints about irregularities during the Nov. 3 runoff election of the District 12 School Board are being studied by the Federal Bureau of Investigation.

Story No. 2

    Washington County extension agent Alan Bergstrom will be speaking at the Monday noon meeting of the Tideland Farm Association about federal tax breaks covering equipment purchases owned by cooperatives.

Story No. 3

    Lead-poisoning cases are on the rise in America's elementary schools, according to the Atlanta-based Centers for Disease Control.

In Story No. 1, for example, who's the actor: the complaints? the election? the school board? the FBI? In Story No. 2, who's the actor: the extension agent? the Tideland Farm Association? the tax breaks? the cooperatives? And in Story No. 3, is the actor the cases? the schools? or the CDC? When you've determined who the *subject* is, you have found the first word of the headline.

To practice finding the *subject,* you'll be instructed to write a headline apiece for each of three stories. Again, the "actor" in these stories should be the first word of the headline.

What to Do When You Hear "Voices"

You now have moved into the area of composition that English teachers call "voice." Voice merely determines who/what is doing the action, and who is on the receiving end. If the subject is on the doing end, the voice is active. For example, the headline "Pope ordains 150 priests" is in the active voice because the pope is the actor. But if the subject is receiving something, the voice is passive. The headline "150 priests ordained by Pope" is in passive voice because the priests are being acted upon by the pope. The copy editor resorting to passive voice in making the priests the first word not only added three characters to the count, but killed the vitality of the headline.

Ideally, copy editors try for active voice in hard-news heads because it gives vigor to a headline. Perhaps the most famous active voice hard-news reporting of all time was Julius Caesar's famous and terse "I came. I saw. I conquered." in his *Commentaries* about the Zela victory in Turkey.[1]

Exceptions exist about using passive voice in headlines because it's used rather frequently in situations like this:

Heart meeting set by Women's Clinic

80 mph limit voted in Montana

The rule of thumb to use when determining whether the head's subject is a doer or a receiver is usually who or what is the element most important to readers (the pope? the priests? the heart meeting? or the speed limit?). Researchers once reported that 20 percent of headlines they studied were in the passive voice.[2] If the leisurely prose in features and opinion pieces had been included, the percentage would have been far higher.

The chief critics determined to choke off passive voice seem to be rigid high school English teachers. Bear in mind that they rarely publish. Ironically, many great authors they cover in literature units, essayists to novelists, used a lot of passive voice.

In short, if you're moonlighting by writing freelance articles or perhaps taking on editing commissions for extra income, "render . . . unto Caesar the things which are Caesar's." But be as versatile as a novelist in composing headlines for feature stories.

The Headline's Second Word: The Verb

Once you've determined the headline's first word—the subject—the next challenge is in finding the second. That word is the verb. It must be tied tightly to the subject because it reveals the action taken by that person or organization (voting, paying, going, winning, meeting, arresting, etc.).

The choice of verb tense is not difficult. Unless a story involves historical or statistical information, copy editors use present or future tense. For example, in the presentation of an award yesterday (or some days ago), the headline would be in present tense: "Cooper wins Palmer cup."

If the award was given as the presses were running—the present—the verb would still be "Cooper wins Palmer cup."

Note that though the event was held in the immediate past, the headline puts it in the present tense. That may trouble you at first if you're fussy about past tense and are tempted to write a headline that says "Cooper won Palmer cup." But if you circle the verbs in today's headlines, you'll discover that all hard-news stories have verbs that either have the word "to" in front of them (the infinitive indicator) or have an *s* attached on the end. It's doubtful in your readings that you spotted a "pure" past tense form of any verb like headline A shown below. But you assuredly saw plenty of examples like headline B. The verb is in what some copy editors still call the "past-active" tense (to distinguish it from the "pure" past tense of the verb):

Kidnapper **seized**	Kidnapper **seizes**
LC bride at altar	LC bride at altar
Headline A (Pure-Past Tense)	**Headline B (Past-Active Tense)**

Two good reasons sparked this "ungrammatical" shift from a verb's pure-past tense to the past-active form. First, a past-active spin on yesterday's event makes it seem fairly fresh. It's good for selling papers. Second, a pure-past tense adds one character to the count. On the American copydesk, therefore, the past is truly the "prologue" to the present, as Shakespeare pointed out to us.[3]

Not that the pure-past tense has vanished. It is reserved for events or data that happened in the distant past: last year's statistics or something happening months or years ago. To use the pure-past tense, in other words, an event or data should be covered by cobwebs, like these:

Floods **claimed**	Senator Norris	Acme's assets
1,200 lives	**saved** Johnson	**frozen** 18 times
in U.S. **last year**	from **1868** ouster	in **3d quarter**

As for the future tense, usage still rests on the count. If that award is to be made tomorrow night and if all know who will get it (the future), a head would be "Cooper to win Palmer Cup." "Will win" is a more definite use of the future tense than the tentative "to win," but "antifuturists" on the rim might argue that "will win" adds a half character to the count. "Will" seems to make them nervous.

What to Do About "Is" and "Are"—the "To-Be" Verbs

A word or two more on that key word "to" when it's linked to a verb form like to win, to go, to love, to *anything:* Grammarians of Romance languages like English, French, and Spanish call a pairing of "to" with a verb the "infinitive." The infinitive works well for future tense with the short count for "to win."

The exception is the irregular infinitive "to be." That form involves the verbs "is/are." The word "to" disappears. But because copy editors argued long ago that the "to-be" verbs were unnecessary props to those of action—and devoured the count besides—most copydesks deleted the words *is, are, was,* and *were.* They are stumbling blocks that interrupt the full force of the main verb. The verb was strong enough to stand alone. See if this isn't true with the heads below:

Texas A&M director **is set**
to explain work-study plan

Texas A&M director **set**
to explain work-study plan

ROTC officers **are enrolling**
for Georgia encampment

ROTC officers **enrolling**
for Georgia encampment

Agreement of Subjects with Their Verbs

It's usually easier to spot subject-verb agreement problems in headlines than in text because copy editors can get lost hacking their way through the jungle of words describing some hard-news event. In headlines, however, the bobbles are glaringly obvious as they stand in type large enough for your retired English teacher to notice.

Matching subjects with their verbs has been drummed into the nation's schoolchildren by every means possible, especially ridicule. Giggles deterred most of us from saying "he don't," or perhaps tart notes in red from English teachers. In the creative passion of a first draft, we probably were careless about pairing singular nouns with singular verbs and plurals with plurals. Professional writers make the same mistakes, especially newspaper reporters on deadline. But the institution of copy editing came about because writers are so close to their work that they rarely can detect errors on the first read.

Knowing this fact may make you less judgmental about reporters' agreement problems in text. The most common errors are in pronouns appearing in the front half of a sentence that fail to match their mates in the second half. You now may not be so hard on yourself when you err—and in 60-point type on Page-1 that may drive legions of English teachers to reach for the telephone. But on the desk, the slot who also missed the error is unlikely to turn scold, and desk colleagues will give you a good-natured ribbing because they too have had their lapses in the heat of deadline and a tough count. Nobody is immune on a desk, no matter how excellent the reputation.

Look at the pairs of headlines below. Grammatical gaffes of agreement between subject and verb are contained in boldface type for those on the left. The correct version is on the right. If you have difficulty in spotting the agreement errors at first, read the heads aloud—still the best technique to find them:

Smith tell Senate unit he shunned subpoena from HUAC in 1957	**Smith tells** Senate unit he shunned subpoena from HUAC in 1957
CIA **chiefs summons** Bush aide in probe on Gulf war action	CIA chief**s summon** Bush aide in probe on Gulf war action

Yet that does not mean you are absolved from making an effort to master subject-verb agreement. If you're unsure of your ground in matching subjects and verbs, draft four or five headlines such as those provided above that will help you practice agreement.

Down Among the Collectives, Agreement Is Still in the Eye of the Beholder: Is It "The Couple Was" or "The Couple Were"?

As usual in the English language, exceptions exist to immutable grammatical rules. Where agreement of subjects and verbs is concerned, the exception occurs when the subject involves two or more people or groups who can be considered both individuals and a collective unit: couple, team, student body, army, etc. These are called collective nouns.

In text, you may have an agreement problem trying to determine whether it is "couple is" or "couple are" or "the family was/were." The choice of whether to use a singular or plural verb may be hidden in the thickets of fact-filled sentences. But in headlines, you're out in the clearing alone, surrounded by the hard eyes of hundreds of grammatical gurus poised to shame you. You may be on a weekly paper, wrestling with whether it's "Couple *visit* Niagara Falls" or "Couple *visits* Niagara Falls." Or on a major daily, the question may be whether to use "Optimist club *see* American Eagle crisis" or "Optimist club *sees* American Eagle crisis."

The decision about agreement of subject and verb in that instance depends on whether the pair or the group, in the "sense of the story" edited, comes off as a collection of individuals or as a collective unit almost welded together. Many hard-liners will never budge from the practice of using plural verbs in heads, no matter how individualistic the activities seem to appear in the story.[4]

If you guess wrong, and in a sizable head, you can always fall back on the copydesk's classic hedge of "the collective noun is in the eye of the beholder." Say it with a smile.

The Verb as the Headline's First Word:
The "Verb Head"

Years ago, sensational newspapers threw a story's action directly into the face of the reader with what were called "demand" or "verb" heads.[5] Powerful one-syllable verbs, seen as appealing mostly to men, occupied the first word of the headline:

Kills 5 bosses	**Cut off gas**	**Lay 202 suicides**
in Sarasota;	**to 200,000**	**to gambling**
17 wounded	**in Great Falls**	**at 4 U.S. casinos**

The main problem with such rat-a-tat banners was that though they sold papers by the millions, many readers were initially confused by the omission of the subject and by a verb that seemingly ordered them to do something. Those still confused by verb heads have a point. A headline in 144-point type that said "Slay 2 politicians" seems to advocate that readers commit murder. But verb heads have been around for decades and newspaper ombudsmen generally declare that critics are dead wrong, judgmental, or jealous, and so the headline style remains. One cogent argument for continuation has been that some readerships don't like tame headlines.

On less sensational publications, verb heads often are used as read-out decks. Copy editors who write them are not likely to admit fondness for them, but anyone who has turned a few knows their attraction: a quirky, unique head style, the tightest fit in headlines, and the ability to read their work from across the street. The pay perhaps is the highest in the business for the head writer who can present spectacle that is readable without spectacles.

If you should be hired by a paper that uses verb heads, the secret in writing those screamers still lies in drafting a brief summation of the story and then deleting the subject along with the articles and conjunctions. So that you have some exposure to verb heads, write two or three that are suited to a big-city tabloid: a 144-point banner of three lines (count 8.5) and another 144-point banner *without* a verb head that has a verb-head deck in 72-point (count 13.5).

7 | Headline Punctuation, Abbreviations, and the Use of Numbers and Symbols

When you're trying to "squeeze" the head count, you'll become grateful for the decades of copy editors who boiled lengthy proper nouns like "Internal Revenue Service" and "Federal Bureau of Investigation" to "IRS" and "FBI." Others cut double quotes (count 1) to singles (count 1/2), and convinced slots that a comma *could* stand for "and," correctly guessing that this saving of three counts would not confuse readers. Skirmishes undoubtedly occurred over borrowing symbols like the ampersand (&) from ads. Although the headlines using punctuation, abbreviations, numbers, and symbols have evolved, readability and grammatical rules still govern how those characters are used. The critical factor always has been clarity to readers.

Periods

Periods assuredly don't appear in main headlines anymore, but some newspapers still use them at the end of decks if the style for those subsidiary headlines resembles the sentencelike decks in Lincoln's obituary.

Commas

Commas are "count savers" regarded with relief when two subjects are involved in one action. A comma is the substitute for the word "and." It also saves you three counts, as shown in the heads below:

Dole and Carter back SS increase

Dole, Carter back SS increase

Semicolons

A semicolon separates two subjects involved in two different actions. The classic use of a semicolon was shown in the *Titanic* headline cited in Chapter 1 with the head writer fencing off all the separate factors from each other. He also used semicolons at the end of each line—poets call this device a "heavy end-stop"—for maximum emphasis *and* clarity. Note the two separate subjects and actions and the end-stopped semicolon in this head:

Classes dismissed;
new regs to hit
graduate students

However, a semicolon is more difficult for the reader to see in a one-line head because it is hidden among words. Could you (or readers) distinguish the semicolon from a colon here:

Classes dismissed; new regs hit grad students

Classes dismissed: new regs hit grad students

If you're confronted with this situation, clarity demands that you focus on just one action; then you won't need a semicolon. But you'll also learn how difficult it is for readers to notice a semicolon or a colon, one of the reasons some copy editors and slots work to avoid both.

Quotation Marks

In the main, headlines have only single quotes—again because the count requires that nonessentials be deleted. That means a count that is half of a double quote.

Double quotes are used only in subheads where a count is not so critical. A subhead's only function is to break up the gray masses of text. It follows the same rule for text that double quotes be used.

Other rules govern quotes.

One rule protects the paper against libel. To put quotes around words that are not uttered by the subject not only is dishonest, but makes it look as if the newspaper is either ridiculing or expressing doubt. Never forget for a moment that ridicule is one of the proofs of libel. Expressions of doubt belong on the editorial page, not in news sections. If no real quote is in the story and if the slot winks at such editorializing as shown in the following headlines, it's only a matter of time until someone sues for libel:

Smith says he 'gave' the money to charity

Council told zone 'won't require' general funds

Quotes don't serve as an attribution to a source, especially when nothing in the story indicates the quoted material was *ever* stated by that source. That's an unethical and dishonest head. Do that to the police and you can expect swift retribution: irate calls to the publisher and editor from those authorities and even heavy monitoring of reporters' cars.

The reporter on the police beat could be the first to suffer the brunt of revenge from this head:

Police say improper-use-of-lane charge 'legal'

Colons

Decades ago, colons were heavily discouraged in heads, mostly because readers either mistook them for semicolons, as already noted, or failed to see them altogether. Colons have that kind of character. Slots told rims to use variations of "says" because the accompanying story usually was about an action urged by someone or by some organization.

But as the evolution of head usage shows, if copy editors are given an inch, they'll take four more, particularly in desperation over a tight fit. Colons seem to have begun seeping into headlines through the backdoor as the pickup tag on jumps from Page-1 (Ike: Nixon will stay on ticket).

The door was thrown open in the last decade and the colon came to life on break pages and front pages as an end-stop, even though it was difficult for many readers to notice it:

Porn, violence:
Is there a link?

Despite the readership problem, the colon made rapid headway into the nation's newspapers, thanks to the discovery that readers love stories about scientific research and polls. They may even peruse them first before plunging into hard news, sports, or the comics. The deluge of such stories presented headaches for the desk because of the long counts for sources that *had* to be attributed. Sources couldn't be trimmed to an acronym unfamiliar to readers, for example, Enormous State University's College of International Agricultural Science (ESUCIAS) or George Gallup's American Institute of Public Opinion (AIPO).

Some nameless braveheart—undoubtedly working nights processing time copy—came up with the solution that quickly swept the nation's copydesks. Ironically, it was a style most readers would have understood when polls and science began appearing nearly a century ago:

Study: Women get higher marks as
Fortune 500 managers than men

Report: Public disgust grows over
pro-sports labor squabbles

Scientists: Gene therapy helps grow
vessels around blocked arteries

When resorting to a "colon" head, make certain the rest of the line is as focused as those above. Also, place the colon after the head's first word if used as an attribution to an individual or organization. Most readers will see the link between subject and statement:

Bush: Public housing wastes tax dollars

Nevertheless, you may wind up with slots who shudder at colon attributions, no matter how lengthy the source's name. They believe the style is lazy or unclear, even if it shortens the count. They also point out that good editors can still fit the story's gist without colons, like this:

Study suggests birth month affects height

Finding indicates moons plentiful

In the middle of what one copy editor calls the "colonic irritation," other slots have championed the dash for attributions, arguing that it is far more visible than a colon:

'I didn't lie under oath'—Livingston

Still other rims have snatched up both colon and dash for attributions because of content in the head. Copy editors use a colon when the subject starts the head, and the dash when the subject is placed at the end:

Miller: 'This will all blow over'

'This will all blow over'—Miller

But for reading comprehension, forget the count and use the colon at the start of the head. Readability difficulty or not, the colon flags the quote's source at the outset and tells the reader that a quote is forthcoming. Most readers know talk is cheap. If you put the source at the end, you may panic some readers who succumb to hysteria before getting to the attribution:

Dollar should be devalued to 25¢ today—Erhard

Dashes and Parentheses in Feature Stories

Use of the dash and parentheses for feature stories generally provides an emphatic interruption in the head's main thought, just as it does in text. In the days when copy editors called the parentheses "fingernails," the use of this piece of punctuation was limited to stories tinged with humor or pathos:

He promised the moon—sun, stars, too—but stole her planetarium

He promised the moon (sun, stars, too) but stole her planetarium

The problem with fingernails is that if people don't spot them in text, they'll miss them in a headline, even if they suggest a fascinating feature story. The eye races through the headline, perhaps the key reason that dashes have replaced fingernails.

As indicated, a dash serves as the strongest and most helpful piece of punctuation for reading comprehension. That is because in both text and headlines, the dash employs typographical emphasis to bring the reader to a full stop. That dash tells the reader that something humorous, ironic, or of great moment is contained in the story.

Apostrophes

Like the other punctuation marks, an apostrophe has the same job in heads that it has in text: It either indicates possession or marks the merger of two words into a contraction:

Barchak's assists make him No. 1

Don't be too talkative on 1st date

Be warned that two contractions are banned from almost all desks: "he'll," "because readers see it as "hell," and "who're," because to some it looks like "whore."

Question Marks

Most readers dislike question heads as much as question leads and for the same reason. They don't buy a paper to be interrogated; they buy it to be informed, edified, or entertained. Annoyance over what is a high school–type headline may mean that the story will be skipped entirely. Avoid such juvenilia. But if you are absolutely certain that a feature cries out for a question head and are determined to use one, at least have the good sense to provide the answer as well:

How many husbands are enough? Liz says '10'

Exclamation Points

Only sensationalist papers usually serve up a constant diet of exclamation points. Readers ignore overuse in text and in heads. Save them for stories of great importance: war, a presidential assassination, peace in Yugoslavia, catastrophes, or major events like this:

Castro dies!

Abbreviations

Abbreviations have been godsends to copy editors confronted with a short count and a long proper noun. But the governing rule is still reader recognition whether used in headlines or text. Perhaps one of the best examples of a clever headline that still might have brought on a double take by readers was crafted off classified-ad abbreviations. The story involved the transporting of the endangered gray wolf from Canada to a preserve in Yellowstone Park:

Fncd Yrd, Grt Vu:
**Wolves get used to new
home in Yellowstone Park**[1]

An abbreviation that could only confuse readers was this headline:

Judge decides against hearing on T-buildings

"T-buildings" is school jargon better suited to education journals and newsletters than to a newspaper. Few outside of education know that a "T-building" is a double-wide mobile home serving as a temporary classroom.

The *Washington Post* stylebook devotes nearly seven pages to rules about abbreviations and acronyms, admitting they are count savers, with some "so well known that they are part of the language and may be used . . . without elaboration"—and without periods (e.g., DDT, IOU, NAACP, AIDS, LSD, PCP, GNP, OPEC, GOP). But its author adds the reality and common sense followed by most editors and slots: "These are judgment calls for editors, and each [department] section's list will change over time."[2]

The AP stylebook author underscores the same main guideline about abbreviations: Don't use those the "reader would not quickly recognize."[3] Within two compact pages, it offers the rules about using abbreviations with names, dates, states, and public agencies. Beyond those national guidelines are local abbreviations and especially acronyms, but they too are still governed by the somewhat capricious "rule of recognition."

States like Texas, for example, easily fit a short count. So does "D.C." But what about Washington, which, if abbreviated, might lead a reader to believe something is being washed? Many newspapers still adhere to the AP stylebook's abbreviations on states, boiling them. They do that on local schools and agencies too—and without the use of periods (ND, SC, USC, NHS, OAS, WPPS). Almost all copydesks waste no periods on the United Nations but paradoxically insist on them for the United States, perhaps only because readers might think the abbreviation stands for the pronoun "us." Some slots today think nothing of passing "AG" for "attorney general" and "SB" for "school board," obviously assuming no reader will mistake the latter for "SOB."

However, other styles are not so liberal and still ban "bobtails" like "N. Dakota" and "W. Virginia." Rearguard purists after the Russian Revolution eagerly trimmed "Communists" to "Reds," yet slots at the Washington *Star* during the Cold War demanded that "West Germany" be spelled out. That space crisis was solved when one staffer set instant precedent with "Bonn," the capital city whose fall from the headlines followed hard upon the fall of the Berlin Wall.

Confusion about "generational legacies" over the two Roosevelts was tolerated in the 1930s by slots so long as *both* audiences were buying newspapers. But our era has a generation gap too. For example, the term "GI" once alluded to soldiers (government-issue supplies). But GI to millions today means a gastrointestinal test. In FDR's time, the NRA was the National Recovery Act, but now it stands for the National Rifle Association. Before you decide to use an acronym, in other words, be sure it's not one with a generation gap.

Names of the weekdays and the months generally are not abbreviated except where dates are tied to months (Oct. 19). "Mon." looks peculiar and "Sun." may look like a stray from the weather column. It's now permissible on some newspapers to use "Q" for "quarter" on *both* sports and business stories—with or without periods:

4th Q. results   **1st Q. slump**
flat for NSP   **buries Bulldogs**

On measurements, readers understand "ft, hr, mph, pct," but many styles require the use of periods to prevent confusion. Similarly, "minute" and "mile" may be spelled out rather than abbreviated as "mi." The exception in measurements is "in." because it could be misread as the preposition "in."

Perhaps the most interesting aspect about abbreviated names is that the nation's copydesks have coined most of them—and solely because of the count. The key factor in the march of nonentities to celebrity status in headlines started and still seems geared to frequency of stories and national affection, as with "Lindy" for aviation's heroic Charles Lindbergh and "Babe" for baseball's Babe Ruth, or opprobrium for those with blackened reputations like "Monica" (Lewinsky) and "O.J." (Simpson). One notable failure was the famous and austere U.N. secretary-general Dag Hammarskjöld. Copy editors wrestled with his activities and prayed for the day when a major tabloid like the New York *Daily News* would begin using "Dag."[4] Most copy editors also were too timorous to call Britain's prime minister "Winnie."

Historically, for editors to reduce presidents to nicknames like "Abe" was unthinkable, although the least that some Confederate editors called Lincoln was a "gorilla."[5]

Most shrank at using "Teddy," but boiling presidents' names to three initials seems to have begun in 1932, when Franklin Delano Roosevelt entered the White House. Copy editors first agonized over the additional count needed to distinguish *Franklin* from *Theodore* Roosevelt, a president then still fondly remembered by millions. But the new president endeared himself to the nation's rims by letting them know he didn't care *how* they *spelled* his name as long as his name was *in* the headlines. FDR knew that constant repetition in the headlines was more potent at the polls than recognition from the expense of buying campaign ads and billboards.

Having set precedent with "FDR," copy editors began using initials on his successors (HST, JFK, LBJ) and undoubtedly thanked Providence for Eisenhower's well-known nickname, "Ike." Affection or awe of presidents, rather than the count, however, seems to determine who copy editors find worthy of initials. They have denied them to Nixon, Carter, Reagan, and Clinton, perhaps because their names were short, but one copy editor explained that too many of his colleagues believed they were "no-counts."

Presidential contender Hubert H. Humphrey was held in such high regard on rims that even before he became vice president, most readers knew who HHH was.[6] The same thing is true for women involved in statecraft, with the exception of affection accorded the late Princess Diana (Di). Most would never have dreamed of using "Eleanor" (Roosevelt) or "Golda" (Meir) or "Liz" for the Queen or "Madeleine" (Albright), but most love to use "Hillary" because of the short count provided by the *i* and the two *l*s.

Sometimes the climb from nonentity to celebrity moves at a snail's pace. But Monica Lewinsky, the world's most famous intern, was catapulted into overnight notoriety and worldwide book sales through knowing how to capitalize on a dalliance with a president.

A nation of copy editors familiar with philandering presidents grumbled about having to shift from the count of 3.5 for White House "aide" to the 8.5 for "Lewinsky" but finally stripped her of the dignity of a last name when she became "Monica."

Again, your guideline for when names of people or groups become "headliners" still rests on your (or the slot's) *sense* of public recognition among the readers.

Acronyms

Franklin Roosevelt and his brain trust have to be the patron saints of acronyms, so that copy editors could abbreviate lengthy agency names like the Federal Bureau of Investigation to "FBI" and call its staff "G-men" despite the thousands of other able government servants.

Roosevelt's establishment of dozens of agencies to bring the nation out of the Great Depression opened the floodgates to an "alphabet soup" whose ingredients were added to the broth served daily to newspapers, actions that made them overnight household acronyms: the WPA (Works Progress Administration), the CCC (Civilian Conservation Corps), the SEC (Securities and Exchange Commission), and the TVA (Tennessee Valley Authority).

The periods quickly vanished from busy key agencies like the IRS and FBI. Wise slots limited acronyms to one per headline, sparing readers from this possibility:

FDR asks AFL, CIO, to get NRLB
OK on ICC, FTC probes

Essentially, constant use *does* breed reader familiarity with acronyms. One recent example, metastasizing out of thousands of health stories, is the CDC, officially known as the Centers for Disease Control and Prevention. Your local newspaper undoubtedly uses acronyms of organizations and school athletic teams once frequency is established. When you join a copydesk, ask the slot about accepted acronyms. Never coin them until you are a staff regular.

If you are in doubt about the recognition factor on national organizations and are unwilling to consult the slot, the AP stylebook offers a compendium of acceptable acronyms.

Numbers and Symbols

The stylebook's rule about numbers also stipulates that journalists spell out numbers from one to nine and shift to figures for those beyond nine. But that rule does not govern headlines, where a tight count traditionally has permitted heads using "9" (with a count of 1.5) instead of "nine" (3.5). Also, numbers are a sensible mix and match as shown in the example below:

Ten die, 119 hurt in Amtrak wreck

As essayist Ralph Waldo Emerson once observed, *foolish* consistency is the "hobgoblin of little minds."[7] Where the count is concerned, foolish consistency can mean being foolhardy. If "consistency of numbers" were followed in the headline above, it would look foolish and, worse, probably would be initially incomprehensible to readers:

**Ten die, one hundred and nineteen
hurt in Amtrak wreck**

As for ordinals (first, second, etc.), they are rarely spelled out and are usually stripped of *r*s and *n*s and handled in this fashion:

Preemption takes 1st as Illinois' top town

2d destroyer launched at Newport News dock

Hansen takes 5th as prosecution cites 3d killing

Symbols are heavily used on business pages and turn up in characters like $, ¢, and %, all of which get a count of 1.5. The ampersand (&) should be reserved for firm names:

**Kleinschmidt & Kleinschmidt
open 2d branch in Honolulu**

The business pages also permit the flexibility of using the dollar sign more than once:

**Hinton loss of $5 million offset
by 1st Q gain of $11 million**

8 | Line Breaks, Decks, Jumps— and Second-Day Headlines

Not counting the makeup and story priorities, another of the most visible differences between, say, Newspaper A and B, and T and Z is in headline styles on "breaks" for the second and third lines of hard-news heads. Differences also exist in the style and content for decks and jumps and, if stories are excessively long, for what copy editors put in subheads. However, little difference exists in the way most papers handle "second-day" heads.

Some newspaper styles may seem fussy about what words can't end the first line of a head (or the second or third line), but other styles are purest laissez-faire. Styles also vary about the content of decks and jumps, but journalistic common sense usually governs second-day headlines because readers look for fresh angles to yesterday's big story. Before you start on the desk, at least read a week of back issues to determine the style on line breaks, decks, subheads, jumps, and second-day heads.

Line Breaks

With a subject and verb packing the first line, the most popular practice is not putting prepositions (at, to, in, etc.), conjunctions (and, or, etc.), or adjectives at the end of any line of the head. When they're orphaned, the desk crew calls them "splits." Avoid them. An example of a split on a word is shown below and is highlighted in boldface:

Ishpeming's mayor set for
Upper Michigan festival

If a noun carries a full backpack of adjectives, including compound adjectives, the reader is faced with an incomprehensible first line. Again, the split words are set in boldface:

Teacher-backed unruly student
bill expected to pass both houses

First lines aside, it is the subsequent lines that raise most copydesk quandaries about splits. As noted, some editors and slots have given up the fight and permit splits, but you may be hired on a newspaper sometime in your career that forbids them.

It was far more than fuddy-duddy obduracy or an aesthetic "sense" of phrasing that instituted and still preserves the rule about where to break the second and subsequent lines. It has nothing to do with abandoning "of" or "and" or an adjective at the end of a line.

The style rule seems to have originated in the time of hot type, when compositors often either failed to set the third line or misplaced it somewhere between galley tray and inserting it into the page chase.[1] In other words, the second line was broken with the idea that if subsequent lines were lost, the head would still make sense, like these:

Elizabeth Dole tosses hat   **Mine-closure demands**
in ring for U.S. president   **rile owners, leaseholders**
at GOP leaders' session   in Montana, Dakotas

Thus the predominant view on line breaks for the last half century has followed the policy that after the first line, all others should be self-contained. In fact, some copydesk authorities have advocated that each subsequent line have a "swinging rhythm" as in "Senators drop/Plan to probe/Movie morals." Some copy editors also have been taught that the "natural pause at the end of each line makes the headline easy to read and enables the reader to absorb its meaning immediately."[2]

Today, the decisionmakers at papers like the *Los Angeles Times* believe readers can do without self-contained lines, especially on one-column heads.[3] That view may have stemmed from the time and energy spent on self-contained heads. Yet you are likely to reach retirement age before this approach picks up many adherents because, carried to the extreme, it leads to heads that split compound adjectives—even syllables. The splits are in boldface:

Canadians warn teachers on **substandard** effort	Two-gun bandit surrenders to **vice-admiral** on Nimitz	Redford **notices dropout rate** rising

To prevent splits and to permit readers to move from line to line without confusion, (1) put prepositions and conjunctions at the *start* of subsequent lines and (2) keep adjectives next to the nouns they modify. The examples below show the difference between splits and good line breaks (splits are in boldface):

Splits	Avoiding Splits
Adjectives	
WSU gets **wild Morgan horse** patient at clinic	Wild Morgan horse WSU clinic patient
Retreat booked at **St. Rita Center** for Jan. 29–31	Retreat set Jan. 29–31 at St. Rita Center
Adverbs	
Rehoboth club **newly decorated** for Easter	Rehoboth club gets Easter redecoration
Patterson seen **'really trying'** on 3-pointers for NBA records	Patterson NBA aim: 'really trying' to set 3-pointer records

Splits	Avoiding Splits

Conjunctions

IRS tells Smith to quit **or** face probe on '95–96 filing	IRS makes audit threat to get Smith resignation
At Lenwear & Dig Court orders strikers **and** bosses to bar 'violent acts'	At Lenwear & Dig Court bars violence between bosses, strikers at Iowa plant

Prepositions

Three coeds hurt **in** crash near Prien mall	Three coeds injured in crash near mall
Temple Israel rabbi visits Jericho **with** UN commissioners	Temple Israel rabbi, UN commissioners make Jericho visit

Decks (a.k.a. RO's or Read-Outs)

The rules about decks are exemplified in the multidecks used in *The New York Times*'s presentation of Lincoln's assassination. They are close companions to the main headline, but offer additional details of the event. Today, more than one deck is unusual for a lead story, but its main purpose is still the same: to add details. A second purpose is to offer a gentle typographic step down for the reader from the 72-point banner to the 9-point text. In terms of content, most decks are almost full sentences and are in active voice.

Another common rule for decks is not to repeat information from the main head or repeat words. Beyond that, decks free you from the bondage of regular styles, with many copydesks permitting verb heads, near-sentences, or even splits. On some papers where the style is formal, decks even end with periods. Decks are also ideal for adding qualifiers that won't fit into the main headline, like this one:

'We're No. 1—Finally!'

St. Leo scoops up 97–92 win from Bozeman to take state title. Evans: 'It was all those assists'

Subheads

A subhead usually is the same size type as text, centered and set in boldface. But some papers like the Minneapolis *Star Tribune* set them in sans serif type to contrast with the text; they use larger type (14-point) and flush them to the left.

A subhead's primary function is to break up the grayness of a long story and also to act as a lively lure preventing readers from quitting a story.[4] The guideline is to place them at the *end* of main topics in a paragraph or a section so the content focus is on the new point in the next paragraph.

Subheads are sprinkled throughout the piece, generally about five inches apart—never too close to the top of a story, nor too close to the bottom. They generally have no more than five words and never less than three.

Most copy editors write subheads immediately after editing a story when the trims and fills have been completed. With a three- to five-word limit, you'll only have space for a subject, a verb, and an object (providing you choose one-syllable words). Verbs, like the story's main head, should be in past-active or future tense. Subheads also should be as specific as the main head. Reader persistence is *not* sparked by vagueness or labels. They should resemble these examples:

Peron seeks new wife

Alligator bite stops career

Garage shop blows up

'Athletes belong in Vegas pen'

If subhead thrusts are tightly tied to the next paragraph, you're unlikely to repeat words from the main headline.

Second-Day Heads

When a story stretches beyond a single day—or goes along for several editions—it warrants as much freshness for the new facts as it did the moment it earned a first-day banner.

Your greatest help will be all the new information that has poured in since the story broke. Under no circumstances should the first-edition headline be repeated because readers will believe they are reading yesterday's paper. A strong reference to the first event is needed to make the story identifiable to readers:

> **Firemen, adjusters sift through ashes of hall for arson; 20 deaths now listed**

> **U of M basketball tutor admits she ghosted all those term papers**

> **Quarter-horse finals lead today's events at Fergus county fair**

> **6 parents charge sheriff, deputies with negligence in school killings**

Jump Headlines and "Continued" Lines

Jump headline styles vary widely, but their function is to help readers quickly locate the remainder of the Page-1 story they were reading. The key word in the jump must be an instant identifier—the more specific, the better. That's why many papers have a policy insisting the first word must have a proper noun that figures heavily in the story:

K-9 corps called efficient ally of sheriff's office

Gingrich: 'I've decided to resign'

Olympics: Tipsters charge payoffs gave games to SLC

Some jump-head styles call for a slight variation of the Page-1 headline. Others demand that after the first-word tag, the rest of the head reflect the jumped material in a declarative sentence—the subject and verb leading the line. Still other papers keep jumps simple by following a tag line either with an ellipsis or a line that says: "Continued from p. 1."

If the Page-1 "continued" line carries a one-word identifying tag—"Provolone, Cont'd., A-4"—some styles use it as the jump line's first word: "Provolone, Cont'd. from A-1."

Let's practice what has been covered in this chapter. Pick two stories; on each, assign yourself a main headline, a deck, a jump, and a second-day headline. That should involve enough headline work to encounter—and avoid—splits.

9 | The Art of Writing Feature Headlines

A common belief in most newsrooms is that *anyone* can learn to write a hard-news head within an hour or so. Feature headlines, however, take far longer. If you had difficulty in putting a feature spin in the headline for that two-way car story in Chapter 1, you'll understand why the writing of masterpieces—like those leading into the first chapter and the one below—cannot be taught. Nor is the most highly competent copy editor capable of producing them. This gem involved a film and book retrospective event about Transylvania's darkest denizen and was voted the headline of the year by the Louisiana Press Association:

FANGS FOR THE MEMORIES

After 100 years, Dracula still sucks[1]

Writing superb feature headlines is an innate gift granted to only a few, usually one copy editor per desk. While their artistry awes even jaded colleagues, these "masters" are often the most surprised of all at headlines that seem to spring from nowhere and need only a tweak or two to lie shimmering in the slot's hand—and with perfect fit in the bargain.

Those trying to teach creativity have made heavy efforts to divine its mystical processes and transplant or replicate it to those with stunted imaginations. When Oregon State University engineers launched such a project of creativity with computer-aided design

(CAD), their subjects divulged the 1-2-3 steps sparking the chain reaction to creativity. Unfortunately, they seemed to have told the
project directors only what they wanted to hear because the circuitry
turned out to be a mystery even to them.

As it was in engineering, so it is on the copydesk: Clever head
writers are born, not made. Be comforted that 99 percent of the features processed never require that kind of mystical creativity.
They're commonplaces about human life: the retiring letter carrier,
sisters separated for 50 years, a new technique tried by a local den-
tist, the couple returning from a Peace Corps hitch in Benin, the parents of four Eagle Scouts, or how Dex and Cyd Broussard escaped
addiction to six credit card companies. Headlines for those stories
don't need genius. They need an eye-catching headline that states
"this is not a hard-news story!"

Readers yearn for the headline that stands out as a beacon of
respite from stories about the darkness of third-world strife and political corruption, of downtown crime, school shootings, and home-
lessness. That beacon may shine because of special typographic
treatment—a kicker, a slammer, a tripod, or italics—but it's the
"plain-vanilla" headlines like these that provide shelter for readers
from life's *sturm und drang*:

Ricky's garage band goes 'uptown' with a Mo-town label

Car-jacker 'mules' earn only $25 on Fords, $100 on Hondas as inventory glut, shoot-to-kill law drop rates

AFTER 4 GENERATIONS
Tim's Pharmacy makes last hot-fudge sundae on Sunday

A feature headline opens the same doors to showcase the liber-
ated prose of a reporter, but it also allows the headline writer to
break loose from the usual terse rule of setting out the facts for all
those hard-news stories. Some copy editors dread them because they
have recognized for years they still don't have the talent to write

them, but for most, a feature head is a welcome break from processing hard news. Deadlines are longer, and they can cast aside the constraints of active voice, past-active tense, correct line breaks—and relax in the sunshine enjoyed by their counterparts in the magazines. They can even use "the," "a," and "and."

A magazine article's "title" still requires a subject and verb and still sums up the content ("How Peggy Lee Changed My Life";[2] "If You Need to Take Something to Stand Life, Maybe You Need to Change Your Life"). But the swing of a phrase is there.

If the content's thrust isn't evident in a feature, and the slot permits consultations with reporters, talk to them rather than slough off yet one more bad head on a poorly written story. Point out the problem areas that make a good head impossible and suggest a rewrite. With a byline on the line and your scalpel poised for "elective surgery," strong motivation exists for the reporter to repair the story.

In return, the reporter deserves that good head and the retention of quotes and paragraphs regarded as essential. Another major commandment is, Never write a head that either hints at a surprise or ironic ending or gives it away.

The Clever-Headline Writer

The more feature heads you do well, the closer you stand to those "masters of the clever head." The initial, hesitant step almost always seems to be using alliteration—a headline of several words starting with the same letter. But alliterative heads are considered by many slots to be a throwback to high school journalism. The stony gaze of slots perusing alliterative efforts has discouraged the fainthearted, even though most readers like that kind of headline. They recognize that some effort went into rounding up all those words starting with *b*s or *w*s. Most important, the head usually signals an amusing feature story.

Once creative energies are unlocked for features, the next step is usually rhymed poetry, despite equally discouraging words from the slot and outside critics of the press. Perhaps the most ferocious enemy of "rhymed" heads was the much-cited word master John B. Bremner, who declared they were the stuff of beginners: "Rarely does a story call for a rhymed head, and then a rhymed head calls for a skilled craftsman," he said. His choice for the worst example involved one of former president Gerald Ford's prayer breakfasts, but a head about foot surgery must run a close second:

Jerry Ford	**Transplanted digit**
begs Lord	**starts to fidget;**
for accord[3]	**toe-talitarian or feat?**[4]

Forced though the humor is and despite the barrage of disparagement from copydesks and Bremner types, the public loves this kind of head too. Every curbside poll on the Jerry Ford head above has evoked smiles. The second received belly laughs. Again, the heads tipped readers that an enjoyable story was at hand.

The Masters of the "Clever" Head

Years ago, "clever" heads were called "blind" or "shrdlus" because no one then or now can explain the blinding yet twinkling force that sparks such inspiration. It seems to occur only when a story collides with the trillion petabytes of data stored in the creator's mind to produce not only a masterpiece, but one custom-fit to a perfect count.

One component in the creative process is the championing by a slot who provides the choice feature story—often humorous. Most slots tend to toss it to the copydesk "master." Another component is an environment cleansed of devil's advocates and "apple-knockers," the jealous archenemies who attempt to strangle all ideas at birth. Yet another component is the stable framework of creative discipline on the desk: read the story, know the count, stay rooted to the desk, and focus on the task to prevent distractions from shutting off the circuitry.

Although the brain's microchip has trillions of bytes available for information storage, most people aren't pack rats. They never fill those spaces with what they perceive as useless. Feature-head masters *are* pack rats, one of the reasons they're experts at board games like Trivial Pursuit and Scrabble. They are open seemingly even before birth to every experience, every piece of data they find interesting: song and book titles, geography, clichés and maxims, sports records, social trends, current events, scientific discoveries, *Beowulf*, famous quotations, politics, and more. New information is constantly being added because of their daily proximity to news sources.

Geniuses like Milton, Mozart, and Einstein have had cerebral warehouses just as full, but they culled and codified the data. The feature masters never do. Aided by an outrageous sense of fun, they open *all* circuits so that the bit appropriate to the story can be released to race down the channel called "inspiration" to VDT screen or paper. The synaptic connections take a nanosecond.

It takes practice to keep the circuitry in superb condition, however; perhaps that's why most masters gravitate to "punning" to stay in shape. Puns are considered the lowest form of humor only by the humorless, who seem jealous of the quick wit that punning requires. Wordplay is hugely popular with ordinary folk who find such cleverness irresistible. In a headline, a pun is comedy relief played on the high wire above a gray world. The punster's rewards are the "groans-and-smiles" reactions, accolades encouraging more (and more and more).

The pun's chief drawback is that the reader must know the frame of reference or the headline will earn the response of "I don't get it." For example, only foreign film fans might "get" the first head below about a once-famous Italian star:

**The end justifies the jeans
in Gina Lollobrigida's case**[5]

Only those who know the adage about "leaving no stone un-turned" would "catch" this head involving a story about a highway department using rocks for rail guards:

No turns left unstoned on Nielson Road

And only those who understand physics would guffaw at the head that counterpuns the work of poet and prime punster Ogden Nash about putting too many ergs in one gasket:

RE-VOLTING!
Bloomington
physicist puts
too many ergs
in one gasket[6]

When masters move from puns to the "clever" head, their debut might mirror the promise of one copy editor who tossed off this headline about a 14-year-old who ran away from home to join a baseball team:

Young fan strikes out for himself[7]

For those budding masters who persist, it is not long before the gems begin to accumulate and proliferate. The result are heads like these:

Disobedience called
wrong way to rights[8]
Canadian club
finishes fifth[9]

When budget cuts gave city hall employees a four-day workweek:

You can't fight city hall—on Fridays, anyway[10]

After the news from Scotland that a female sheep had been cloned:

Scientists find way to double ewe[11]

And here are the two classics from headline lore geared to song titles. The first was for a Christmas feature about a homesick soldier stationed at the Panama Canal:

He's dreaming of a wide isthmus[12]

The second head was a play on "Stars Fell on Alabama Last Night," a tune popular when a wrestler named Ali Baba was hospitalized after being tossed on his head:

Stars fell
on Ali Baba
last night

For all of this marvelous creative electricity, for all of the creators' astonished delight at the phenomenon, and for all the well-concealed admiration of rim mates, the reality about "clever" heads is that perhaps they have nothing to do with amusing the readers. Those sparklers usually go over the heads of most readers. It appears to have everything to do with copy editors themselves. Those heads *do* inspire secret pride in the craft and its stars. The compliments that pour in from counterparts around the nation, the $5 weekly awards, the thousand uncredited reprintings, and the covert pleasure when one of their own wins a state prize are all indicators of respect from the hardest-to-impress fraternity in the news business.

The headlines of fun and genius indeed may be what keep many copy editors at their posts, despite being taken for granted and often being stretched to the breaking point. The women and men of the rim have always spent nine-tenths of their shift refashioning, resuscitating, and rescuing the copy of reporters. They are well aware that hard-news headlines sell papers from the newsstands and compel subscribers' attention as they move the morning edition from front door to the kitchen table.

But it is those clever heads that bring them notice from the profession of words. Their largest and most enthusiastic audience are what one veteran calls "the joyless sourpusses" on the copydesks around the English-speaking world. For those who have never been able to write clever heads, it is the ones spun by the masters that spark them to remain in the copy editing profession for another week, another year. To write yet another 2/24/2 Helvetica for an annexation story or yet another 1/36/4 about the United Way's final take. Every day.

10 | Different Papers, Different Head Styles

The previous chapters will get you probation status on a copydesk. But staying there depends on fine-tuning your editing skills and having an attitude of teachability. Teachability involves your reaction when you discover that you have been hired by a paper with different rules about headlines that range beyond giving a space one full count rather than a half, as was the case on your previous copydesk. Or time spent in fuming when the slot bounces your head for using "Y2K," the abbreviation for anticipated computer problems after the year 2000.

The slot is adhering to what is called "style," or a newspaper's preferred treatment of everything from acceptable pictures and comic strips to acceptable news stories and typographic dress for the local readership. Most of the nation's publishers are not turning out *The New York Times* or *Willamette Week*. They play to their publics and, whether you consider their style timid or tasteless, publishers are not about to risk even a small-scale revolt from offended readers ("cancel my subscription") just to demonstrate that they are standard-bearers for your brand of liberality—or conservatism—on news and its packaging. Because advertising depends on circulation, unofficial boycotts and disinterest have killed hundreds of papers.

It's in the "packaging" of news that style impacts the copydesk. It's manifested, as previously noted, in preferences on abbreviations and acronyms, forbidden words as well as punctuation, spelling, and capitalization. Add to that the treatment of crime news, prominent citizenry, and the powerless, as well as local business and industry interests. In other words, be flexible enough to shift from one paper's style to another without those plaintive fulminations of, "But on the *Pittsburgh Press*, we . . ." or the snide remarks in the canteen. The ability to quickly conform to a newspaper's editing and headline style is the mark of a professional.

Boning Up on Style Before Starting on a Copydesk

If you aren't able to obtain a month of back issues of the paper that just hired you, at least cut some stress from your first days by studying its stylebook or style sheet to master the characteristics unique to the paper. Beyond the AP stylebook, almost every newspaper has its own stylebook for area idiosyncrasies. It may be in hardback, like that of *The New York Times,* or in a loose-leaf notebook (for ease in updating); some are stipulated informally on signs taped to walls ("It's St., p.m., low Mass, and 2d District court").

Many style mandates are unwritten local prohibitions about verbs. They become unforgettable when hurled at a new hire by an old slot: "Even if the kids lose by 100 points, we don't use *negatives* around here!" and "Never use 'comes' or 'plays' in ANY head on this paper!" The decibels in which the instructions are delivered are in direct proportion to the amount of ridicule or rebuke suffered in the past at the hands of readers or after a brush with libel.

No copy-editing textbook or 10 years of back issues can prepare you for such local taboos, unfortunately, until *after* you have "eaten of the tree." Stylebooks deal principally with text, although they'll keep you from writing headlines mistaking "parole" for "probation" or from assuming "habeas corpus" involves a "corpse."

At least you know better now than to exaggerate the lead's main point or write a "bait and switch" tease banner for the newsstands if your publisher isn't a Hearst or a Pulitzer. The paper may have subscribers who abhor supermarket tabloids and will complain to the publisher or to the circulation department about what they perceive as sensationalism.

Where society news, food stories, and obituaries are concerned, the head style on most papers is to play them straight. Forget about lively headlines for Toastmaster or Soroptimist meetings or jazzing up stories about engagements, weddings, anniversaries, births, or deaths. Concern yourself only with ensuring that names are spelled correctly when you move from text to drafting the head. And be certain that weddings *were* double-ringed or candlelit, and that the plural of "candelabrum" is spelled correctly ("candelabra").

Counts Too Short or Too Long?

When your count is too long, you at least have a decision of what words to cut. But what if you have a count *beyond* 20 and the paper's style demands nothing less than 2 counts from the maximum? Give the story one more read to see if you can't fill that line with something far more specific. Even a one-paragraph brief has a name or activity in it to keep you from writing "dead heads" or "labels." If not, then and then only should you resort to the classic giveaways of padding: adding words like "here" and "now" and spelling out the numbers. The first "say-nothing" label head below is an example of "dead heads."

The specifics on the second headline could bring out a larger audience to hear this particular professor or the topic:

Professor speaks tonight

Kudzu talk set tonight

Most copy editors have no trouble being specific with major wire stories or with a shattering bit of local spot news, even on the tightest of deadlines ("Gore sides with AFL demands"; "6 die in Maple St. collision"). But many *without* deadline pressures complain about short counts on two-liners when they are forced to write an "umbrella" head for a roundup of wire items, or one for a lengthy piece of dull "time copy" for a news release from the chamber of commerce that nobody has had time to rewrite.

Those who love the language and read constantly to expand their vocabularies find the hot pursuit of specifics to be exhilarating and addictive. That might explain copy editors' traditional penchant in lulls between editions for crossword puzzles and syndicated features like "Jumble."

The difference between the two sets of heads below is that the vague variety is on the left and interesting ones are on the right. The copy editor obviously regarded the effort on the right as a wordsmith's Mount Everest. She packed up the proper nouns (and facts) and picked her way to the summit through the intricate route of a 15 count on 2/36/2 head orders:

Label (Dead) Heads	Specific Heads
Heat wave sweeps most of country	**18 die in U.S. from heat wave**
Travel increases off beaten track	**Tunisia offers beaches, bargain**
Many new shops set to open here	**Hallmark among 5 store openings**

Another common style rule bars "long" words. These so-called five-dollar words are stoppers to readers with basic vocabularies and, surprisingly, also to the highly educated. Let's not forget that both Plato and Lincoln found that simple words were the most powerful. Only elitist exhibitionists such as William F. Buckley, publisher of the *National Review*, deliberately court the "select" and small circulations by using words like "anfractuosity," "phlogistonic," and "otiose."[1]

A copy editor on a medical tabloid once hotly defended his choice of a Buckley-like verb by saying he found it in the dictionary and, besides, weren't doctors the best-educated readers of all? The terrible-tempered slot snapped, "We're not driving doctors to a dictionary!" His view has been supported by famed usage gurus such as columnist James J. Kilpatrick who, though fascinated with Buckley's writings, still urges journalists to:

Use familiar words—words your readers will understand, and not words they will have to look up. . . . When we feel an impulse to use a marvelously exotic word, let us lie down until the impulse goes away.[2]

Another style problem involves ambiguous words. Most university newspaper copy editors may never have worried about common headline words like "body" or "tests," but your new slot may note that those two words are among the most ambiguous terms in our language—as well as those most likely to be used in headlines. "Body" has at least six main definitions in some dictionaries. These range from the physical substance of plants to a group and the viscosity of grease.[3] "Tests" can suggest "examinations" by teachers and physicians, but also projects of scientists or engineers or those producing goods or services.

Copy editors looking for a good mix of headline words never repeat words or even close cousins in the same head, for example, "Iowa educator says education reserved for wealthy." Nor are they likely to double up on terms that are interchangeable nouns and verbs: "Vermont rule on breath test ruled out by court."

In addition, red flags should go up about "occupational hazards" that are not just style issues, but points of accuracy. "Jurists" can be lawyers, judges, or virtually any expert on the law. Be careful not to use "realtor" in a business headline as a short-count synonym for a real-estate agent because "realtor" is an official designation awarded by the National Association of Realtors. You may have no reservations about using "Dr." in headlines, but some styles ban that title for osteopaths, chiropractors, veterinarians, and especially those holding an academic doctorate.

Names in Headlines

Few headlines have space for long titles like "UN Secretary-General." As you edit a story, you'll need to pick through identifying clues to determine exactly what the person does. With some, the job title may be deliberately obscure, but if they're worthy of headline notice, boil the position down to one or two words. Or use the company name. For example, a Jane Smithers, vice president of interstate banking loans and intrabank investments for Duluth's 1st Federal Bank, could be identified in two ways:

**Banker Jane Smithers   Duluth 1st Federal official
to talk on credit union bill   to talk on credit union bill**

You may not be allowed to shorten the names of the mayor or other political entities, but most styles are now liberal enough to permit public bodies to be reduced to the essentials. "County" can stand for "county commission," and "city council" has been telescoped into "city." The state's administrative offices can be shortened to "state."

In foreign news, a few newspapers have a style forbidding copy editors from using a nation's name as an adjective. That rules out "Spanish crisis" for "Spain crisis," even though historians, politicians, and television news analysts refer to a "Chinese war" or a "Nigerian economic upheaval." To separate a populace from its nation and write headlines like "Germany crisis" and "France crisis" instead of "German crisis" and "French crisis" may seem illogical, but follow the paper's style; it might even provide a shorter count.

Foreign news has one more style mandate for headlines: Our globe has always been riven with the rise and fall of colonial empires and coups and countercoups. "Balkanization," the breaking up of colonial empires into new nations, has kept cartographers busy over the centuries and has forced copy editors to introduce the new country to the breakfast table.

That *does* confuse readers—at first. Fortunately, newspapers are aided today by the wire services' splendid infographics and backed by the morning television news shows, radio drive-time programs, and now the Internet.

For instance, few Americans had ever heard of Kosovo before 1990. And when the Soviet Union cracked apart, copy editors knew readers would be baffled by the names of the new nations that formerly had been provinces. Some desks still hedge the recognition problem with "Soviet state," but most copy editors use the new terms hot off the wire. This may annoy you, just as yesteryear's copy editors were irked when Indochina became Vietnam, or decades before when Bohemia and Slovakia became Czechoslovakia. Is it Myanmar or Burma? And what about the switch from Cambodia to Kampuchea—and then back again to Cambodia? If your predecessors could cut a 13.5-count nation to "Czechs," have faith that copy editors—maybe you—can do the same on emerging nations.

No study is available to measure the time frame in which an unfamiliar foreign name or foreign term achieves reader recognition. But Europe's new currency, the 4.5-count euro, required sixteen days in late 1998 to go from "Europe's new/currency means/creation of new/institutions" to "euro rates locked."[4] The foregoing indicates some slots perceive that the best course for introducing a new nation or term is to do it immediately and risk baffling readers for a few days. Readers seem to class infant nations with Timbuktu anyway. After all, a wire editor on *The Chicago Tribune* many years ago spoke for millions (and irritated only hundreds perhaps) when he uttered the unmentionable: that most American readers still care far more about a missing comic strip than news about *any* foreign country. His successors know it's still true unless a president sends ground troops to that land.[5]

Headline Styles for News of Fires, Accidents, and Major Disasters

When fires, floods, accidents, or major disasters happen, the prevailing headline style follows the acronym "DI$": the dead, the injured, and, if available, the dollar damage.

The damage is often included in the deck along with other crucial details like the location and the apparent cause (if authorities are willing to second-guess insurance adjusters and government officials). The result generally is crafted this way:

203 die, 830 injured in Petrolco explosion

Maintenance in cracking plant
blamed for $11.5 million fire

An accident or a house fire gets the DI$ approach:

5 teens die, 2 hurt in   **Family of 8 dies**
head-on collision   **from heater blaze**
in downtown Salem   **in Otis trailer park**

Incidentally, don't confuse the word "damages" with "damage." "Damages," according to the AP stylebook, "are awarded by a court as compensation for injury, loss, etc."[6]

One thing to be noted about major disasters is that both editors and slots usually turn into Carr Van Andas in dividing up the reporting and copydesk duties for several stories. What is paramount for copy editors to know in advance is the content of the banner and, if possible, the deck so that heads for subordinate stories won't repeat those words. So ask. Fortunately, a banner headline—often picked off the wire service slug—usually is written early to avert repetition in heads. But decks may be written just before the presses roll to incorporate the latest facts like the casualty count, so you'll need to see what will be used.

Subordinate stories spun off that Page-1 account will have different angles and thus different headline focus. But it's still a good idea to alert colleagues on words you're planning to use and to get reciprocity. That cooperation will save everyone time, eliminate squabbles and repetition, and, most of all, produce an edition like a precision watch. Such situations require that copy editors function with that Hemingway "grace under pressure."

Some papers' style is to ban negative heads for such stories. They insist the positive side can be found even in horrendous events rather than just the chill of the facts-only (5W) approach. If you find yourself on that kind of copydesk, this is the style you'll encounter:

**All 72 passengers survive crash
of Iran airliner near Baalbek**

**2 tots found alive
after water drowns
75 in S.D. village**

The various styles of newspapers may initially aggravate beginning copy editors whose frustration levels indicate their need for security. Such infantilism subsides for those recognizing that flexibility and respect for various styles are the price for being upwardly mobile and being able to work on several desks in a lifetime. Local style also means the paper is not a "cookie-cutter-carbon" or a boilerplated publication.

PART II

COPY EDITING

11 | An Overall Look at Copy Editing Today

After working on headlines, you already know a lot about editing copy, especially hard-news stories. The lead has to be meaty to generate specific nouns. Content has to be accurate, be written in active voice, and use mostly past-active verbs. A headline's singular subject has to have a singular verb. And the prospect of misspellings or punctuation errors being set in 72-point type with a 36-point deck should have made you careful about mechanics. Your heads also have to reflect a story's tone and demonstrate fairness to avoid a lawsuit.

You've also been exposed to copy editing's other vital steps.

By taking notes during a "first read" to create a headline, you develop a good sense about a story's content and organization. A beginning reporting class undoubtedly taught you that a hard-news story must be constructed like an inverted pyramid so it could be trimmed from the bottom if space was short. If heavy surgery was required, the lead could still stand alone.

By jotting down the names of people and entities cited initially—because reporters tend to spell them correctly in the first two paragraphs—you are able to spot misspellings farther down in the story.

Additionally, the sections on headline writing should have provided you with the ability to question copy, AP to *The New York Times* News Service, and particularly stories from staff reporters or stringers. The presumption at this point is that you're used to reaching for reference tools, such as the dictionary, the *Britannica,* or the AP stylebook, and hunting for a law case on the Internet. Because you've experienced the lash of deadlines, quick turnarounds on all kinds of stories probably will come easily.

In short, you know far more about copy editing than you think you do, something to remember as you begin editing a story set in hard copy or one that appears on the lab's computer files or in a newsroom's queue. The cardinal rule for editing *all* copy—be it hard news, features, columns, or editorials—is the same as for headline writing: *Readers must be attracted and retained and must understand every word in a story.*

Part II of this book follows recent and strong recommendations from editors, copy editors, and editing coaches at press institutes. The first section covers "substantive" editing, what these experts call the "least practiced, most needed" in copydesk training. Substantive editing involves close attention to a story's lead, its organization, tone, completeness, accuracy, and fairness, as well as sound judgment about relegating paragraphs to the cutting-room floor.

The second section emphasizes the "technical" side of editing, the area perceived as the "most practiced, least needed" in a deadline crunch. Technical editing focuses on grammar, style, spelling, punctuation, and an economy of words that are precise and clear, but are also in the "bricklayer's English" that sells newspapers. Resist the temptation in a "first read" to fix errors in spelling and punctuation rather than those in content and organization.

If sizable chunks of copy have to be killed to fulfill a trim order, the effort spent on the "technicals" will have been a waste of skill and time. Technicals are essential, but they are the polish applied *after* the substantives. Like car care, a story's "motor and transmission" take priority over a wash-and-wax job.

The Impact of the "Maestro" System and Pagination

When you start on a copydesk, expect the excitement and chaos that have been part of the newspaper business since the fifteenth century, when Gutenberg's movable type put scriveners out of a job. Only a century ago, Mergenthaler's linotype machine did the same to those setting type from the font case. The electronic age has had the same impact on the news business, except that epic changes in software, hardware, and systems sometimes seem to turn up within weeks. Never get cocky about computer proficiency because change can come instantly and trigger the same kind of shock and fury in a newsroom staff as did Gutenberg's new process. Focus instead on the fact that no matter what new gizmos churn out the printed words, copy editors will always eat.

The next few paragraphs are intended to prepare you for stepping into the electronic whirlwind swirling around the copydesk— and surviving *every* generation of gizmos.

In the early 1990s, the big dailies began instituting something called the "maestro" system to counteract what one newspaper consultant called the "disturbing trend [of] quality people being stretched to mediocrity."[1] Magazines such as LIFE, almost from its founding in 1936, called such weekly sessions "staff meetings." A senior editor would gather everyone from reporters and photographers to subeditors and the art director (even trainees from the clip desk and photo lab) to select stories mostly suggested by the staff and then decide on a story's treatment.[2] On newspapers, top editors *might* listen to ideas from a few outspoken staffers, but, like military commanders, they were the only decisionmakers.

As at LIFE, maestro-system conferences involve managing editors and section editors gathering reporters, photographers, designers, and copy editors to orchestrate the handling of major day-to-day news and special editions. Sessions focus on staff views about the *why* of doing a story and include advice from photographers and designers on the *how* of capturing readers' interest, from pictures and infographics to pullout quotes. Copy editors might chime in on the *why,* but you're there principally to understand what content will be coming across the copydesk and to produce "quality, errorless text."[3] Above all, staffs are expected to "view the story from the reader's perspective,"[4] to treat stories with proprietary care, and, in this cooperative process, to develop a sense of esprit de corps.

Your newsroom may shun the "maestro" term for "team" with subsets of "topic teams" that extend to the copydesk in terms of co-operative operations. At some big dailies like the Portland *Oregonian*, the slot may assign cover stories for the A and Metro sections, but on all other stories the copy editors reach into a community basket. Custom and courtesy dictate that each takes the top-of-the-list story so that the story roster gets whittled down during a shift's three editions.[5]

Predictions that the newsroom's territorial "detachment" would vanish, and especially that the "traditional copy desk [would be] gone,"[6] have failed to materialize. Many reporters have not shed ingrained habits of rarely reading their work in the paper.[7] Add to all of this the fact that at some papers, trims and adds are determined not by editors and slots, but by paginators, who then send the remaining material to copy editors.[8]

As for that "quality, errorless text," the pagination duties have guaranteed stories of diminished quality with multiple glaring errors, judging from the frequent appearance of "payed" and "tryed." One failure to distinguish between the National Rifle Association and the Equal Rights Amendment meant that a syndicated columnist's blast at the gun lobby in one daily carried the six-column head, "Voters must make ERA endorsement the kiss of death." You still need to do an exemplary job. Make certain that a group photo has *four* names for *four* people and that everyone is correctly identified "from left." And look out for pronouns coached into contractions (e.g., "they sent *they're* employees to a diversity-awareness program").

Maestro or "team" concepts notwithstanding, outside critics and overly sensitive writers still upbraid copy editors about having the taste of philistines when they sneer and slash material written in the literary journalism style of a Norman Mailer or a Tom Wolfe. Reporters never tire of grousing that they work on the run under often hostile conditions and bad weather; without their labors, copy editors would be teaching English at some high school. One pair of observers did recommend that copy editors attempt to be aware of the challenges to reporters: "[Copy] editors must be sensitive enough so they can appreciate what the reporter is trying to achieve, yet wise enough to question writing that is overwrought or wrongheaded."[9]

Yet that does not mean abandoning Van Anda's extraordinary news sense and his almost matchless editing skills.

Attitude and Editing

A compelling interest in news is required for careful examination of copy—paragraph by paragraph, sentence by sentence, and word by word—under deadline pressure. That attitude makes great editors. A lack of interest in news and feature stories can end your career on a desk. You must have a lifelong curiosity about all stories, pride in the paper, or pride in the craft of editing. As noted, another major motivator is the recognition that copy editors are essential to writers and play a major role in great stories that win prizes. But so does ensuring accurate obituaries because they are treasured forever by ordinary people.

Reporters often are so caught up in the creative process and with juggling the facts they've gathered that they may veer off course at considerable length or dump entire notebooks into what was supposed to be only a 10-inch story. They may be oblivious to gaping holes and missing facts, not to mention lapses in attributions, dates, and times. They may omit a closing quotation mark or start a sentence with one person and end it with "they." Few writers are capable of editing their own output because, like loving parents, they perceive their progeny to be perfect. If you have avoided subsequent drafts on your own writing, you have an idea of how strong the urge is to "be done with the damned thing" on the *first* try. Onerous as rewriting is, professional writers know that each draft polishes the raw material contained in the first effort.

Copy editors confront those "first-try" stories on every shift. But unlike despairing English teachers grading poor compositions and wondering where they've failed, most copy editors realize that rough drafts, carelessness, and ignorance are their bread and butter.

Many copy editors delight in correcting copy. Others get a lift from "catches," whether pronounced or picayune. One copy editor sees the "catch" of an error as the "brass ring" on a merry-go-round. As he once put it, "Others may not consider a catch valuable, but grabbing it is the best part of the ride for the copy editor. The bigger the error, the bigger the brass ring."[10] (Not to mention the sheer relief of the erring reporter.)

Boredom with copy also can be overcome with working to get interested in the story's content or a determination to unsnarl confusion for the average reader. Copy editors are desk-bound explorers who generally savor learning something new. They are also the third (after the editor and reporter) to know about the great deeds (and misdeeds) of the high and mighty, or that the better mousetrap is a building in a local garage. That's why copy editors often know more about city hall than the people who work there, more about the law than many on the local bench, and much, much more about how teams become champions in many cases than their coaching staffs. That's how copy editors become "Renaissance types," human encyclopedias about their communities or experts on the 1932 season of the Chicago White Sox, and worthy equals of the best English teachers in spotting technical errors.

12 | The Editing Routine

This chapter will introduce you to a suggested routine of editing copy, whether it's done on a computer or on hard copy. Hard-copy editing is still alive and prevalent on thousands of major and minor publications, so you need to know how to apply what you've learned on both systems.[1]

The headline routine introduced you to a copy editor's regimen, beginning with a quick scan of the story's content so you could write the headline. In copy editing, you'll bear down much harder on that text for substantive and technical reviews. The first step is to note the headline order, to be sure, but also to mark down any orders to cut ("trim") or to add lines before that first overall reading.

As late as 1982, when many copy editors were doing two or more reads before "surgery," beginners were given these still excellent editing guidelines and admonished to be "methodical and merciless in rejecting unsatisfactory copy; discriminating in editing out weaknesses and enhancing strengths; and compassionate in preserving the author's original ideas."[2]

Today's read-and-take-notes regimen has to be done at a "gallop," as one Wisconsin copy editor put it, strongly indicating the frustrations in trying to uphold the copydesk's high standards. That advice was considered valuable enough to be reprinted in many state press association newsletters to help the nation's copy editors and those just learning the craft:

When a piece of copy comes up on your screen, put on your running shoes. Give yourself a maximum of two minutes, a minute-thirty is better. . . . When you finish your reading sprint, ask your-self: What is this story all about? And write your answer. . . . A nut-line . . . one line, 80 characters—until you know what the piece is about. . . . If it needs rewriting, talk to the writer and let him or her rewrite it. That way, he will learn. If the story needs cutting, let the writer cut it. And learning takes place. Later, the copy gets better. Finally, edit the story in detail. Organization? Length? Unan-swered questions? Tone? Good taste? Jargon? Does it have all the necessary information? And ask yourself: Am I trying to fix it when it ain't broke?[3]

Make the first read from an ordinary reader's viewpoint, with an eye to all the facts above, plus some not mentioned: clarity, bias, and technical errors. That read will also indicate places for trims or adds.

"Adds" ideally require asking reporters to furnish new material for the required lines, but if they're not available and the deadline is nigh, make paragraphs out of the sentences *within* the paragraphs.

A simple "trim" involves selecting expendable sentences and paragraphs. Quotes go first usually, unless they're earthshaking ("I'm not a crook"; "I will not run for reelection"). Quotes should add color or flesh out character *if there's space,* but if they don't, those four or more lines will help fulfill a trim order.

The second target requires "killing from the bottom," literally deleting excess lines from the *end* of the story. This will train you to "hard-edit" stories, bearing down *hard* on every paragraph, every sentence, every word to determine what's excess baggage, what can be rephrased, what needs clarification. Hard-editing tends to be bru-tal to improve stories. Hard-news stories should be structured in an inverted pyramid—major points on top, minor ones below. One warning: Be sure that the surviving copy doesn't have allusions to something or someone trimmed from the story.

Next, polish the prose and tackle technical editing (grammar, style, punctuation, spelling). Then do one more read *after* all surgery to see if the repair operation is a success.

Into Action

Let's start off with an imaginary wire service story set in a computerized format. Teletype hard copy would be set in all caps—saving the wire service operator the effort and putting it on the copy editor. So the formats are different, but editing is editing. So is the underlying rule that as long as humans are filing wire or feature service stories, their material is no more sacred than deadline copy about the local Friday night football games.

These examples also are designed to train you to do substantive editing—editing for *substance*—before you rush in with technical editing. That urge to "fix the commas" can be overwhelming at the start. Many veteran copy editors admit to it, but they've learned to postpone it for two important reasons. First, a trim order might mean cutting so much copy that the time and effort spent on technical editing are wasted. Second, fixing technical errors means missing the story's gist and doing yet another read.

In the example below, do first read at a gallop—*and take notes.* Set a five-minute deadline. Also, write down the answers to some crucial questions: What's the story about? Does the lead have *all* 5W's (and an *H*—how)? And because a hard-news story requires active voice, who's the "actor"?

Forget about editing for organization until you've read the next chapter. Make sure your notes also track the organization, as that Wisconsin copy editor suggested. Although you might not know anything about the novel *Gone With the Wind*, even its acronym GWTW is famous to film fans and the movie industry. Try to determine the story's accuracy, fairness, and completeness. If it were a feature or opinion piece, you'd also be asked to determine its *tone*.

> A10:14
> PM-GWTW Plagiarized, 176
> Eds: New lead to kum on
> outrage of Georgia/Atlanta
> delegates

MINEAPOLIS (PA)—An uproar over "Gne
With the Wind" broke out yesterday at the the
American Writers convention wheeen a member of
the Minneapolis grope charges that Margaret
Mitchell not only plagarized the plot of Willaim
Thackerays "Vanity Fair and characters like Scarlett
O'Hara but even purloined dialogue for that classic
Civil War novel ("she's so mealy mouthed she
wouldn't say 'boo" to a goose)"; Mitchell's Melanie
Wilkes was almost an "exact duplicate" of
Thackerey's frail steel-magnolia Amelia Sedley,
including blind loyalty to her double-dealing
schoolmate. "Mitchell knew exactly what she was
doing, Lenmark said, noting she had Melanie say at
the Twelve Oaks barbecue that she disliked
Thackeray. "No wonder she hid the manuscript for
years "

A paper of B. G. Lenmark, a Minnasota novelist,
noted Thackeray's 1848 worke involved Napoleon's
campains, particularlythe battleofWaterloo. His
heroine, Becky Sharp, was the same hard-headed
baeuty as Scarlet, she said. Becky's frenetic search for
a hearse and buggy in Brussellls paralelled Scarlettt's
on the eve of Atlanta's fall. . . .

BGE1031ACS

Now that you've read this version at least once, did you spot the
flawed organization, that the second paragraph needs to be re-
versed? Did you determine the story's tone (hard news? feature? editorial?)? You don't have to be a Margaret Mitchell fan to recognize
that the story is far from being complete, accurate, or fair. If a deadline precluded waiting for rebuttal from an angry Georgia delegation, you might still champion GWTW. One solution to eliminate
the bias would be adding a sentence pointing out that William
Shakespeare also "borrowed" plots, characters, and dialogue from
the ancients. He improved their moldering works, made money, and
achieved immortality besides. When you have presented both sides,
let the reader draw a conclusion.

The main problem with the story centers on accuracy from familiarity with *both* novels. For instance, if you know *Gone With the Wind*, has the reporter erred on plot, characters, or dialogue? The Thackeray novel may be unfamiliar. Still, first-rate copydesks generally have a list of local consultants to contact. In the real world, letting that quote stand without checking will unleash uncomplimentary letters and calls. The story will not suffer from the quote's omission, by the way. The publishing date of *Vanity Fair* can at least be verified from basic reference tools such as the unabridged Merriam-Webster dictionary.

Move now to technical editing.

Assume that the slot has assigned a trim order cutting all but the lead. On hard copy, you would draw a box around the trimmed paragraphs with a pen stroke and add a large *X* so that the dead material would not get set. It would look like this:

MINEAPOLIS (PA)—AN UPROAR OVER "GNE WITH THE WIND" BROKE OUT YESTERDAY AT THE THE AMERICAN WRITERS CONVENTION WHEEEN A MEMBER OF THE MINNEAPOLIS GROPE CHARGES THAT MARGARET MITCHELL NOT ONLY PLAGARIZED THE PLOT OF WILLAIM THACKERAYS "VANITY FAIR AND CHARACTERS LIKE SCARLETT O'HARA BUT EVEN PURLOINED DIALOGUE FOR THAT CLASSIC CIVIL WAR NOVEL ("SHE'S SO MEALY MOUTHED SHE WOULDN'T SAY 'BOO" TO A GOOSE)";

MITCHELL'S MELANIE WILKES WAS ALMOST AN "EXACT DUPLICATE" OF THACKEREY'S FRAIL STEEL-MAGNOLIA AMELIA SEDLEY, INCLUDING BLIND LOYALTY TO HER DOUBLE-DEALING SCHOOLMATE. MITCHELL KNEW EXACTLY WHAT SHE WAS DOING, LENMARK SAID, NOTING SHE HAD MELANIE SAY AT THE TWELVE OAKS BARBECUE THAT SHE DISLIKED THACKERAY. "NO WONDER SHE HID THE MANUSCRIPT FOR YEARS "
A PAPER OF B. G. LENMARK, A MINNASOTA NOVELIST, NOTED THACKERAY'S 1848 WORKE INVOLVED NAPOLEON'S CAMPAINS, PARTICULARLYTHE BATTLEOFWATERLOO. HIS HEROINE, BECKY SHARP, WAS THE SAME HARDHEADED BAEUTY AS SCARLET, SHE SAID. BECKY'S FRENETIC SEARCH FOR A HEARSE AND BUGGY IN BRUSSELLLS PARALELLED SCARLETTT'S ON THE EVE OF ATLANTA'S FALL. ...

On computer copy, you would highlight the designated section to be killed and then tap the delete key.

The final step would be to attack all the technical errors in the remaining paragraph. Here's a second look for that kind of editing:

> MINEAPOLIS (PA)—An uproar over "Gne
> With the Wind" broke out yesterday at the the
> American Writers convention wheeen a member of
> the Minneapolis grope charges that Margaret
> Mitchell not only plagarized the plot of Willaim
> Thackerays "Vanity Fair and characters like Scarlett
> O'Hara but even purloined dialogue for that classic
> Civil War novel ("she's so mealy mouthed she
> wouldn't say 'boo" to a goose)";

Let's look at the mistakes: The wire service reporter, obviously rushed, had difficulty spelling even the dateline city. A letter was omitted in the book's title, and two letters were transposed so it became "Willaim." Too many letters were included in "when," and one too many and one too few in "group." And "the" got a double mention. If you caught the misspelling on "plagarized" for "plagiarized," you may well develop into one of those crack copy editors who see errors like "miniscule," "judgement," and "goverment" leaping off a page even in leisure reading. That skill comes from a lifetime of heavy reading.[4]

Punctuation problems include the omission of an apostrophe (indicating possession) before the *s* in "Thackeray." The common error of forgetting to close quotes turns up with the omitted quotes after "Fair." Today's popular "not only . . . but" construction may or may not require a comma before "but," depending on a newspaper's style, but purists will demand a comma. You'd probably remember to tuck quotes *inside* the parentheses enclosing "mealy-mouthed" and to change that semicolon to a period. With computers, the small screen makes it difficult to differentiate between a semicolon and a colon, and a comma and a period.

The grammatical error of tense on the verb "change" was the reporter's failure to stick to the past-active tense demanded in hard-news stories. Blame the reporter's love of a packed lead. That pattern led to two subjects ("uproar" and "member") and two verbs ("broke" and "charges") that could make all but grammar sticklers stumble. Fifteen words separate the first verb from the second, or the writer surely would have used the form "charged."

That error points up a writer's common failing: long sentences lead to forgetfulness and carelessness, as is shown above. Cut them in two (or three), and grammar improves markedly. The word "purloined" would be a show-off stopper to most newspaper readers and isn't warranted even in a story about literature. Simple words may bore the sophisticated reader, but they are a minuscule segment of any newspaper's circulation.

Editing Features and Opinion Pieces

A feature story and an opinion piece require somewhat different handling because they are not framed in the inverted-pyramid style. The points and examples of an editorial, for example, are like an English theme: they hold a composition together and are followed by a snappy ending or a restatement of management's view. But even if the author permits some tinkering with mechanics, the copy editor who goes beyond that point and removes key sentences or entire paragraphs risks a tongue-lashing and possible termination if the author is the publisher. Prudent copy editors call or visit the chief editorial writer or publisher to raise issues perceived as erroneous or likely to invite trouble from readers.

Fine-tuning a feature—killing quotes or *any* paragraphs, *particularly an ending*—may well cause the entire story to wither, wander, or halt abruptly. Experienced copy editors know the basics of storytelling, but sometimes their perceptions of what is unnecessary don't mesh with the writer's view. Again, professional courtesy demands that you at least talk to the reporter and raise issues of clarity, content essentials, or structure. Reporters may not like rewriting stories, but if your questions are valid and your judgment respected, they'll make the changes.

A final word on the GWTW examples: Wire services for generations found it less expensive to put the burden on copy editors to capitalize proper nouns, so teletyped stories were set in caps, including dateline and wire service credit. Today, only news flashes get that kind of treatment, but it is still useful to know this form of editing. Everything not to be set in type—including wire service codes and instructions—is either circled in hard copy or deleted in computer copy; otherwise, that material will turn up in the story and mystify readers.

So much for the bare bones of the editing routine. Subsequent chapters will flesh out both substantive and technical editing areas. The remainder of this chapter is divided into the particular needs and problems of those working on computers and on hard copy.

Editing by Computer

Different computer systems and software use different coding, so be prepared to see changes from newsroom to newsroom. On many papers, the slot's orders for heads and trim/adds come to the copy editor from a code (the "notes mode" or "header") located at the top left-hand corner of a computer screen. Whether your newsroom has a state-of-the-art software system or hasn't been upgraded since the dawn of the Information Age, such notes contain vital information for each story.

Codes differ around the country, but their instruction content is much the same. Elaborate codes like the examples below include the name of the writer or syndicate. The dates and times the story "moved" are essential in determining its current status, as is the story's number and the key word, or slug, summing up its content. In addition, some codes contain the headline order, including cuts and adds and the font.

These data are followed by the page or section designations (called "baskets" on some papers, "queues" on others), the copy editor who is assigned the story, and head and trim orders. Some codes look like this:

Entered 3/17 at 10:15a by SMITH   NYT NEWSSERVICE
Changed 3/25 at 3:18p by SMITH   MIAC-Rome/bribes
moved 4/20/6:30 A   basket/page 1
Story #518 Keyword 4 CONVICTS   copy editor: Benjamin
QUEUE DEMORRIS   lucida 5/48/1-RO 2/24/2
HEL4/36/1-TRI   overset 18
ADD 4

At one West Coast daily, copy editors work on a "first-come, first-pick" communal system off the slot's list of stories for all but the main stories in the A and Metro sections, as has been noted. So the coding has no copy editor designation, story number, or identifying summary word (a.k.a. slug). Instead, the codes focus on head orders. Copy editors put their initials atop the code so the slot knows who processed what story. The trims/adds have already been done by the paginators. After the copy editor completes processing a story and initials it, a click of the slot icon speeds it to that designation. The slot sees something like this atop the screen:

hst
[/hedr,4,36,1]   Forest Grove, Hillsboro merge
[/decks,11.03]   Historic rivals
                                                merge services,
                                                cut costs, taxes

[/by] R. GREGORY NOKES
[/staff][5]

When you begin editing copy—electronic or hard versions—remember to make note of the head and the trim/add orders and to check the key word, or slug, for the story's gist before the first reading.

Many desk staffs, experienced in editing *both* hard and electronic copy, tend to prefer hard copy despite their familiarity with screens and "cursoring and clicking." Their chief complaint about editing on a screen is not being able to see the entire story at once.

Yet generations of copy editors who grew up with typewriters dealt with fast-breaking stories written with a paragraph per page (a "take"). The takes were split among a half dozen compositors in time for the press deadline.

The answer to this current complaint is the same as in the days of a paragraph-per-take: Make meaty notes as you scroll down through the story on the first read so you'll know what's in the *entire* story. Scrolling, in fact, should give you a feeling of control over the story.

Writers and editors who exchanged typewriters for computers generally prefer the latter. One major advantage of word processing software is its capacity for reorganizing a story with some form of the cut-and-paste feature. On the Microsoft program, for example, the material to be moved is first highlighted. Then, with nearly simultaneous taps of the Control and *X* keys (C+X), the selected text is extracted. Tapping the Control and *V* keys (C+V) puts the material where the copy editor wants it located.

Take a moment to flow some text onto the screen and practice moving it by this system from one spot to another. If you should bobble the experiment, press C+Z and the page will revert to what it was before you began the cut-and-paste experiment.

Another welcome feature permits deleting large chunks of excess copy with the taps of those Control and *X* keys (C+X). If you change your mind, return the material with a tap of the Control and *Z* keys (C+Z). The Find feature (C+F) permits you to comb through a story in seconds to see if the reporter has a case of the "howevers" or starts too many sentences with the word "and" or "but." Equally, if the reporter has repeatedly and unintentionally misspelled a word, the C+H keys will replace the error with the proper spelling *throughout* the story.

Heated quarrels have erupted between language purists and newspaper practitioners about the laziness of those using the spelling- and grammar-checking features instead of turning to the dictionary or grammar textbook. But the need for speed and the popularity of these two features in the newsroom have largely snuffed out complaints that these "lame-brain gadgets," as one veteran copy editor has dubbed them, cripple journalists. Yet anyone making a living in the writing field also knows better than to trust a spell-checker for *everything*. Spell-checkers bypass words of two letters and pass "your," say, for "you're" and thousands of other words that look or sound alike. Such errors, often set in poetry, adorn a thousand newsroom bulletin boards. Few copy editors tend to use the grammar-checker feature because most have the rules packed firmly in their heads, which provides faster access than highlighting and searching.

Among the computer's disadvantages are frequent "crashes" stemming from electrical outages or even broken cooling fans. But newspapers were paralyzed by press breakdowns in the days before computers, albeit not a half dozen times per shift, as is often the case today. Another drawback is that copy sometimes is not totally deleted from a story, as staffers have discovered to their horror when "reminder notes," space-holding heads or their private mutterings about content turn up in the first edition.[6]

The most serious disadvantage of computer editing involves vision problems, something more frightening than carpal tunnel syndrome or backaches, because copy editors' livelihoods depend on eyesight. These range from tired or watering eyes to double vision.

Short of making an anonymous call to the Occupational Safety and Health Administration (OSHA) or the publication's group insurance carrier about the work environment, most copy editors haven't been able to do much about improper lighting or nonadjustable chairs, desks, or computer monitors. Complaints about eyestrain or being unable to see punctuation marks are common, but remedies exist: If your computer system permits it, highlight the entire story and raise the point size to a comfortable reading level—12- to 14-point—sufficient to see whether a comma or apostrophe is *next* to an italicized word. When you're finished, remember to reduce the type to the default point size, of course.

It's not just copy editors nearing 50 who complain about readability. Many teens and twenty-somethings have trouble seeing a colon or semicolon, let alone recognizing their subtle differences. The copy editor on a major daily who closed an editorial—set in 10-point, one point size larger than news text—let an extra period mar that superbly edited paper: "If he can't convert the Bronx Bombers into the West Side Whackers, well, he'll move the team to New Jersey.."

You probably could pick off those two periods in this book, but pity the copy editor working at a screen that makes 10-point look like

8-point. If that staffer had a computer system permitting highlighting and enlargement of the text, say, to 18-point, as shown below, the extra period probably would have been noticed and deleted:

If he can't convert the Bronx Bombers into the West Side Whackers, well, he'll move the team to New Jersey..
18-Point Type

When eyes water, optometrists warn that the muscles are tired from continuous, close focus on a screen after two or three hours. A return to normal vision requires at least an hour's break. In addition, the recent enlargement of screen sizes beyond a 10-inch width has triggered a proportional increase in the incidence of such fatigue because peripheral vision is taxed to its limits. Officials at Apple Computer say that "although eye fatigue is annoying, there's no evidence [thus far] that it leads to permanent [physical] damage."[7] But fatigue *does* adversely affect the quality of editing. Some daub eyes with a dampened washcloth. The wise blink for a full minute.

Eyedrops specifically developed for "tired eye relief" are being marketed as an antidote,[8] but the latest research indicates they may damage vision—as may massaging tear ducts. Blinking is still the most natural antidote.

Probably the best remedy for watering or tired eyes or double vision comes from optometrists and Apple, a company with every reason to monitor eye problems. Among its current instructions is the warning to "give your eyes frequent rest breaks by looking up and focusing on distant objects. Remember to have your eyes examined regularly."[9]

Hard-Copy Editing

Editing hard copy has almost none of the physical problems associated with processing computerized stories beyond the traditional backaches from being hunched over copy and writer's cramp from clutching a copy pencil. Hard copy provides plenty of opportunities to relax eye muscles when shifting from copy to making notes about the story, looking around the city room, or just gazing off into the mind's creative zones for a headline. Time was when glare from newsroom lights forced prudent copy editors to wear green eye-shades and all sorts of brimmed hats to ease vision problems.[10]

Hard copy allows most of a story to be seen at a glance, whether in teletype form or manuscripts from local reporting, or news releases. Head and trim/add orders are still placed above the text.

Orders for trims and adds are usually based on inches, although some slots may specify them in lines. The formula on most copy-desks for text is: Four lines usually equal a single inch of typeset copy. Thus the slot's instruction for a copy editor to "trim 1" means finding four lines to delete. Again, quotes are killed before copy editors cut stories from the bottom.

Unlike computerized editing, the hard-copy variety looks untidy, littered with copy-editing symbols used to indicate paragraphing, inserted words, and punctuation. Paragraphs to be shifted have to be boxed and marked "Insert A" (or B, C, D, etc.) with a corresponding arrow indicating the new spot for "Insert A" and its brethren.

Because compositors look *under* the lines for corrections, copy editors insert a caret mark (∧) there to get their attention. As you'll note from the editing symbols (see inside cover), a corresponding upside-down caret indicates where to insert words or punctuation marks. Photocopy a pair of hard-copy stories and practice using the symbols.

Copy-editing symbols are ancient and are used around the globe wherever type is set in a Roman alphabet (English, French, Spanish, Italian, German, etc.). They are designed for optimal editing speed and require only a flick of the wrist even in jotting the word "stet," the Latin abbreviation for *stet processus* (let it stand) to restore deleted words or paragraphs.

13 | Editing for Organization

In that *Gone With the Wind* example in the previous chapter, poor organization turned up in a two-paragraph hard-news story. Imagine the poor organization possible in a story of 15 paragraphs. Add to this the potential for disorganization in feature stories or a series of articles filling several pages. You'll begin to understand the copydesk's frustrations about the organizational skills of some reporters, even on prestigious dailies; these writers continually rely on copy editors to be "story doctors" and rescuers. But expertise in organization is part of a copy editor's job description.

Sometimes the emphasis might seem eccentric or outlandish. For example, you might be puzzled about why a Montana daily gave so much footage to the 50 dogs brought to a city council meeting to lobby against a $10 increase in spaying fees instead of the expenditure of $1.7 million for street repairs. News values may seem skewed, but not in a town where dog lovers are far more interested in a spaying spike than in streets.

Acquiring such knowledge and wise judgment about the arrangement of news content takes time and experience. When you're hired, read at least two years of back issues of the paper to see "what's hot and what's not" in town. Further, it requires a thorough grounding in public finance, business world maneuvers, and local politics masterminded by the "good-ole boys and girls." Above all, it takes just keeping your ears open in those first months on the desk.

A New Method for Editing a
News Story's Organization

While you're acquiring that seasoning, you can become a quick expert in discerning a story's organization (or lack of it) on the first day. This chapter is designed to help you do that by providing a method new to journalism for editing organization.

The method is fast and easy to master and is immediately applicable.[1]

If you've been making notes about story content in the first read for headlines, as is *strongly* recommended, you're already using a scratch sheet by the keyboard or making jottings in the hard-copy margins. The only new wrinkle is to code *paragraphs* for content on that scratch sheet. Select a word, a letter, an abbreviation, a symbol—or a combination of these choices. You decide your code.

Coding enables you to see—instantly—whether the reporter has been "hopscotching" or repetitive in the story. It also detects whether the footage devoted to one issue or event is lopsided. Once content coding is complete, consult the slot about what items are crucial and how the remainder should be ranked.

Coding is applicable to virtually *every* newspaper story or magazine article of today or yesteryear, something that also shows the competence of an editor or a copy editor. Take the organizational challenge faced by *New York Times* editor Carr Van Anda when he had to merge into the main story the work of several reporters covering the Triangle Waist factory holocaust of March 25, 1911.[2] Coding the main sections reveals how he organized all the data pouring into the newsroom for the lengthy main story on Page-1, with only one lapse.[3]

However, Van Anda had years of experience and superb natural instincts for story organization—as well as subeditors—to determine the positioning of material. He repeated this feat a year later in the masterly organization on deadline for coverage of the *Titanic* sinking. You are just acquiring this skill. Although you aren't yet able to judge the *importance* of the data in the paragraphs,

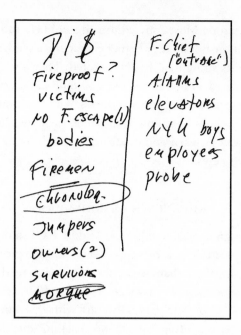

coding will enable you to at least spot the disorganization and re-peated data.

The Basics of Newspaper Story Organization

Before you begin coding, remember what you were taught in your introductory newswriting class about the organization of material. Hard news was supposed to be organized into an inverted pyramid: the first paragraph must contain the 5W's, followed by the stacking of subsequent paragraphs providing details in *declining* importance to the story. If space was limited, you were warned that copy editors might have to apply the "cutoff test" and delete paragraphs, starting from the bottom and working up to the lead.

Feature stories were the exception to this structural pattern, but, like short stories, they still had to be organized to retain reader interest from start to finish. As for checking organization in editorials or opinion pieces, know that copy editors generally leave them alone, even though some may be softhearted enough to fix misspellings or grammatical errors. Most copy editors are unlikely to fix the boss's poor organization, nor do they bother contacting a syndicate to set famous columnists straight, as has been noted. They also tend to leave reviews untouched, although the pieces should have a structure that includes a synopsis, a price, and an address. The common view is that opinion writers should be allowed to fall on their swords.

The best way to learn about editing a story's organization is to start with hard news.

Hard-News Organization

On many foreign dailies, notably the Middle Eastern ones, the local hard news is written in a blow-by-blow (chronological) sequence. Coverage of, say, the Lebanese parliament session reads like one of Scheherazade's stories: "Parliament opened at 10 this morning, followed by . . ."[4] Beginners generally start with that same organizational structure, including the sin of "backing into a lede" (also "lead") a story's first paragraph; for example, "At a meeting yesterday afternoon of the Student Government Association . . .". Usually, a professor or snappish slot will point out a newspaper's space limitations and then lecture them about the inverted pyramid. The chronological structure is reserved for features, opinion pieces, and, on weekly newspapers, the chatty, name-filled "country correspondence" that boosts and maintains circulation.

Meeting stories usually are major offenders in disorganization, but the worst may be speech stories because speakers can meander down so many provocative paths (a.k.a. "bunny trails") that the bewildered reporter may become unable to determine priority items.

Most veteran copy editors therefore tend to approach any hard-news story longer than two paragraphs with a suspicious eye about its organization.

To illustrate hard-news organization, let's begin with the most common and numerous stories written in that genre. Examine three examples: a business brief, an engagement, and an obituary. These stories could be cut back to their leads and still contain the chief points. Even the sentences tend to place the most critical information in the first few words, with the rest organized in declining order of importance, like this:

Standard Insurance Co. has named Dietrick W. Benedict to manage its Jackson group office, effective Aug. 1.

Benedict has been the manager of the life and annuity carrier's Denmark office. He joined the company in 1991. He will head an office of nine sales representatives and five service representatives.

Benedict holds a BS in public relations from Louisiana State University and an MBA from the University of Alabama. His Chartered Life Underwrite designation was conferred in 1996.

Mr. and Mrs. Ronald R. Loam of Macon, Ga. have announced the engagement of their daughter Lori Anne Loam of Macon, Ga., to Sean W. Smith, son of Mrs. Sharon Hodges and Kyle E. Smith, both of Detroit.

The wedding will be held at 10 a.m. on Dec. 26 at the Cathedral of St. Mark in Minneapolis. They will honeymoon in Hawaii and make their home in Savannah.

The bride is a teacher at Holgate elementary school and the bridegroom is a coach and history teacher at Savannah high school.

A graveside service will be at 2 p.m. Wednesday, May 18, 2000, in Evergreen Memorial Gardens Cemetery for LaToya Sonnier, who died May 13 at age 38.

Mrs. Sonnier was born April 13, 1962 in Harrisburg, Pa. Her maiden name was Isles. She lived in Harrisburg until two years ago when she married Jared Sonnier and moved to Milwaukee. She was a systems analyst for Brown Electronics Company.

> Survivors include her husband, daughter Traci
> Lee, her mother, Sarah Leeds Isles, of Chicago, and
> several aunts and uncles.
> The family suggests remembrances to the
> American Heart Association.

Organization problems usually start when hard-news stories outgrow a two- or three-inch newshole. Yet the story should be written with the inverted-pyramid structure no matter what the length.

The reporter decides the ranking order of what is less important in the paragraphs contained in the pyramid. Some stories, like those above, have such a standard organization that the reporter can whip off copy by formula. Lengthy hard-news stories about fires, disasters, and accidents have that same inverted-pyramid structure, but many reporters err in determining the order of major and minor elements.

The lead in such spot-news stories should enumerate the dead, the injured, and the damages (DI$)—and in just that order. The remaining 5W information follows. The second paragraph adds details on the condition of the injured or survivors. The third paragraph might sum up the impact or meaning of the event:

> The blaze, reported at 5:37 a.m., destroyed an
> entire block within 40 minutes as four fire companies
> struggled to keep it from spreading beyond Zarthan
> Avenue.

After that, the paragraphs can be a compendium of chronological events, eyewitness accounts, or factors *unconnected* to sidebars if the event is major enough to warrant that kind of treatment.

A crime story, no matter how lengthy, should follow the inverted-pyramid organization that is shown in the coded example below. The first two paragraphs could stand alone if space was tight. Or the copy editor could delete the last paragraph—or the paragraphs describing the chase. In the crime story below, the coding displays each paragraph's content. That enables the copy editor to check the organization and identify potential deletions at a glance:

A gunfight and an 80-mph car chase across the Central bridge by state and city police Monday evening ended a six-hour hunt for a man suspected of involvement in two recent local shootings. Officers reported he fired shots at his pursuers, but no one was injured.

Victor M. Smith, 28, may have been wounded in the chase and finally surrendered at 11:30 p.m. to a special-weapons unit after spike strips laid by state police on the highway blew out a tire, and squad cars forced his north-bound vehicle to the shoulder of U.S. 171.

Smith was being sought in connection with a late Monday afternoon near-fatal shooting of a 69-year-old woman inside a residence in the 5800 block of South Jefferson Avenue. The shooting victim, as yet unidentified, is in a Seattle hospital.

Smith is also one of three persons charged with attempted murder in the of shooting at Marquette county deputy Lonnie Gallaway on July 4 when he pursued their vehicle on Washington 104, Interstate 5 and through downtown Seattle, according to Loretta Betteridge, a sheriff's spokesperson. Thoroughman was uninjured.

After the shooting, police spotted Smith who fled on foot near Southeast 30th Ave. and Bayshore Street. From 6:15 p.m. on Sunday to to 7:30 a.m. Monday, police, dogs and an state police helicopter combed the area. A tipster spotted Smith and a passenger in a car around 7 p.m. in East Seattle.

With squad cars in hot pursuit, Smith sped across the bridge at 70 mph, stopped to let out the passenger and zoomed up the highway at 80 mph, police said. The punctured tire dropped his speed to 35 mph and police forced him to the shoulder where he was surrounded.

A woman, Mary D. Jones, 41, has been charged with attempted aggravated murder in the county case. She will be tried May 5. A third suspect, Jack B. White, 31, faces the same charge and remains at large. Police suspect Smith and Jones also stole a truck earlier Monday from a Northeast Seattle home. The vehicle has been recovered.

How to Code a Story

Meeting stories are an excellent place to learn coding for organization because most sessions follow agendas. Such stories have elements that are fairly universal, such as money, history, background, examples, and quotes, plus a lead and a "nut graf" (a paragraph following the lead that sums up the story's gist) and a close. Those common factors can also be coded by a word per paragraph. Or a code could use letters, or a symbol, such as a dollar sign. Or a specific word. For instance:

$=money	**H**=history (or **B**=background)	**Ex**=example
T=items tabled	**L**=lead	**NG**=nut graf
Q=quotes	**P**=items passed	**D**=description
Bio=biography	**F**=future prospects	**C**=closer
NP=items not passed		

You'll be shown exercises for coding a meeting story, but the example below demonstrates how to code a city council story set in hard copy with a combination:

Your scratch sheet (or Post-it Note) for that story might look something like this:

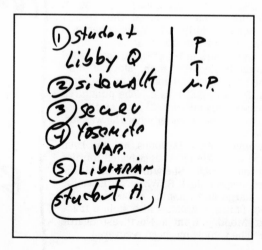

Adding a college student to Lexington's 10-person city council will be up to local voters in the Nov. 3 election, according to action taken last night by an 8-2 vote of the council. The vote will amend the city charter to include a student from East Maine State College, and candidates would appear on the ballot.

student

Council member Elizabeth Libby predicted the change would pass overwhelmingly because EMSC is the town's largest employer and at least 53% of students were eligible to vote. Libby and John Alden opposed the measure. Alden said students: "know nothing and care nothing about the town except who sells the cheapest six packs and pizzas."

Libby view

The issue was among a 17-item agenda in which the council:

• Awarded the low bid of $89,000 for 10 blocks of sidewalk on Xenwood Avenue to Fred Stickney Construction company of Standish. Work will begin June 1 at Xenwood and Lake Streets and is expected to be finished by mid-August, city manager Rex Pickett told the council.

sidew.

•Transferred $17,000 in general funds to the water department for enhancements to the sewage plant.

sewer

•Tabled approving two building-code variances approved by the zoning board to permit property owners in the 3200 block of Yosemite Avenue to add second floors to their homes.

Yosemite variance

•Approved a raise of $1 per hour to town librarian Abby Watson that expands her salary to $5.75.

Librarian

EMSC's student government has worked for a decade to put a student on the council and finally submitted a petition with 1,500 signatures for that action.

(H.)

Spearheading the drive was Eben McGibbon, an EMSC junior, who told council members last night that unlike high school students, EMSC students paid property taxes through rent, utility and sewer bills, bought groceries and clothes, and were registered voters. "Townies make fortunes off students and give virtually nothing back except insults like that pizza remark," he said. "It's time we got representation along with the taxation."

In other action, the council approved zoning permits to H. Z. C. Veterinary Clinic and Clarke's Pharmacy, spending $200 for town square Christmas lights, and a maximum of $800 in repairs to a police cruiser, hiring of an additional part-time constable at $4.75, per hour and posting of "no-entry" signs in the one-block alley between J. C. Penney's and the Coast-to-Coast hardware store.

(P)

Members tabled action on changing hours of the municipal pool from 7 a.m. to 10 p.m., and adding a clerk to the city manager's office. They voted against buying wood for the public skating rink, buying a pumper for the fire department, annexing Saco, and renewing the liquor license for Easy Aces tavern.

(T) (N. P.)

When you finally *do* learn the readers' prime interests, coding obviously will enable you to determine stories organized by their interest values. You'll know when and where to relocate paragraphs or which items will have to be ganged in the story's final paragraph ("The council also tabled ordinances on noise abatement, borrow pits on Lake Street, and the teen curfew").

Coding "Delayed" Leads and Discovering Buried Leads

A delayed lead lures readers into a story by first piquing their curiosity or ire with a fascinating anecdote or outrageous scenario that could involve a second and even a third paragraph. It is followed by a paragraph that encapsulates the overall point of the story, the thrust in a nutshell. For that reason, such a paragraph is called the "nut graf." A coding system makes it possible for the copy editor to quickly see that the "delayed" lead might take too many paragraphs before readers arrive at the nut graf. Coding would be like this:

> East Maine State College students may finally get turned on to voting despite an abysmal average turnout of 5% for their own university's government elections.
> One Lexington city council member forecast that instead of the usual 500 who vote in the annual student government (SGA) elections, nearly 5000 may get to the polls if one of their own gets a seat on the council. But maybe only if beer and pizza issues are on the agenda, another member indicated.
> Adding a college student to Lexington's 10-person city council will be up to local voters in the Nov. 3 election, according to action taken last night by an 8-2 vote of the council. The vote will amend the city charter to include a student from East Maine State College, and candidates would appear on the ballot.
> Council member ...

Nut ⎤

By coding, you'd also have little difficulty deciding that this "anecdotal" lead is too lengthy and perhaps needs only one example to hold reader interest:

> When the landlord failed to provide heat for two weeks in winter two years ago, Eben McGibbon and four fellow students at East Maine State College organized a Tenants Association and the furnace got fixed. When voters went to the polls last November to pass a 1.5¢ special sales tax, McGibbon and his roommates voted against it—unlike most of Lexington—and saw their weekly grocery bill edge upward. And when the rent went up to $50 for their new digs in January, their newest landlord blamed the hike on increased property taxes, including the expected special assessment for sidewalks.
>
> The 25-year-old had enough. He got 1,500 signatures on a petition that probably could put an EMSC student on the city council.
>
> Adding a college student...

Another advantage of coding is that the "buried" lead can be seen immediately. Buried leads occur when the reporter misses a major element or event that should have led the story in the rush to deadline. Or because news judgment is awry. Or from stringers assuming the paper will cover the big event. The example below, so common in weekly newspapers over the decades, contains a major event in a small community—a fire. But the correspondent buried it deep in the news items probably because she was focused on inserting scores of names in the newspaper. These, she knows, sell many duplicate copies of the paper and expand the inches for which she will be paid. Long paragraphs of names often sell more papers than a five-day blizzard. Coding this story should unearth a buried lead within seconds:

By ETHEL THOMAS
Gazette Correspondent

HERNANDO—Several Hernandoians attended Thursday's covered-dish supper feting the 50th anniversary of former and long-time residents Ralph and Doris Eckles, staged by their four children and grandchildren at the Commerce community hall.

The Eckles lived at Hernando from 1945 when he was discharged from the Army until last year when they moved to Miami. Their sons and daughters John, Calvin, Mary, and Susanne all attended Hernando public schools and gradually moved to the Commerce and Grenada areas in the last 10 years.

The couple repeated their vows before officiant The Rev. Harry Woods of the Hernando 2d Presbyterian church who married them a half-century ago. Other events included the presentation of a scrapbook of letters from family, friends, and neighbors, and showing movies of the Eckles in their Hernando days. An ensemble from the Commerce high school band played for the dance and reception, and included the couple's favorite songs.

Sandi and Marty Cope and children Sean and Candi went to Detroit over the holidays to take delivery on a new pickup. Enroute to Hernando and stopped in Cairo, Ill. to visit her sister, Mrs. Shane Wilcox, and family.

The roster for the American Legion baseball teams will be announced May 15. Signups at the Gem Bar and Grill will close Saturday evening. Company teams are welcome. Call Paul Cameron, 239-8632, for further information.

The county courthouse burned to the ground Monday. Seven people died in the 3 p.m. blaze, including Hernando mayor Margaret Miller, and Philip Scarston, judge of the probate court. Fifteen people are in serious condition at DeSoto Memorial hospital. The blaze was blamed on aging wiring, according to fire chief Felix H. Walker. Damage is estimated at more than two million dollars, according to the adjuster from Travelers Insurance.

Girl Scout Troop No. 3456 will be going to Memphis from Friday until Sunday to visit Graceland and other sights. The troop will be accompanied by Mrs. Floyd Davis, troop leader, and Mrs. Ernest Monson, Ms. Nikki Olmstead, and Mrs. Jason Pooler.

Feature-Story Organization

Feature stories often have a Scheherazade structure of chronological order, especially when the reporter presents background information. A story on how to build a deck or on successful fly-fishing must use a step-by-step chronological organization scheme.

Yet all features—heartbreakers to travel pieces—must have an engaging beginning, a meaty midsection, and an obvious ending. None should be cluttered with irrelevant details or digressions. Coding will uncover these flaws immediately.

The crucial caveat in editing feature stories for organization is to remember their creative nature, something that requires a copy editor's careful thought and *restraint*. Before attempting a reorganization, remember that the world-famous short stories of Nathaniel Hawthorne, Anton Chekhov, and O. Henry first appeared as newspaper features with a limit ranging from 800 to 1,200 words. If some copy editor had pruned the life out of them, reorganized factors, or given away surprise endings, the world of literature would have been the loser.

So instead of rewriting the piece, the copy editor should point out the flawed organization to the writer for revamping. A scratch sheet coding the story's organization should be the most convincing evidence (and helpful tool) for that rearrangement. As one copy editor explained her technique, "I either start or end with a buildup and then lay the [rewriting] on reporters. Fastest lesson in organization most [of them] ever get."

Question-and-answer (Q&A) interview stories are another form of the feature, but the only reorganizational touch might come with a trim order. Even then, editing requires a sure sense of what questions are vital to the content's overall thrust. Again, a consultation with the reporter is essential, augmented by the coding scratch sheet.

Organization of Second-Day Stories and a Series of Articles

Follow-up stories require extra work with or without coding for organization. For starters, ensure that the reporter has included a paragraph high in the story encapsulating the previous account. Reporters often are so consumed with adding fresh information to a second-day story that they assume the reader remembers all the details of its first run. This is particularly true in court stories because months or years may elapse between the incident and the trial or the appeal. In coding court stories, be certain that this brief recap is included.

Obviously, you'll need the first-day story as a point of reference for what must be resurrected and what can be omitted. Coding will prevent nonessential repetitions from the previous story (or stories if several follow-ups are involved) and guarantee that vital data are carried from story to story.

Editing a series of articles for organization follows the same rules and has the same problems. For one thing, it's essential that each person on the rim be familiar with *all* previous articles because it's unlikely one individual will edit the entire series. So never assume the cup won't pass your way. Read all articles in a series, even though they may not interest you.

A series should have a "standing" paragraph near the start of each article that sums up its overall thrust. Coding prevents the omission of that paragraph on subsequent articles.

Problems other than organization generally surface when a series is closely monitored. Writers often err on repeating names, dates, or facts as they move from article no. 1 even to article no. 2. Book authors are notorious for such "second-reference" mistakes, as when the heroine's blue eyes in Chapter 3 turn brown by Chapter 23. And they generally have far more watchdogs perusing their manuscripts than a series writer. The *New Yorker* magazine used to delight in unveiling such lapses in its "Our Forgetful Authors" fillers. But newspaper readers generally aren't amused. They rightly conclude that although much time, money, and effort have been spent for a series, minuscule errors indicate the reporting or the editing was sloppy, and so *any* future series will be of questionable value.

Some Last Words on Editing for Organization

Know that even great reporters on the nation's greatest papers sometimes fall into "hopscotch" organization and may blur or repeat major and minor elements of a story. Those slips may happen because of arrogance, befuddlement, or sloppiness, or because they believed yards-long anecdotes humanizing even a drainage board story would win more readers than a facts-only 5W lead. Extensive cutting-and-pasting on computer copy also might be blamed for poor structure, even though that usually reveals a reporter who spent little time organizing the story before doing the first interview and disdained a compass.

Other organizational errors get by copy editors awed by the reporter's reputation who forget their role of being a "scourge to the scribes," as one editor put it. Most copy editors are too busy to be charitable to ace reporters. One at the *Star Tribune* in Minneapolis shakes her head about the repairs she's had to make for a quarter of a century: "Some reporters who write 40-inch stories *never* get to the point," she said. "There's *never* even a nut graf."

All these causes for disorganization, however, are givens. The fact is that the copy editor's job is "to catch and repair" poor organization. Begin coding long stories by content and you'll see what a fast and effective editing technique it is to retain.

14 | Editing the Lead

Dead.
That was what the man was the
police found in an areaway last night.[1]

Brutal though the first sentence in the above example might seem, it's what the puckish James Thurber submitted years ago when the managing editor of *The New York Evening Post* commanded one-word leads on hard-news stories. He wanted them to have maximum impact on readers.[2]

Thurber became a famous author and illustrator of dry-humored books, and that *Post* editor relented *slightly* under a deluge of imaginative single-word leads.[3] Nevertheless, Thurber's lead became an indelible lesson to two generations of newspaper people: *The first three to five words* of a hard-news story should contain its gist, including a verb strong enough for that maximum impact on readers. A second sentence—or a second paragraph—should carry the attributions and identifications of sources. Then the story can unfold.[4]

Thurber's editor was on the right track. Readers may never get beyond the fifth word if the opening isn't meaty. Except for board members or environmentalists, how many readers will persist after encountering: "At a meeting yesterday . . ." or "According to one of Johnson County's Waste Water, Contamination, and Environmental Purity board members Mary Jane Eades and McKean County's Environmental Protection and Action Association president Claude B. T. Thibodeaux . . ."?

Editing Hard-News Leads

Seasoned copy editors know that a reporter who wastes those precious three to five words drives readers to other parts of the paper, to the 10 o'clock news, or to the Internet's 24-hour cable pages. In fact, with the increasing use of "infographics," readers may read only the bulleted and boxed nutshells of facts.

One solution to readers' short attention spans, born in the 1970s, has been the extended or anecdotal leads. But soon these "feature" spins were so overdone that some copy editors, tired of searching for headline clues, predicted they would be used on obituaries.[5]

Instances of literary leads, followed by even windier paragraphs, are not difficult to find. One copy editor, evidently worn down by bromides, wearily let this one slide by:

> There are times when truth really is stranger than fiction, says Police Capt. Howard Ralston.

The nine-inch account that followed could have been boiled to a two-paragraph summation of the arrest of a husband for hitting a police officer, disturbing the peace, and setting fire to his house, followed by the arrests of two men for battering him and another officer and "interfering with medical treatment."

The next example is a classic stopper, a lengthy "mare's nest" likely to confuse the most avid police-blotter readers:

> The former girlfriend of a man charged with killing a Middletown bar owner almost four years ago testified Monday that she had never seen another man who claims he killed the victim and that she was with him that night.[6]

A good copy editor would have cut through that tangle with something like this:

A man's assertion that he—not John Doe—should be on trial for murder was contradicted yesterday by his girlfriend.

Fortunately, the increasing number of blotter items and trials, even in small towns, has forced many copy editors to boil items to one or two paragraphs. This kind of "hard-editing" needs to be applied to all news. To combat escalating paper prices, publishers have begun saving their supplies by narrowing columns so that subscribers can be expected to demand "less art and more matter" that they can't see on TV or the Internet. A sharp copy editor, facing silly and biased delayed leads like these,

> All they wanted were a few good men.
>
> Five years ago the demand was for women, but having more than filled their affirmative-action quota within a few hours by January 1997 when new laws were in place, the county's voting registrar office began experiencing an exodus of men when eight out of the 18 on staff began agitating for transfers to other county offices, especially as deputies in the sheriff's office and on both the transit agency and water department.
>
> The office had a reputation of being a "chick place," according to Registrar Nona Petersen.
>
> Thanks to $384,912 in federal funds earmarked for the registrar's budget, that was reported at yesterday's county commission meeting, expansion of the office may attract 10 more men.

would cut to essentials in the lead's first three to five words, perhaps like this:

> Ten new positions will be available in the county registrar's office, beginning in July, thanks to $384,912 in federal funds reported at yesterday's county commission meeting.

Less *is* more. In the early 1990s, copy editors and a host of writing coaches like Jim Stasiowski began to make headway in urging a return to 5W leads (who, what when, where, why—and sometimes how). You might be hired by a desk demanding "immediate" leads that lay out the story's gist in the first three to five words. In features, the overall point needs to be foreshadowed in those openings, whether the reporter gets down to business at the outset or spins an enthralling feature lead told in the style of a Scheherazade tale.

Immediate Leads

"Immediate" leads in hard-news stories require most of the 5W's and should be set in the active-voice word order of subject-verb (e.g., "The Park board dedicated . . .").

The "what" tends to predominate as the first words in most immediate leads: "The Supreme Court left in doubt Tuesday the fate of . . ." "Fill dirt no longer will be sold by the . . ." "The Western Conference finals don't resume until Friday . . ." "Sarcasm in advertising was outlawed Tuesday by . . ."

A "who" lead should involve fatalities, crime, or celebrities known to the readership. Readers have few problems understanding these leads: "Cocaine users are 24 times more likely to have a heart attack . . ." "A ninth-grade dropout was executed Tuesday night . . ." "Hillary Rodham Clinton interviewed potential staffers Tuesday . . ."

The use of "where" in the first three to five words generally is reserved for major events like catastrophes or bombings, or acts of countries, public entities, or communities: "Morocco suffered its second earthquake Friday . . ." "A Bulgarian village was hit by NATO aircraft Wednesday . . ." "Portland will host the next Democratic convention . . ."

The "why" and "when" elements of the 5W's are almost always overshadowed by these three other W's in an immediate lead. The why generally is placed in a second paragraph if the who, what, and where pack the opening sentence.

The when element is seldom used in the first two or three words, but is present in that first sentence, as shown in the previous examples. Copy editors recognize that even veteran reporters sometimes either forget to include the when in a lead sentence or are unsure about its placement. The standard practice is to insert the when factor as close to the verb as possible.

Decades of readership studies warn against reporters using more than *20 words* in the lead's initial sentence. To retain readers, the best length is from 16 to 19 words of simple English—about 1.5 lines for copy set in 10-point type. But again, such brevity demands that the story's point be captured *in the first three to five words.*

If meat is provided in those initial words, a copy editor should examine the rest of the opening sentence to ensure that the other 5W's are set out in compact, declarative form with the attributions ("according to . . .") placed at the *end,* like this:

> A 5% tax break will go to property owners in the Overton subdivision next year if they can show at least $50,000 worth of improvements, *according to Friday's announcement from the Tax Assessor's office.*

Readers lose interest when a "straight-shot" sentence is interrupted with an attribution or comma-packed qualifiers:

> A 5% tax break, *according to an announcement Friday from the Tax Assessor's office,* will be given to property owners, providing they are in single-family residences, in the Overton subdivision.

The worst construction, and one guaranteed to drive readers straight to the comics or crossword puzzle, is for a reporter to snuff out the story's content with an attribution:

> *According to an announcement Friday from the Tax Assessor's office,* a 5% tax break will be given to prop-

erty owners, providing they are in single-family residences, in the Overton subdivision.

The copy editor's next priority is to ensure that a lead contains *strong* verbs. Considering that too many reporters lack the time, inclination, or vocabulary to select them, that job of energizing pallid verbs usually falls to the copy editor. The dull verb "set" in the following example

> The Vermillion Parish School Board is *set* to consider a mandatory-uniform policy for all public schools at its 6 p.m. meeting today.

can receive a boost if a copy editor selects a vibrant verb like "dressed." Selecting verbs with power or pizzazz provides this kind of vitality:

> The Vermilion Parish School Board *may be dressing* students next fall if it approves a mandatory-uniforms policy today at its 6 p.m. meeting.

Complex leads, such as those involving ordinary deeds of Congress, seize readers' attention if they have a touch of power or color. This example not only has two strong verbs, but both are backstopped by a carefully selected adjective and adverb:

> WASHINGTON (AP)—A $3 billion pool of federal money to help the welfare recipients with the toughest problems *break* into the work force has barely been tapped as states *scramble* to find clients who fit the strict rules.[7]

Adverbs, used with restraint, also can add life, as shown below:

> The defense rested *quickly and quietly* Tuesday in the trial of four police officers charged with beating of a Haitian immigrant.[8]

Editing Other Styles of Immediate Leads

Immediate leads that pose questions or use quotes have irked copy editors for generations because they are leftovers from high school journalism (as equally resented by many students for generations). They also steal space from other stories. The question, "Have you ever wondered why this school is so tough on hooky players?" is not too far afield from a professional reporter leading off with, "Ever wondered what goes on in the minds of court reporters as they transcribe testimony?" or the threatening "Have you looked at your IRA lately?" If question leads were tried out on colleagues *before* publication, reporters might learn that the universal response to this overused invasion of privacy is either a resounding "No!" or "What's it to you?"

An effective quote lead requires someone of celebrity stature saying something monumental. The famous quote "I came. I saw. I conquered." from Julius Caesar qualifies.

So does a former president's snappish "You won't have Richard Nixon to kick around anymore." But a quote by lesser lights insisting that "we need to think about the future" does not qualify.

If a quotation summarizes a story better than a paraphrase, it merits the lead's first five words. But content analyses generally reveal that most quotes are space wasters. Instead of being intimidated by exhibitionist writing, a fearless copy editor should have axed this unnecessary start and let the second paragraph serve as the lead:

> "Laissez les bons livres rouler!"
> "Let the good books roll" is the theme for the
> 1999 summer reading program beginning Monday,
> according to Barbara Mauseth, the parish librarian.

Some newspapers ban negative leads, believing the columns are so full of upsetting news that readers need a glass that is half full rather than half empty. Others, however, believe readers can stand unvarnished truths. A story reporting that a heavily used bridge would be shut down for the first three days of the week was deftly changed from negative predictions of a massive traffic snarl by a copy editor's positive spin:

> The Flagler Street bridge will reopen Thursday, following three days of repairs.

Delayed Leads

A delayed lead takes a paragraph or two to get to the nut graf that contains the 5W's ("Mary Rice's struggle to get off welfare is reflected in the federal report sent to the White House yesterday. She is among the thousands who . . ."). From there, the patient reader is transported into the body of the story.

The delayed lead was an outgrowth of feature stories that editors knew had high readership, especially if most of the news budget was grim. Readership studies in the late 1940s asking whether people had *seen* a story, read *any* of it, or read *all* of it seemed to reinforce the feature's popularity.

When studies in the 1970s suggested that news was very complex and needed interpreting, or at least less bluntness than the 5W's, the feature lead was "borrowed" for hard news. Part of what was called the "new journalism," such a lead provided the added flavor of a fictional writing style.[9] Never mind that most news was no more complex than it had ever been or that the preliminary studies for launching *USA Today* showed that readers wanted *shorter* stories with unadorned facts.[10]

Scheherazade's storytelling style was thus unloosed in the American newspaper, often by an anecdote ("explanations for dummies," one editor called them), to entice a reader into complex stories, like this one about molecular damage to spacecraft:

> Imagine you are whizzing through space on a peanut-butter-and-jelly sandwich. But just when you are settling in for the ride of a lifetime, you notice

that little critters are nibbling away the edges of the sandwich.

That's what engineers are rushing to combat before the next generation of spacecraft is lofted. And that's what was in the extra budgetary items for the space program that Congress approved late Thursday night.

Coding a story's structure reveals whether an anecdote is making speedy passage to the nut graf, mandatory for wire stories. Code the following example:

> **By MINERVA CANTO**
>
> TIJUANA (AP)—Nearly $200 worth of prescription drugs bulged from Barry Villafana's backpack after he left Farmacia Americana, one of a dozen drugstores drawing elderly Americans across the border.
>
> He drives 480 miles round trip from his Santa Barbara home to Tijuana every two months to stock up on medicine for his high cholesterol and arthritis.
>
> "The amount of drugs I could have bought with this money back home would barely fill a fanny pack," the 69-year-old retired factory worker said.
>
> Americans have long crossed into Mexico for inexpensive car repairs, discount clothes and cheap liquor. Now they're driving over the border to fill prescriptions, too.[11]

In the hands of gifted reporters, the delayed lead certainly has its place, but newsrooms often lack such talents, as most copy editors can attest. By the mid-1980s, when "literary journalism" was in flower, some editors feared slashing the fat lest some budding Norman Mailer huff out of the newsroom. The shrinking newshole has ended "pap attacks."

The "You" Lead

Delayed leads are not going to vanish overnight, though readers puzzled about a story's destination generally quit after the first sentence. The solution seems to be the use of the you-lead, which combines the best elements of the immediate and delayed forms.

A you-lead involves the reader in the first three to five words. It should swiftly dramatize the story's gist and rush the reader to the *second* paragraph for the 5W nuggets. Irreverently called the "you-hoo" lead by some copydesk wags, it's still the fastest getaway to a nut graf yet created, as the following two AP examples show:

> The cost of flying to your favorite vacation spot is up almost 11 percent this year after another fare increase from the major airlines at the start of the summer travel season.
>
> The third fare increase of 1999 is expected to stick since Northwest Airlines Corp. has gone along with a 4 percent increase levied by Continental Airlines last week.[12]

> If you join the staff of the new community college system at a salary of less than $50,000, you must be a clerk or a secretary.
>
> Even the clerks can make up to $32,000, the Senate Finance Committee was told Tuesday. Administrative secretaries can make up to $34,000.[13]

Editing Feature Leads

Writing consultants and coaches have escalated their war against the wordy lead, turning from hard news to features. Feature leads now need to be "short, sharp, and snappy," as one coach put it. These critics are as intolerant of massaging tender egos as Thurber's editor was. They have been instructing copy editors to warn reporters who refuse to tighten copy that the desk will pinch hit and turn that balk into a home run of brevity.

Released from the constraints of the 5W's to the spaciousness of a feature lead, many reporters still believe they have license to lolly-gag. In the example below, readers had to wade through three bloated paragraphs to learn that the story was about cemetery caretakers:

> Once they walked among us, laughing, yelling, whispering, keeping watch. We knew them. We spoke to them. We took them by the hand. We loved them. They were our friends, our families, our heroes. Now, in the crumbled earth, they are our memories, remaining in this world, if not visible to it.

Most copy editors would jump-start such leads to something like this:

> When you lay flowers at the gravesite of a loved one on Memorial Day, the only reason the grass is freshly mowed and the coffin hasn't been despoiled by vandals is because of those sentinels of the stone gardens: the cemetery caretakers.

The cemetery lead appeared in an alternate biweekly newspaper whose editors were desperate for free local features. But they're not alone in permitting bloat to float. A copy editor on a prestigious eastern daily seemed to be so intimidated by a junior Tom Wolfe's pseudocleverness that this confusing and patronizing lead appeared:

> Compatibility. That's a big word in computers, especially to novices who forever find themselves, hexagonal peg in hand, steam emanating from ears, staring at an octagonal hole; and who, in having the effrontery to think they can download with the big boys and girls, continually get messages like: "You just made a type x2z46tf error, you numskull!"

One newsroom sign says "The Lead Must Make the Reader Read," strongly emphasizing to *both* reporters and copy editors that a direct correlation exists between circulation growth and the lead, whether it's hard news or features. Reporters might have a thousand excuses to justify a slow trot into a feature, including their perception that readers actually like verbosity or the yarning of literary journalism. But copy editors know better. Most teach reporters that "more is *not* better" by using the delete key down to the nut graf.

15 | Editing the Close and Quotes

Little attention is usually paid to the "close" of a story in the training of copy editors. Some focus is placed on quotations, often because they are the first target for deletion when copy editors cope with a trim order (a.k.a. overset) from the slot.

During the Civil War, the wire services learned that editors refused to pay 10 or 12 cents per word for hot air, especially quotations. Today, AP watchdogs take a dim view of bureau staffs that "featherbed" by moving words seldom used by subscribers. Despite decades of complaints about AP style turning American newspapers into cookie-cutter products and about its periodic errors, its great contribution to the profession has been in offering copy editors and reporters the best and most inexpensive daily short course on editing staff-generated stories, from both substantive and technical standpoints.

One of the most subtle AP lessons to the nation's copydesks involves closes and quotes.

In wire or syndicated material from major newspapers such as *The New York Times* or the *Los Angeles Times*, copy editors for generations have relied on the judgment and efforts of Associated Press staff, scattered all over the globe, to assume responsibility for these two elements of stories. Harassed and shorthanded AP bureau staffers at least know better than to move an ending that's a variation on the old travelogue closer: "As the sun slowly sinks behind beautiful Tahiti . . ." or the bathos of: "After all, tomorrow is another day."

The Hard-News Close

Whether a close is in hard news or features, it must provide a sense of finality to the story. It can't seem to be the last paragraph before a jump. In this regard, that organizational coding system described in Chapter 13 is the best tool to determine if the reporter has written a close.

Because of the inverted-pyramid structure, a close in a hard-news story should contain the least important factors detailed in the copy. Coding will instantly reveal whether the reporter has conformed to that structure. Formula closes are dictated for several types of stories: obituaries, weddings, anniversaries, crime, lotteries, accidents, or future meeting items. All numbers should be double-checked—telephones, streets, zip codes—lest contributions go astray or someone be deluged with wrong numbers. A sampler of formula closes is below:

> The next Lotto Texas game will be held Saturday night for an estimated $18 million jackpot.[1]

> The woman, who was not identified, was brought to a hospital and treated for unspecified injuries, officials said.[2]

> For information or to pick up an application and rules, stop at the Carnegie Library, 830 N. Jefferson Ave., or call 475-5290.

Sports closes tend to provide period scorings or background material:

> Malone is the first MVP in nine seasons to fail to take his team to at least the conference finals. Magic Johnson's Los Angeles Lakers also were upset in the second round of the playoffs in 1990.[3]

A story about a job promotion should end with a sentence or paragraph that includes *minor* attainments or data not particularly related to the new position, as well as what happened to the person who had the job. If reporters don't recognize the *least* important factor in biographical data, a copy editor must. Profile closes usually are handled like this:

> Rivlin was nominated to be vice chair of the Fed by Clinton in 1996. At the time, she was serving as head of the president's Office of Management and Budget, where she had the reputation as one of the administration's leading deficit hawks.[4]

> Smith succeeds Joel P. Campo, who held that position from 1996–98, and will head the San Pedro agency.

Public meetings with lengthy agendas pose a major challenge for both reporter and desk in determining the close's content ("In other business, the board approved . . ."). With the inverted-pyramid structure, minor items generally are grouped in the close. A copy editor must be familiar with the community and its priorities so that items in the close are indeed *minor*. That knowledge can be obtained only by staying current with public issues and expenditures. As already noted, a new copy editor needs to read a few months of back issues to learn about those priorities.

For reader comprehension, no more than four items should be included in a sentence. Use the items that were *passed* to lead that closing sentence. The second sentence lists the *rejected* items; the third, the items that were *tabled*. In case of a tight trim, the sentence with the tabled items can be deleted. The following example shows how to do it:

> The commissioners also approved inviting bids for a woodchipper, and an ordinance forbidding county property owners to permit or allow the growth of noxious weeds or grass on vacant lots, and tabled a hearing request for obtaining a variance to change a residential zone to a business zone at 143 S. Washington Ave. They rejected liquor licenses for

KC's Quik Grocery, the Tack Room, and the Blue
Heaven cafe, and unanimously refused to accept a
quitclaim deed from the Union Pacific Railroad for
its station on Dover St.

The same criteria are applied with wire or syndicated copy covering the state legislature or congressional news. The close on an
overall agenda should gang "other key bills." If separate issues warrant separate paragraphs, the close might be written like this:

The vote comes a month after the House approved
a $12,000 annual raise for Louisiana sheriffs. HB1405
goes to the Senate for consideration.[5]

Closes for all other types of hard-news stories will stop being a
dilemma when you realize that minor factors usually involve at least
four things: history, future significance, tidbits of extra information,
and warnings, as the following examples demonstrate:

The Past
The fatalities are the first aboard a U.S. air carrier
since turbulence aboard a United Airlines 747 killed
a woman Dec. 28, 1997, over the Pacific Ocean.[6]

The Future
If the Ahtisaari-Chernomyrdin peace plan is
eventually put into action, the NATO-led peace-
keepers will face a difficult mission, from coping
with chancy Russian participation to demilitarizing
ethnic Albanian guerrillas and avoiding land mines,
U.S. officials said Sunday.[7]

The Tidbit
The new cathedral in the northern farming
community is the seventh largest in Europe and
towers over the rolling countryside. Longer than a
soccer field and as tall as a 30-story building, it is
being constructed at an estimated cost of $50 million,

all coming from donations, to honor the church's 2,000 years of Christianity next year.[8]

The Warning
Fannie Mae is giving mortgage companies until January 2001 to implement the change. Homeowners should still check with their lender to see if they can cancel PMI when equity reaches 20%.[9]

Feature-Story Closes

The French writer Anatole France built his famous story "The Procurator of Judaea" around an imaginary windup quote of Pontius Pilate. Most of the plot involves fictional reminiscences between the aging Pilate and an old friend who meet at an Italian coastal resort. In the final paragraphs, the friend inquires about the troubled days in Jerusalem and a "young Galilean thaumaturgist" from Nazareth named Jesus. "Pontius, do you remember anything about the man?" he asks. Pilot "probes the deeps of memory" and then the author stuns readers with this ironic closer:

> "Jesus?" he murmured, "Jesus—of Nazareth? I cannot call him to mind."[10]

Talented reporters also have an uncanny sense of whether to leave readers laughing, crying, or thinking, or to give them a visceral blow to heart or the intellect. Careful editing and a sense of literary style must be accorded feature stories, as has been mentioned, because hard editing *has* destroyed many articles, especially in giving away surprise endings.

A gem usually will travel well, with no need of editing, straight onto a page. But a poor close requires either refining or telling the reporter that "it just doesn't come off," followed by laying out the array of known choices appropriate to the article's content or tenor: the strong statement, the firecracker, the tieback anecdote paired to the lead, or the splenic punch.

Unfortunately, many features close with a quotation, that over-used tool of amateurs and the unimaginative or lazy. Anatole France probably would have shunned this familiar, callous, and inane quote about the upside of downsizing:

> "We believe that we need to streamline our operation and make our organization more effective," he said.[11]

Far tougher to create are strong statements ("If you're home alone, you're probably sitting with a killer") or snappers like "Hayden had seen the pillar of salt and found he preferred a little pepper." Tieback closes take some skill in designing the bookends of connective anecdotes for lead and close:

The Lead
Marisa Coupe was the kind of A student who stole reserve books out of the library and complained violently about cheating whenever anyone threatened to surpass her overall GPA of 3.9.

The Tieback Close
These days, Marisa Coupe is just grateful to be able to put a small string of words together, but she still speaks up when she suspects cheating.

Editing Quotations

For well over a century, most copy and wire editors have counted on those unsung journalists to sort through a mountain of quotes and select only the most significant. The AP rarely moves copy that is more than 15 percent quotations unless it is a major document, like the text of a president's speech, or it concerns sports.[12] In disasters, AP might send client papers tired and obvious quotes ("A lot of the roads are closed in different areas because of low-water crossings").[13]

But most of its fare is rarely bromidic unless the quote is from a Miss America winner or from a coach like Mike Ditka, as shown below:

> That's when I knew that God was teasing me, and that I could possibly achieve the title of Miss America.[14]
>
> **(Miss Florida)**

> "I think we're a better football team. I keep saying that every year because we are," Ditka said. "We have the best receivers we've had in three years here. I think running backs are better than we've been in three years. Offensive line: I know we're better than we've been in three years. I see a lot of good things happening on this team. You can see body changes in people. The attitude is great. Now we've got to take that to the playing field."[15]
>
> **(Mike Ditka)**

One cardinal rule in writing and editing is that quotation marks should never be placed around an indirect quote, no matter how much stronger or brighter the copy would be if the reporter (or copy editor) put words in a source's mouth. The newspaper business has had trouble enough over the years with sources falsely shouting that they were "misquoted" or "quoted out of context" after their loose lips got them in trouble. Adding quotation marks where they don't belong will only prove them right.

Most reporters work hard to obtain direct quotes and to ensure that they are accurate. Sadly, more than 95 percent of those remarks could be paraphrased or omitted. It's one thing when a national or local figure resigns with a paragraph-long explanation, but too many of those statements, especially at the local level, resemble clichés like this:

> "It is with the greatest regret to my constituents in the 4th ward and to this city that I find I must resign

from the council at this time. I know the ward's needs of solid representation are great, especially for the 12th Street pocket park and resurfacing of Broad Street. My constituents know I have put every ounce of my energies into serving their needs. My record over the last six years shows how hard I worked to try to represent my people. I believe I can say I "have fought the good fight and I have kept the faith in being the 4th ward's good steward.

"But the needs of my job, family, and health need to be placed ahead of such important civic duties. I regret deeply that, effective October 19, I will no longer be your strong voice on the council. But I am sure that my successor will carry on my long tradition of service to the 4th ward, something you have a right to expect."

This story could be pared to the bone and lose nothing in the translation, like this:

> Council member Lydia Tanner-Sjelbostead, of the 4th ward, resigned this morning citing job, family and health reasons.

You don't have to be a crusty copy editor to recognize that politicians, in particular, should buy an ad for their arrivals or their swan songs. If a reporter permits any story to be consumed by self-serving or say-nothing platitudes, a copy editor's obligation, to space and readers, is to delete or paraphrase. Quotes should never consume more than 15 percent of a story and should meet three qualifications or else be paraphrased or deleted. To survive, a "hot" quote should be:

- Earth-shattering—or at least significant and meaty
- Something said in a colorful or an imaginative way
- Illustrative of a source's personality

Quotes in wire copy generally meet these qualifications—except in sports stories. But staff-generated copy too often contains quotes that are nothing more than padding or are banal, obvious, or just plain awful. When sources say, "You just have to believe in yourself and start to do it," or "We need to do some long-range planning," or "Our bench has been an important part of the team effort," these quotes aren't earthshaking, colorful, clever, or illustrative. Repetition over the years has rendered them meaningless.

The tradition of the copydesk has been to cut the puffery and padding furnished by quotes, whether in wire copy or generated by staff and stringers. Readers paying nearly half a dollar for a paper should get wheat, not chaff—and they *do* know the difference.

Content analyses of many papers probably would substantiate copydesks' abdication of this mandate, if a monthlong study of one daily is any indication. The results showed that an average of 18 percent of hard-news and feature copy was allotted to quotes, largely provided by regional reporters. Most of those quotes could have been paraphrased or omitted. In local sports, 21 percent of stories were expended on quotes, making that department the biggest offender in letting bloat float. Local hard-news stories had an average of 16 percent of the content devoted to quotes, but a significant 30 percent was contained in local features.[16] If you circled quotes in your local paper for a week— an excellent assignment for both beginning reporters and copy editors—you would undoubtedly gather similar statistics.

Moreover, quotes cripple writing because accuracy forces reporters to carve copy to fit *around* the statement, creating awkward writing and organizational problems and often losing control of the story altogether. That tempts writers to change the quote "slightly" to fit a point, which in turn justifies complaints of "I was misquoted."

Detecting "Phony" Quotes

Another test of the copy editor's experience and intuition is detecting phony quotes—remarks never uttered. Phony quotes usually appear in features and in series, most often penned by arrogant reporters or freelance writers, many clinging to the "artistic license" of literary journalism. Habitual quote fabricators often are so forceful or so articulate that they make cowards of some copy editors fearful of newsroom scenes. One such reporter justified phony quotes and names by saying he couldn't get his sources to verbalize the tenor of a situation and claimed a famous editor once told writers to "never let a name stand between you and a good quote." Only when that reporter became a professional writer and a magazine's researchers reported difficulty locating his sources did he mend his ways.[17]

This practice was spotlighted in a 1991 landmark lawsuit—*Masson v. The New Yorker*—when writer Janet Malcolm was sued by psychiatrist Jeffrey Masson for putting words into his mouth. He charged that they were inaccurate and libelous.[18] In the Malcolm case, the Supreme Court ruled against her defense that it's permissible to put quotes around a source's words if they are "rational interpretations of ambiguous" statements that don't "alter the substantive content" of what's said. Noting that she "deliberately or recklessly altered" five out of the six quotations at issue, the Court sent the case back to the lower court.[19] Two subsequent trials (1993, 1994), however, appeared to give her and all other writers the right to coin phony quotes.[20] Yet the case is not closed. Aside from the ruinous legal expenses to the publishers and Malcolm, the Supreme Court's ruling gave a clear warning of how it will rule in quotation questions in the next go-round:

> In general, quotation marks indicate a verbatim reproduction, and quotations add authority to a statement and credibility to an author's work. A fabricated quotation may injure reputation by attributing an untrue factual assertion to the speaker, or by indicating a negative personal trait or an attitude the speaker does not hold. . . . Malcolm's work gives the reader no clue that the quotations are anything but the reproductions of actual conversations, and the work was published in a magazine that enjoyed a reputation for scrupulous factual inquiry. These factors could lead a reader to take the quotations at face value.[21]

The only "researchers" on a newspaper are copy editors, and nothing will stop the habit of phony quotes faster than a request for contacting the source to verify a quote. If you encounter a defensive writer, chances are you have detected a phony quote. Bear down and ask why a *named* source cannot be contacted about a quote. If the writer persists and gets threatening, back off, but clear the quote with the slot to protect the paper. You may stave off a lawsuit or the embarrassment of a Masson-type situation.

Editing Quotes from the Unschooled or Foreign Born

When one Confederate editor finally tired of an unschooled general like Nathan Bedford Forrest who had a godlike reputation, alternately thrilling Rebels and terrifying Yankees, he sought to tumble and humble the fierce and boastful cavalry raider by the cruel technique of having a soldier correspondent quote him verbatim in a fiery pep talk to the troops.[22] Clearly this was no gentrified West Pointer like Robert E. Lee speaking:

> Well, soldiers, I came here to jine you. I'm gwine to show you the way into Tennessee. . . . I come down here with three hundred and fifty men. I got thirty-five hundred conscripts. Since May I have fought in every county in West Tennessee. I fought in the streets of Memphis, and the women run out in their night clothes to see us, and they will do it again in Nashville. I have fought a battle every twenty-five days. I have seen the Mississippi run with blood for two hundred yards, and I'm gwine to see it again. I've captured seventy-eight pieces of artillery and sixteen thousand Yankees, and buried twenty-five hundred of them.[23]

Forrest's publisher friends and civilians and Confederate troopers rose to his defense with a thunderous "so what!!" response. As for that army correspondent, he was killed in Forrest's next battle, and perhaps not by Yankee bullets. That might not happen to the reporter or publisher who decides to ridicule a public figure's poor language skills, but even opponents cry "foul" by letters to the editor, calls, public attacks, and cancelled subscriptions. Attempts to blemish reputations by the device of verbatim reporting—including all the "uhs," "y'knows," and misuses of "I" for "me"—generally backfire into sympathy for the victim. Readers will tolerate it for hot news such as the tapes from a crashed airliner's black box or a president's recordings, but not when meanness is intended.

The general rule on thousands of copydesks is to fix *minor* errors in syntax and grammar, whether it's an unlettered council member or a star athlete. But if *major* plastic surgery is required, copy editors generally remove the quotes and paraphrase the remarks.

What about quotes from a foreigner newly arrived whose command of English is minimal? Again, fairness and common sense should come into play through the use of paraphrasing and partial quotes if the reporter fails to make those changes. Copy editors ought to be able to refashion remarks about, say, the eleventh hole. "Difficult." What does the exchange student like best so far about the States? "Disney World."

Which Quotes Should Be Killed?

Where space is at a premium, a quote from the fire chief or police shouldn't crowd out vital information. Most of these statements are made under duress anyway and usually are of the "this-is-the-worst-[fire, disaster, crime]-I've-ever-seen" genre. Unless officeholders confess to crimes or suddenly resign, their statements tend to be timeworn ("It's time we tell Washington where to get off"; "We all need to pull together on this problem").

AP keeps quotes to a minimum unless they involve sports[24] or statements from world figures. Pope John Paul II's remarks in his homeland (Poland) did consume 35 percent of one story. But his remarks warranted that space, given that the pontiff announced the church's epochal, if hedged, turnabout on Copernicus's view that the

Earth revolves around the sun instead of the church's ancient view
that the reverse was true:

> "The discovery made by Copernicus and its
> importance for the history of science, remind us of the
> ever-present tension between reason and faith. . . .
> This progress gives rise to both wonderment and fear.
> Man is becoming ever more fearful of the products of
> his own intelligence and freedom. . . . Concern for the
> moral conscience and the sense of individual
> responsibility has today become a fundamental
> imperative for men and women of science."[25]

When an American president or a celebrity is known to speak
with a "many-forked tongue," the wire service does supply the seemingly mundane words so that readers can examine them minutely.
Copy editors for years have delighted in boiling the two or three
paragraphs of "gas" into two or three words rather than permit national or regional politicians to use the newspaper as a free forum.
Some copy editors just vaporize the wire service quotes entirely.

How different things are with stories involving local windbags or
opportunists when the authors are only a few steps away from the
copy editor. In fairness, many cub reporters are unfamiliar with platitudes and can be taken in by smooth talkers or motormouths who
are in public life or private charities. Some cub reporters believe such
utterances are monumental, and their naiveté can be forgiven—at
the start. But when they persist in using quotes similar to those
below, a copy editor needs to explain to them why they were deleted:

> "This is a city in which I chose to live and raise a
> family. I see this as a chance to serve the people of this
> city, to help the city move forward. I look forward to
> working with the other members of the council."

Sports departments have sources that supply colorful quotes,
many because they are uninhibited or unlettered. Some athletes like

Dizzy Dean, Mohammed Ali, and Casey Stengel have made state-ments so memorable that they're in quotation anthologies. Their successors can offer just as much "good copy," but wire and local re-porters seem unable to kill quotes that had whiskers decades ago, like these:

> "I felt good out there. . . . I was able to throw strikes and the defense was there behind me."

> "We're real excited about the condition of the course. The players are going to have a golf course that is in premier condition. It's never been better."

In sum, where quotes are concerned, the copy editor must be able to recognize pap even without the goad of a trim order. Either kill extraneous quotes or paraphrase them. As one copy editor put it, "When I see quotation marks, I ask myself, is this quip hot or nec-essary?" Paired with the three qualifications for retaining quotes, that's good advice.

Partial Quotes

Some desks ban partial quotes (a.k.a. fragmentary quotes of one word or one phrase). They look like this:

> The mayor said that he would "fine-tune" measures planned for that exigency.

> The first-time angler said this event constituted the "happiest" day of her life.

> He told reporters he "found" that pension funds had been automatically siphoned into annuities with no notification to recipients.

Some editing experts see nothing wrong with partial quotes, es-pecially if the words are not simple or they either give the flavor of the occasion or fulfill the same qualifications for full quotes. Yet if a partial quote qualifies, why not use the full quote?

Most partial quotes stem from reporters' attempts to paraphrase while giving readers a taste of statements. Readers don't interpret things that way, however. Most conclude that quotation marks on plain words give a special meaning, something significant—or insidious. Partial quotes also open newspapers to the charge of taking statements out of context, and rightly so. Beyond all this, partial quotes prevent readability. The antidote is simple: Delete the quotation marks on partial quotes. Only a scholarly work has quote marks on single words.

Partial quotes also can lead to awkward second references. A classic example involved President Harry Truman:

> Mr. Truman smilingly conceded that he "feels more kindly toward newspapermen, now that one is about to become a member of his family."[26]

In other words, the reporter had Truman saying, "I feels more kindly toward newspapermen, now that one is about to become a member of his family."

Placement of Quotation Attributions

The worst placement for an attribution such as "he said" is in the middle of the quote because it short-circuits the power of a sentence, as shown below:

> "We have never," Ernst said, "knowingly shipped any guns that must be assembled to teenagers."

For maximum clarity and effective presentation of a short quote, put the attribution *after* the statement:

> "We have never knowingly shipped any guns that must be assembled to teenagers," Ernst said.

Where long quotes of one paragraph are concerned, readers have a right to know at the outset who's being quoted as well as that person's authority to make such statements.

Place the attribution at the start of the sentence leading into the quote, like this:

> Even when Civil War generals like Sherman and Bragg were trying to cover up mistakes obvious to soldiers and civilians by gagging the press, *The Memphis Daily Appeal's* great owner and editor thundered: "The public actions of public men are public property, and those who would censure the press for a candid scrutiny and a fair criticism of those actions has lost his allegiance to liberty, and has a forehead ready for the pressure of the despot's heel."[27]

If the paper tolerates long-winded quotes by more than two individuals, reporters might know who said what, but the reader doesn't. Again, the rule speaks to clarity: Give the attributions of both at the start of their quotations.

16 | Adds and Trims

In some parts of the world—the Mideast, for example—compositors believe that output is of such a creative and sacred nature that even a comma should be exempt from being trimmed. In Beirut, during the days of "hot type" and the Linotype machine, the Western world's "hellbox" was unknown, that wooden box into which left-over lead type was tossed for remelting.[1] Also unknown was "over-set," the unused type from a story, or a "bank" lodging preset material to use at a later date or to fill space.

At the Beirut *Daily Star,* when I first inserted a new lead from a wire story and marked the former one for deletion, the shop foreman refused to make the change and, eyes blazing, screamed, "Men set!!" To kill their creation was appalling and spoke to the usual wasteful practices in American shops. The "dead" type began appearing as space fillers that convulsed our readers, and the men darkly hinted at revolt if this lack of planning continued. To comply meant exactitude in estimating how much type equaled a centimeter and not using stories that didn't fill the finished pages exactly.

Stateside, editors try not to have the local staff write more copy than can be fitted into the newshole. But even with this saving of energy and even if a major story doesn't "tear up" the pages, copy editors still need to obey orders for adding or trimming stories so that paginators or those who paste up pages won't have either yards of overset or big holes to fill. Fudging a trim or add order creates problems in production. Don't do it.

Your job is to note that trim or add order and to determine what material in the copy must be killed or how to add material. Most newspaper staffs, including the printers, recognize that copy editors are the "supreme court" on what *is* essential to a story. So valued is their judgment about writing, in fact, that their decisions concerning adds and trims are rarely questioned. You need to think about that factor instead of perceiving that adds and trims are irksome forays through copy.

Determining those adds and fills involves basic knowledge of typography or just a good "eye." Copy set in 10-point type for 12-pica columns may require a ratio of four or five lines per inch.[2] Raw typed copy, set with margins of 10–80, also tends to measure out to four or five lines per column inch. These measurements depend on the type's design as well as the number of thin letters like *i* and *l* and thick letters like *w* and *m* are included in the paragraph.

The popular Nimrod font's *m,* for example, has a different width than, say, an *m* set in Ionic or Caslon. The difference between paragraphs heavy with thin and wide letters is shown below. Three lines include nine sets of *i, l,* and *f,* but seven sets of *m, w,* and 4:

> This is a line of type loaded with the letters i, l, and f, and more i, l, and f, i, l, and f, i, l, and f, i, l, and f, i, l, and f, i, l, and f, i, l, and f, i, l, and f, i, l.

> This is a line of type loaded with the letters m, w, and 4, and m, w, 4, and m, w, 4, and m, w, 4, and m, w, 4, and m, w, 4, and m, w, 4, and m, w, 4.

Adds

Adding copy generally is done by *reparagraphing* to pad out the fit— depending on whether the story is hard news or a feature.

Hard news requiring only an additional inch means careful examination of one or two paragraphs containing material that can be *logically* reparagraphed. If the slot's order calls for adding three or four inches or more, the copy editor's chief recourse is to target additional paragraphs and make new paragraphs out of the sentences. That technique may puzzle English teachers and some readers insisting a para-

graph contain only one thought. If an add order is even more extensive, ask the slot to find another story to fill such a hole.

Because reparagraphing can destroy a feature story, either show
reporters a printout of your reparagraphing or ask them to do the
adds. They alone have the data and sources to provide the additional
information.

Trims

"Country correspondence," the chatty news used in weeklies and
small dailies, is perhaps the only copy exempt from "trim" orders.
Newsroom beginners laugh—initially, anyway—at this marginally
written, name-pocked copy submitted by stringers (usually elderly
women at the center of village life). However, publishers, editors, and
circulation departments know that names not only make news, but
sell papers by the score. Hundreds of rural subscribers will buy extra
copies containing names or events involving the friends and relatives.
Publishers like Ken Byerly at the Lewistown (Montana) *Daily News*
saw correspondents as gold. He staged annual Correspondents Day
luncheons to honor those "circulation builders," offering plaques and
praise along with sessions on news-gathering techniques and writing
tips. Only the foolhardy would ever hard-edit this kind of name-
filled copy. The correspondents are responsible for the correct
spelling of those names, but you need to double-check them, letter by
letter, from copy. The story below will sell extra copies:

By GRAYCE PRICE
MILLIKIN's BEND—The Carl Sonnier family
just returned from Detroit where they took delivery
on a new Ford Escort. Betty and Carl took their two
grandsons, Kyle and Bobby Branson (children of the
former Keri Sonnier, who's now Mrs. Bradley
Branson, Jr.) with them.

They went through Vicksburg and met with their
daughter Keri which is where they picked up the
grandsons. They had a grand time, they report, and

the new car, which grandson Kyle drove behind them—he got his license in January. And he drove well, Grandpa reports.

Visitors at the Voight Broussard home for the Easter holidays included her aunt and uncle, Martin and Mary Kleinman of Bismarck, N.D.

The valedictorian at Millikins Bend Consolidated High School No. 102 will be split this year between Chad Bouvier and Juli Anne Talbott. They both have maintained a 4.0 grade-point average since they entered Millikins Bend Junior High School.

The overall guideline on trimming *all* other stories—hard news or features, wire or local copy—requires coding for organization to detect extraneous areas that can be deleted without harming the content. Many writers admit having difficulty discerning excess baggage because of their parental role in creating the stories. They generally accept (and often never even notice) the judgment of copy editors who have no compunctions about ruthlessly trimming "fat" from a story. They recognize that space is expensive and to be conserved for substance.

The order of trims generally begins with "surgery" on *paragraphs,* then *sentences,* and, last, extraneous *words,* especially if their deletion will kill short last lines ("widows").

Major Trims

The first target for major trims in *all* stories should be quotations, as emphasized in the previous chapter. Coding certainly will reveal whether the story will fall apart if certain quotes are removed. Deleting quotations is a fast and simple method of fulfilling a trim order because they often consume an inch or two. However, make sure that the quoted material—especially in features—is either paraphrased elsewhere or is totally unnecessary. In controversial issues where fairness is essential, both sides should have "their say," not necessarily in length, but in the heft of what is said. For features, show the authors your cuts or let them make the trims.

The next major target in hard-news stories involves "cutting from the bottom." If 20 lines of overset are indicated, either kill the last 20 lines or hunt through the story for paragraphs, sentences, or enough words to kill "widows," those short last lines of a paragraph.

Reporters should be structuring the story in an inverted pyramid so that it *can* be cut back to the lead and still stand as a 5W news brief. But before performing radical surgery, scroll up and down the screen or scan the hard copy for the targeted area to ensure that the trimmed material *is* unnecessary to the story.

Hard copy offers the advantage of allowing you to see the *entire* piece at a glance before slashing material or marking every sentence for paragraphing. Don't render a cut illegible by countless strokes across the copy because you or the editor may have second thoughts. Or the dead copy may need to be resurrected for another edition and compositors won't be able to read it. If that section is to be restored, box and mark the entire area "stet" (Latin for "leave [the copy] as it was") for resetting.

A computer kill on a system such as Atex "grays out" (or dims) the deleted copy so it's still visible. The material can be restored for those second thoughts or second editions.[3]

Features should not be hacked so brutally that the story's heart and soul shrivel. Don't kill the throb of cadence and style that's attained by repetition of words and phrases, especially when followed by a powerful end-stop like the following lead by a famed Confederate correspondent cataloguing Civil War devastation to his state:

> The condition of North Mississippi is deplorable. Mention the name of a town in that raid ridden section, and I will tell you it is burned. Ride with me twenty miles south of the Memphis and Charleston railroad, and I will show you charred chimneys, and little fields of luxuriant rose bushes; nothing else remains of all that made that section as prosperous

and pleasant as any spot in the Confederacy. The
Yankees have been there, and it is a wreck.[4]

Notebook Dumping and Stray-Fact Hitchhikers

Few copy editors feel guilty about savage trims to wire or syndicated
hard news or features written by faceless reporters across the nation
or halfway around the world. Wire service reporters know client papers don't run everything they write. Their output may be trimmed
back to the leads, or data that were difficult or expensive to obtain
may be expunged. But desks also have experience with wire or syndicated reporters "dumping their notebooks" or sneaking in what
writing consultant Jim Stasiowski calls "hitchhikers," the "stand-
alone stray facts" that have little to do with the story's thrust.[5]

How different it is for copy editors to process the work of staff
reporters who have the same habits, but sit at keyboards just across
the newsroom and socialize around the canteen coffeepot. Super-
sensitive to trims of "my best stuff," they make their displeasure
known to editors and publishers. Happily, they are usually all bark
and no bite and *do* trust a copy editor's judgment. In hard news,
notebook dumping or trivia hitchhiking ends only when copy editors consistently kill sections that may be highly interesting or en-
tertaining, but are also highly irrelevant space wasters.

Moreover, because of the brevity of newspaper writing, readers
seeing a stray fact such as "the Sistine's fresco has 343 different
faces," cannot help concluding that piece of information *must* have
some major bearing on the rest of the feature. When it doesn't, they
get irked. One irascible deskman used to sting perpetrators by asking, "What's this [the stray fact] got to do with the price of milk?" A
kinder and far more productive response to notebook dumping or
trivia hitchhiking is to acknowledge the reporter's research, but to
point out that the "factoid" doesn't fit the piece and should be saved
for another story. Most professional writers *do* sense nonpertinence
and have a file drawer or two full of data for future stories.

Minor Trims

When trim orders are minor (an inch or so), copy editors generally tighten the story by focusing on sentences and replacing long words with short ones.

One helpful feature of some computer software that hard copy doesn't offer for tightening sentences is the grammar-checker tool. It has been programmed to catch strings of prepositional phrases ("Smith said he was going *to the station in the main square at the Market Street entrance of the downtown area*"). The grammar-checker also warns that phrase-laden sentences present readability problems. When it "bells" the prepositions, recast the sentences containing this flaw.

Another technique for fulfilling trims is finding a sentence over-packed with information, much of it involving those hitchhikers. We can criticize authors of science and mathematics textbooks when they cram so much material into a single sentence that students can't understand it. But some reporters are just as guilty. Their sentences are called "portmanteau" (a large traveling bag) by newspapering's master grammarian, James J. Kilpatrick. He chose the word "portmanteau" perhaps because it certainly applies to a sentence like this one:

> She was shot through the right lung after confronting a woman married to her ex-husband inside the Food World Store on Bankhead Highway shortly before 1 p.m.[6]

Portmanteau sentences also include noninformative wordiness and gobbledygook that a copy editor must rewrite. Take this sentence of 15 lines from a school board story:

> It was the considered opinion of the superintendent of schools when he addressed the board that the proclivities and predilections of eligible faculty

> affecting to elect the option of the district's current rest
> and relaxation program made it mandatory for the
> administration to implement with all deliberate speed
> a mandatory policy of surveillance with regard to
> utilization of this period of non-teaching.

That sentence can be trimmed drastically by eleven lines if a copy editor translates it into a compact, uncluttered, and meaty declarative sentence in the first three to five words:

> Faculty rest-and-relaxation leaves will be moni-
> tored by the administration.

This system works well also for condensing stories concerning legislatures, commissions, or councils. Reporters often get entangled in the language of a bill or ordinance and fail to make its gist clear, like this:

> The council voted 7–6 to oppose the zoning
> board's approval by 4–1 last week in recommending
> that St. Barnabas hospital be permitted to buy the
> 150-acre site on Airport Road.

The copy editor's rewrite cut one line and even clarified the issue:

> The council voted 7–6 against Mercy hospital's
> plans to buy 150 acres on Airport Road despite the
> zoning board's approval (4–1) last week.

Gobbledygook and insider jargon are used either because reporters don't understand what their sources have said—the verbatim approach puts the burden on readers—or because they've stopped being the public's watchdog and have become a lapdog of the public group they're supposed to be covering. In short, when combing through sentences to fulfill trim orders, boil them back to the basics for reader comprehension.

Lancing the Boils and Bloodsuckers in Sentences

The average line of type in most 12-pica columns includes about four or five words. "Microediting" it may be, but copy editors know that if they can delete those few words, they've trimmed a line. More than this, they often undergo an awareness of what one writing coach calls "the bloodsuckers of a good sentence." Another coach says that copy editors have an obligation to "lance the boils" in a sentence. This kind of awakening means recognizing the clutter of meaningless terms like "in order" and unnecessary qualifiers like "very," "really," and "extremely," or expletives like "there is/are" that slow down the action. Examine the familiar "boils" and "bloodsuckers" in this short list below and get out the lancet because they weaken sentences:

a lot	in reality	little	truly
extremely	in short	pretty	very
in fact	in sum	rather	when asked
in order	kind/sort of	there are/is	which are/is

Be warned that the word "very" used as an adverb has vociferous defenders—but few on copydesks—who argue that it has been adding muscle to verbs since the fourteenth century. Opponents urge selecting a verb strong enough to avoid this adverbial bodyguard. Some slots train rookies to substitute "very" with "damned" to see just how unnecessary "very" is.

Taut editing means that copy editors can also prune some articles (the, an) as well as prepositions (e.g., on, at, and in) and conjunctions (e.g., and, or, and nor). Other unnecessary words contain the two suffixes—"ize" and "wise"—that used to make slots apoplectic. Yet

several have wormed their way into common usage today: hospitalize, traumatize, internalize, maximize, and personalize. Suffixes such
as "wise" that have made end runs around too many copy editors and
are now firmly cemented into the language are clockwise, lengthwise, likewise, streetwise, and otherwise. AP warns copy editors
about "contrived combinations such as moneywise, religionwise."[7]

Awareness of redundancy, even if it appears picayune, also will
aid a trim. When a reporter ends a news brief with "The public is
invited (urged/welcomed)," change the story to indicate, perhaps in
the lead, that the meeting is "open." When you list the names of participants, does the story need an enumeration? ("They included the
five children, Matthew, Mark, Luke, John, and Carter.") And is
"four" necessary in the following: "Among the *four* classes participating were freshmen, sophomores, juniors, and seniors."

So when doing a trim, make sure every quote, every paragraph,
every sentence, and every word are vital to the story. If not, wield the
scalpel or the axe.

17 | Editing Stories Involving Numbers

A fear of mathematics—mathophobia—afflicts many reporters and copy editors, especially stories about taxes, stocks, banking, and utility-rate increases. Some pray that the wire services and Federal Reserve Board spokesmen never err. Yet press-association workshops on "numbers for dummies" have few attendees, because of either pride or a lifetime intimidation about math. Yet database resources are providing statistical records that must be translated for readers.[1] One professor noted that the potential for any change seemed discouraging:

> Colorado State University requires every student to complete three credits of basic math—just three. Yet some journalism students have failed to graduate because they couldn't whip the math. Others put it off as long as possible, dreading any number manipulation more sophisticated than counting their change at the local coffeehouse.[2]

Admittedly, math too often has been imparted by teachers and textbooks catering to the few who instantly grasp abstract concepts. One grade school teacher gave a rough estimate that her arithmetic "whizzes" constituted only 5 percent of her classes. Their memorization powers were awesome, and their hands were always the first raised when asked to solve problems in their heads. By contrast, most journalists seem to have been part of the schoolroom masses who could think only in tangibles and could never solve even relevant problems under stopwatch conditions. Nor would they memorize anything perceived as nonessential. Add to this an impatient math teacher's ridicule, and it's no mystery why so many still believe they are math dunces. Worse, they carry this view into newspapering.

Few are really dunces, however. It's just that math teaching is not geared to mathophobes, and no revolt is yet in sight about rigid, age-old teaching methods. Yet mathophobia can be overcome with a determination to defy past bad experiences and with an open mind for unorthodox approaches. You could be part of the first generation of copy editors to master "newspaper math." We'll start slowly with stories involving suspicious numbers, especially statistics.

Suspicious Numbers

Many "numbers stories" require only suspicion and common sense rather than a calculator. Sometimes all it takes is finger counting. When a sentence refers to the "four candidates" or "five subdivisions," count them. Perhaps the most common numerical errors involve ages contained in obituaries, often flubbed by funeral homes, distracted families, or reporters shying away from basic subtraction. The person born on July 4, 1950, who dies on July 5, 2001, is 51 years old. But if the death was on July 3, 2001, the age is 50. Because families treasure obituaries and pass them through the generations, pay them and the deceased the respect of taking two minutes to subtract the month, date, and year of birth from the month, date, and year of death.

Another story that should arouse suspicion is one stating that a woman aged 24 is the mother of a 16-year-old. Giving birth at age eight is possible, but not probable. Ask the reporter if the teenager may be identified as a stepchild, an adoptee, or a foster child. With any story involving noticeable age discrepancies, ask for an explanation. Readers have sharp pencils.

Business stories are rife with suspect numbers. For instance, when a labor story marks steep drops in the unemployment rate for the fourth quarter, a copy editor needs to add the information that many retailers hire temporary workers for the holidays. Steep increases in unemployment from January to March may correspond to the common practice of "cleaning house" for the first quarters of the year. Third-quarter increases may reflect the influx of teenagers and teachers seeking summer jobs. Be aware, too, that labor statistics may include part-time help; many people need two or even three part-time jobs to survive. A company doubling its 1991 labor force in 1998 may have achieved it by hiring two part-timers for one job.

Explanatory insertions are not new, by the way. When the federal government helped farmers keep growing food after the Great Depression with subsidies to offset low market prices, the payments were decided on the basis of parity. The word "parity" was constantly used in farm stories, usually followed by an entire sentence, such as "Parity is the difference between a farmer's current purchasing power and the purchasing power determined by the federal government for a selected baseline period set to support commodity prices."

Wages often need explaining. Part-time employees usually receive no benefits, but executives do, plus stocks and golden-parachute options. So a $15-per-hour part-time job and a $90,000 annual salary are both illusory unless the copy editor adds a line pointing out these factors.

Also, be wary of the word "average" in wage stories for either employees or bosses because, like the grade curve, that number is skewed by extremes on each end. The "median" is the midsection number that gives a far more accurate picture of a range than the "average."

For example, one syndicated feature about wages was based almost entirely on the averages given in an institute's report on what bosses earned. A key section claimed that the "average annual compensation for a chief executive of a large company was $10.6 million."[3] Aside from the reporter's failing to include the span and worth of companies measured (was it only Fortune 500s?), that figure certainly was not an accurate picture of CEO salaries because it encompassed a range of those earning far less and one who might have earned $90 million.

A "median" might have been $100,000 or $75,000. At the least, a copy editor can add a phrase or sentence pointing out the limits of the "average," or that the "median," a far more accurate portrayal of those surveyed, was not included in the story.

What about the "phased-in" salaries in stories about labor, entertainment, or sports? These salaries are spread over a period of contractual years ("the $90 million is a five-year net of $18 million paid annually"; "the 18% increase will pay out at 6% per year on that three-year contract"). Insert an analogy as you would for lottery winners. Most readers know that lottery winnings are reduced by taxes and are often paid out over several years instead of in a lump sum. Fairness in reporting eight-figure earnings of celebrities also should involve adding a line that large sums are deducted by the IRS, agents, other handlers, and bodyguards, as well as for promotion and medical insurance.

Stories about strikes and settlements should contain information about the percentage of a benefits package in wages finally set after negotiations. Escalating health insurance premiums paid by employees, for example, may wipe out gains from wage increases. Likewise, ask the reporter whether a company has cut its contributions to insurance or pension plans, data that should be included. The addition of dental benefits may make good copy and indicate management benevolence, but employee contributions or deductibles may be so high that few sign up; ask the reporter for the enrollment percentages.

Inflation must be factored in to any story comparing wages from one time period with another. For instance, the minimum wage may have increased from 50¢ per hour in 1945 to nearly $6 in 2000, but if you consider the price of bread in 1945 and 2000, you'll see the impact of inflation on wages and prices. A more official way to measure a dollar's value is the federal government's consumer price index (CPI), provided annually since 1913.[4]

Recognizing Statistical Bias

The foregoing indicates that the reliability of statistics depends on the reporter's source and the eye of the beholder. Even reliable statistics can be twisted by virtually anyone. That's why astute professors of research and statistics recommend students purchase that humorous, timeless little book *How to Lie With Statistics*. Or perhaps one that is sports specific on the statistical jiggering used to canonize stars and to make records sacrosanct.

Some sources are unmasked as especially adept in shifting baselines for measuring sports records. Another pundit described techniques used by some sportswriters to bias results:

> Say the New York Mets lose four games, win the next four, then lose two more. Want to make them look bad? Just write, "The Mets have lost six of their last 10 games." But if you'd like to make them look good, that's just as easy: "The Mets have won four of their last six games."[5]

Others citing dubious numbers culled from even more dubious sources may be politicians, lobbyists, religious zealots, publicists, and writers and speakers with many axes to grind. Include also unscrupulous or lazy researchers who shift baselines, dates, and other numbers in journal articles that later appear at the bottom of bibliographies for other articles, steadily building credibility because few journalists rarely examine the first articles for flawed research. At least one famed feminist writer has been called to task for citing unsubstantiated statistics about anorexia deaths ("150,000 per year"). She used data from an eating disorder foundation despite a 1991 statistic of only 54 deaths reported by the National Center for Health Statistics. Can one year reflect many years? A decade-long epidemic?

Beware of politicians playing with statistics who claim real wages are declining or increasing. One writer declared that take-home income has increased because the "average-size house built in 1970 had 1,500 square feet and in 1997 had 2,150 [square feet]."[6] Note that word "average" once again. Aside from insisting that the size of a home is directly related to wages or neglecting to use the latest data on U.S. median wages, where were those 2,150-square-foot houses? California? Mississippi? Maine? Were mobile homes included? Can the worker drawing the nation's median salary afford to buy one of those houses?

When editing volunteerism stories, get suspicious about a company reporting that 100 percent of its employees contributed to a fund-raising campaign. Overt coercion usually is forbidden, but some companies mandate contributions as a hiring condition. Ask the reporter if this situation exists. Also, if totals appear sensational, fairness to other companies and the area's workforce demands inclusion of the percentage of contributors or the median contribution.

Participation percentages will reveal whether employees were fired up about a cause or the company gave most of the dollars to keep its good-citizen image shiny—and to take a tax write-off for charitable contributions.

In real estate stories, inflation and supply and demand are always governing factors in property market values. Many stories are variations on a county pioneer paying only 10¢ per acre in 1847 when he built that 40-room mansion for $15,000, but the property just sold for $1,000 per square foot and the mansion fetched $15 million. Population density and housing shortages also drive up values. So do people coming from areas like California, where properties fetch significantly high prices.

Copy editors rarely have access to blueprints of proposed apartment complexes or malls or downtown buildings. But the reporter writing a story about them does have access through a zoning or planning board. Ask her or him about the details. When a developer desperately needs tenants (subcontractors are vocal), remember too that the number of units or square footage may be exaggerated to attract occupants. Don't let them use the news columns for free advertising and promotion.

Many copy editors comb budgets from schools, cities, and counties and are not averse to getting out the calculator to see if the line items equal the debts and revenues announced at meetings and press conferences. Many copydesks keep budgets within arm's reach to verify the figure in a story stating that the park board director's salary is $64,534.28, or that the per-prisoner revenue yielded from renting jail space to other counties is accurate.

Budgets bring numbers to life and reveal the true priorities of school districts and all other public entities, no matter what their spokespersons intone for the 10 o'clock news. Sometimes it takes a good memory. For example, taxpayers in an affluent Minnesota suburb paid for a domed football stadium for its high school, but two years later school officials were begging voters to approve millions for books and faculty. If you work on a newspaper that fosters exposés by close monitoring of line items, you'll need to become familiar with that formidable-looking document to verify a reporter's figures in that story on street maintenance by neighborhoods. Or the salaries of librarians and police officers. Or what the sheriff spent to redecorate the office. You especially need to know that school officials usually conceal expenses for varsity athletic programs within the expenses under other large or expensive programs. In retrenchment, that makes athletic expenses difficult to find.

Suspicious Research Numbers

The proliferation of research stories presents opportunities almost daily for catching suspicious numbers. The chief suspect is the size of experimental groups. As the broadcast business and trustworthy pollsters have proved, researchers don't need to interview millions for a survey, especially for a project that doesn't involve life or death. In education, social studies, and psychology, 30 is considered a minimum number of people to be studied or interviewed. Medical research, however, should include far more people than that, but a landmark study on fetal alcohol syndrome had only eight.[7]

Many editors and slots have begun to discard poll stories unless they contain the source (to determine reliability), the number of subjects, and the margin of error. If a story lacks these components, either point out to the slot the need for such a qualifying paragraph or call the pollster to supply the missing data for the story; if your request is refused, the study is suspect.

Be particularly suspicious of mailed questionnaires (a.k.a. self-reports), no matter how reputable the institution or investigators.[8] Many recipients hedge the truth, usually out of pride, moral scruples, a need to be mischievous, or a desire to please the researchers. In this respect, ponder a recent self-report by 72,488 women nurses (aged 40–65) indicating a 30-minute brisk walk was equal to aerobics and jogging in cutting the risk of heart disease.[9] How researchers obtain the final portion of any study to fulfill the required 70 percent response rate (e.g., reminders by telephone, postcard) may have skewed results because if people are nagged, their responses may come from irritation. If long-term results are essential, as is the case with any medical study, self-reports are questionable. If college alumni offices have difficulty tracking down graduates after just two years, how can researchers locate, say, 112,432 subjects five or ten years later? Or trust that they are truthful?

Reporters will become careful about data once copy editors start questioning them about factoring in elements such as inflation, part-timers, wages, and dwindling benefits, or demanding blueprint data and double-checking budgetary figures. That kind of accuracy will be achieved by such interrogations and requests to either recalculate figures or ask harder questions of sources about the numbers they're providing. To obtain and retain reportorial vigilance, just keep after them to use a calculator or double-check numbers.

Understanding Property Taxes

Most readers understand that taxpayer dollars fund municipal services: street cleaning, sewage plants, drainage and mosquito control, schools, police, and fire protection. However, most don't understand who determines the taxes and how they are calculated. The public agency or unit decides what revenues are needed to pay the bills, and the assessor then sets the property tax rates to bring in most of the funds. The rates are based on the "assessed" values of land and property, not the market value. Fail to pay up and the taxing entity puts a lien for the tax amount on the property; flout it too long and that entity can condemn and take the holdings. Most people grumble, but they pay up, accepting property taxes as the price for government services.

The rub is that the cost of those services always seems to go up, never down, something reflected in property tax bills sent out each November. The tax increase is stated in "mills" even though the tax bill sent to property owners is stated in dollars owed as well as mills.

Let's say that you own property assessed at $90,000 and the county commissioners are debating putting a one-mill increase to the voters. That means for every $1,000 of that assessed value of your property, you might have to pay $1 more in taxes. So a one-mill increase will raise your property taxes by $90. If the total levy proposed is three mills ($3 per $1,000 assessed valuation), you'd multiply $3 times 90 and pay $270. Four mills would be $360, and so on. Every property tax story should contain an explanatory example about millage that's applied to the median-priced property in the area. Don't use either the high or the low end.

Bear in mind that property owners are already paying for past millage increases, one of the reasons for "taxpayer revolts" demanding ceilings on property taxes or the defeat of many school levies. They've also voted down floating long-term IOUs—municipal bonds for major projects (capital expenditures) such as bridges, roads, and stadiums that can't be paid for immediately from annual revenues.

Be aware in any story involving the floating of municipal bonds that the county, city/town, or school district may have a low credit rating and thus be unable to attract bond buyers willing to lend millions for streets, domed stadiums, or schools. Low credit ratings indicate a treasury that lacks taxpayer dollars and tip bond buyers they may lose their money by a default. Low ratings usually are boosted from, say, a B to an A– or an A– to a AA by bond insurance. But bond insurance premiums are included in the "indebtedness" part of a budget. A sharp copy editor calls the entity to get the credit ratings and the amounts of the annual insurance premiums so that they may be included in a sentence on a bond-floating story.

Editing Percentages

When stories state that 50 percent of those getting divorced are women or that in the past 30 years, 50 percent of those getting married for a third time are men, you know that some percentages can be glaringly flawed, even humorous, but also can be manipulated. In the case of science or medical studies, inadvertent or deliberate mistakes can maim and kill. Mathophobia or gullibility in reporters and copy editors can add a false sense of reliability to such data.

The copydesk may be the first protector of the public health that the reader ever encounters. Even though a story may have been based on a prominent professional journal, its editors and peer reviewers can be biased—or fooled—about procedures, devices, or medications, as I learned as a medical editor. The last few decades seem to have reinforced the view that living is better through chemistry. But remember that many readers, no matter how well educated, still believe ad testimonials that are a variation on that statement about "nine out of ten doctors . . ." They imply that 90 percent of a sizable number of physicians agreed about a medication, a device, or a treatment. Didn't many doctors and women patients believe that breast implants and the intrauterine contraceptive device (IUD) were safe, that muscle relaxants such as Valium were nonaddictive? Television audiences are bombarded about medications ("Ask your doctor about . . .") that cannot, in a 15-second spot, reveal all the side effects and contraindications or the longitudinal results of clinical trials or data about the research methods, subjects, and caliber of researchers. Some physicians may be steamrolled by patient demands from such ads into prescribing medications before trials are complete. Some universities recently admitted bias in results for company-paid research.

The copy editor has an important role in detecting false claims and deflecting such stories because many readers' information comes from the media, particularly the newspaper. The adverse or fatal reactions in tests must be reported in any reliable study, and when lives are at stake, such data must be included in the story. Most stories are abstracted by a wire or syndicated service, but an astute copy editor who processes them can still serve as a gatekeeper, as explained below.

One vital factor for inclusion involves longitudinal results (5–10 years), something the Food and Drug Administration monitors where medications are concerned. Class-action suits about breast implants and IUDs and the highly addictive nature of some medications such as Valium might be nonexistent if physicians had resisted prescribing such items until longitudinal studies had turned up the results now detailed in litigation involving thousands. In view of the trend of pharmaceutical firms using the media to sell new medications lacking long-term studies, a copydesk should have at least two well-known reference books available so you can check adverse reactions, side effects, and contraindications and, by the debut date, determine whether longitudinal results are complete. The books are the *Physician's Desk Reference,* published by the pharmaceutical industry, and *Worst Pills, Best Pills,* published and updated regularly by Ralph Nader's citizens' research group.

To understand how to apply these instructions, let's take a fictional story with a lead reporting a medical "breakthrough" (no such thing exists) that was successful for 90 percent of the patients tested. You scan the story and see nothing about longitudinal studies or about who funded the study (a firm making the medication or device?). Red flags should go up. At least a paragraph, often buried at the bottom, does state that the study included only 25 people, all men, aged 18 to 20 (or 45–50). Publicists, especially former reporters, know that if a copy editor has to make a trim, that last paragraph probably will be deleted—possibly harming those who believe that something printed by a newspaper must be true. Move that paragraph near the lead.

This example has other gaping holes aside from the major flaw of too few study subjects. It included only men and omitted vital variables such as their ages, the pretrial state of their health, and lon-gitudinal results—all essentials for evaluation of any health product or device. Unfortunately, real-life stories just like this one about "wonder" drugs and devices get past copy editors who fail to see those initial red flags: the size of the study group, and whether test subjects are mice, men, or women. Other factors can flaw results too, as indicated. Be aware, by the way, that some researchers who doubt peer reviewers will ever pass their work, send stories to the media. And unwitting copy editors pass them.

If you don't have time to research the omissions, at least include a sentence that notes these vital components ("No information has been provided as yet about longitudinal results or the study's spon-sor"). If complaints result from the university or institute or com-pany involved, the spokesperson should have no difficulty providing that information. If no information is instantly forthcoming, report this fact to the slot and request that the story be killed. You may have just protected the public's health and, down the road, staved off a class-action suit.

How to Calculate Percentages

You can challenge or at least verify a study's numbers, particularly percentages. Fight the fear about figuring percentages by attacking them boldly with a calculator and by applying some new 1-2-3 in-structions designed for mathophobes. We'll start with the fictional study that includes the misleading 90 percent success rate.

To figure how many cases (not percentages) were successful (or unsuccessful), punch in the number "25."

Then, punch the multiplication key. Next punch in ".90." Be sure to include the period because you're exchanging the percent sign in the story for the decimal point.

Finally, punch the equal-sign key (=). The answer should be "22.5." And because statisticians usually round off fractional num-bers above ".5" (and anything below it), that additional "half person" identified as ".5" would be rounded up to 23 people. If the answer were 22.4, you'd round down the percentage to 22 people.

Translate the results for readers by deleting the 90 percent and add "that 23 out of the 25 people tested had favorable reactions" (or 2 out of 25 had adverse reactions). That will expose the small sample group and permit readers to judge the study's real value.

Here's another way to check percentages. Suppose a school story says that the superintendent's self-report study mailed to parents and guardians revealed that 49 percent would like to enroll their children in private schools. The second graph says that results were based on responses of 30 percent of the 5,001 parents and guardians.

Forget that only those most interested might respond by the deadline. Forget also that the survey was a "mailer" with all of its skewing factors—or that the kids might throw it away before their caretakers saw it. Most of all, forget that surveys are expensive, especially one involving 5,001 households, so the superintendent must have had strong reasons to resort to a survey. Instead, focus on those numbers. The calculator will unveil misleading percentages.

This time, you'll do something different in math calculations, something helpful and unorthodox: Write the number "5,001" on your scratch sheet and circle it before punching it into the calculator. Don't scoff. That number is the "baseline" of percentage calculations. Circling that base number emphasizes that fact and also makes it highly visible for later reference.

Next, punch in the number "5,001." Then, punch the multiplication key. Punch in the decimal point (and number) of the percentage of responses (".30"). Finally, punch the answer key: 1,500 out of 5,001 caretakers mailed back the survey.

Now you'll need to tell readers how many caretakers out of those 1,500 respondents constituted the 49 percent used by the reporter in the lead. Once again, circle this new baseline number ("1,501"). Multiply it by ".49." The answer should be 735 respondents.

The last step reveals what percentage the 735 people represent of the 5,001 caretakers. It surely isn't the 49 percent hinted at in the lead. The baseline number now shifts from "5,001" to "735" because that last number is the story's real focus. Circle it.

Feed that baseline number ("735") into the calculator.

The newest step is to punch the key with the division sign.

Then, enter "5,001." Follow up that step by punching the answer key. You should have "0.1469706." Drop the "0" and retain only the first two numbers (".14"). Exchange the decimal point for the percentage sign ("14%"). To be fair to the superintendent, include the third number ("6") from the total answer. Because "6" is a number larger than "5," round up the final percentage to "15 percent." In short, only 15 percent of those polled said they would like to enroll their kids in private schools. That 15 percent is a far cry from the startling 49 percent in the lead and provides a more accurate picture about the issue. The edited lead could be something like this:

> Only 15% of parents and guardians in the Lake City district, 735 out of 5,001, would like to enroll their children in private schools. That finding was reported Tuesday in a survey by Superintendent D. S. Woods who wanted to test the strength of private-school appeal.

Figuring the Percentages of Increases and Decreases

Figuring percentages will be invaluable because public officials—for example, police and fire chiefs, the water and street managers—tend to vigorously defend proposed increases in budgets to fend off decreases. Let's say the sewer department manager begs to expand the facility by a 23 percent increase to last year's allocation of $115,321. Circle that baseline number and multiply it by ".23." How much money does that increase involve?

On decreased percentages, assume you're processing a school story that fails to mention the number of students lost to a district because of the state's "early enrollment" plan at public universities for high school seniors. The reporter repeated the superintendent's "scare" percentage of "9 percent" out of the district's 7,891 seniors. Because translating that 9 percent to numbers will calm the excitable, how many seniors will you include along with that percentage?

Circle that baseline number, of course. But in multiplying one-digit percentage numbers ("9") against it, slip in a zero ("0") directly after the decimal point and before a one-digit percentage number. Your multiplier then should be ".09." If your answer is 710 students, you've mastered calculating increases and decreases of percentages.

Let's now work on percentage increases and decreases over periods of time, essential for editing budget stories to prevent deliberate distortion by sources. If officials fear that a 10-year chart will show recently skyrocketing numbers, many provide budgets with only two-year comparisons (current and projected) and hope the public forgets the past decade and doesn't see the increase as a mismanagement spurt. Likewise, if officials believe their projected budget will be perceived by the public as extraordinarily high, they use 10-year comparisons to show that the increases have been small. If percentages might appear to be exorbitant, officials often resort to dollar figures; equally, if numbers might cause outrage, they shift to percentages.

Suppose a sheriff uses that two-year comparison to soften the blow to taxpayers by saying next year's budget would be "increased by only 14 percent." The copydesk policy on that paper is to provide both dollars and percentages, however. Calculate the dollar increase off this year's allocation of $115,803.20 by multiplying that circled baseline by 14 percent. Add the dollar difference to the baseline number ($16,212.45 + $115,803.20) to get the final dollar figure of $132,015.65.

But what if a highway department superintendent provides the estimate of the dollar increase only, believing the percentage number to be damaging? If the reporter doesn't include the percentage, copydesk policy mandates it. At hand is the current year's allocation of $250,729.14, compared with the projected $338,484.33. The story says the rise is attributable to frost-heave damage on 80 percent of the county's roads, repaving a dozen, and filling potholes.

The percentage increase is computed by first entering next year's proposed allocation into the calculator.

Then, punch the subtraction key (–).

Enter this year's allocation and, because it is the budget baseline, jot it down and circle it because that is the pivotal number that will determine the percentage.

Next, punch the answer key to get the difference subtracted between the two sums.

If you got $87,755.19, you're literally "on the money."

Punch the division key.

Enter the circled baseline number (this year's allocation: $250,729.14).

Punch the answer key. The sum should be 0.3499999. To round off the percentage, drop the 0 and decimal point and place a percentage sign after the first two numbers (".34" becomes "34 percent"). The increase is 34.99 percent but should be rounded up to 35 percent, an eyepopper for taxpayers.

To figure a percentage decrease, you'll use the same formula. The county librarian, who put up a ferocious fight to win an allocation of $71,943.18 for the current year, is depicted in a story as weeping when she heard the Citizens Budget Review Board would be recommending that next year's allocation be trimmed to $33,623.16. The reporter has omitted the decreased percentage, perhaps believing readers can figure it out.

Here's how to calculate the percentage of decrease.

The baseline number circled is this year's allocation ($71,943.16). Subtract next year's proposed allocation ($33,623.18) from it. Then, enter the "difference" ($38,320) into the calculator. Divide it by the baseline number. The percentage that emerges (0.5326428, or 53 percent) is something that might goad library patrons into rage and, perhaps, action.

A warning about rounding off percentage points: Never round off fractional points in money stories ("the interest rate is 1.89 percent) because the content involves millions of dollars for investors or financial and real estate institutions. For instance, if a payday loan shop lends you $750 until your next paycheck at a monthly rate of .3211 (i.e., 32.11 percent), you'll pay $240.83 per month in interest. But if the rate were .3297 (32.97 percent), interest would be $247.28. Expand the example by loans of thousands or millions, and you'll see why fractional points must not be rounded off on money stories.

Stock Market News

One rule many slots impart to new copy editors before they process financial news is, "Change nothing until you understand it." When you do, you probably will think twice before passing wire service stories or writing a terrifying headline implying that because the Dow Jones industrial index has dropped, the Great Depression is about to reappear. You'll also be wary of number stories about stock payouts (dividends) unless the reporter stipulates which kind of dividends are involved (e.g., regular, special, extra, increases, interims, or parallels).

You'll begin that education if you compare the market to the lemonade stand across the street. Their start-up month was June, and promotion and hustle enabled them to clear $55 after expenses. A stifling July brought them a stunning net profit (after expenses) of $160. Because you now know how to do baseline comparisons by percentage, you are astonished to find the kids' earnings for July have hit a staggering 191 percent. You talk them into "going public" to sell stock so they have more capital to buy more supplies. They sell you three shares at $1 each.

The lemonade stand grows into a major industry—Neighborade—and your three shares are soon worth $77.50 each. Eventually, the kids' chain of street-side stands lets them join the 2,000 companies that buy and sell shares on the New York Stock Exchange. A day's stock trading data for the company, as reported in the daily newspaper, might look like this:

Name	PE	Sales	Last	Chg.
Neigh'ade	11	200	87	+9$^{1/2}$

The "PE" stands for "price earnings," the price of a share of Neighborade stock, divided by the earnings per share. "Sales" alludes to the number of shares traded per day and is stated in hundreds (i.e., 200 = 200,000 shares traded). "Last" means the closing price of the stock when the exchange closed at 3 p.m. (EST). "Chg." is the stock's price change from the previous day. The "+" means a stock's worth is going up; the "–", it's going down.

When you get a tip that the weather for the coming summer is going to be cold and rainy, you contact your brokerage account executive to sell your shares. Alas, you and the weather forecaster prove wrong. And a gigantic food conglomerate stages a "hostile" takeover of Neighborade by promising shareholders a 3–1 stock "split" if they vote them control of the company. That moves the share's price to $90. Had you hung on to those three shares, you'd be holding nine shares; if you'd sold them minutes after the deal boosted their worth to $90, you would have made $540 off the six extra shares, plus the difference in price ($87–90=$3 per share) when shareholders voted for the takeover.

Editing the Market's Ups and Downs

The major stories of the financial page focus on the market's daily "health." That health is measured by a handful of scorekeepers called "indexers" who each day monitor a particular segment of the market's stocks (a.k.a. securities) for what's traded (bought or sold) and for how much. They then average all the trading for an index that's based on a system of "points."[10] A point traditionally was equal to $1 per share traded—not for every company in the exchange, but only a small, key number that the indexers considered good barometers of the American financial climate.[11]

Despite the nearly unshakable, yet mistaken belief of the public and many in the media that "as the Dow index goes, so goes the market," the Dow industrial index tracks only 30 companies, albeit "blue chippers" like AT&T, IBM, and Wal-Mart, but late in 1999 it added some high-technology companies. Some indexes monitor a far broader spectrum of companies and also include the blue-chip firms tracked by the "Dow." Knowledgeable financial reporters and copy editors know that before they pass a story or write headlines likely to cause a panic in next-day trading, they need to check a cross-section of the major indexes—not just the Dow.

So follow the path of newspapers like *The Oregonian*. On the day after the Federal Reserve Board raised the interest rate from 5 percent to 5.25 percent, it carried a headline and deck based on a careful reading of several indexes far more reflective of the market than that the Dow's points fell 16.46. Standard & Poor's index was up by 3.28 points, Nasdaq's by 32.80, and so on:

Fed's rate increases depress only Dow

The blue chip average loses
16.46 points, but broader
gauges of stock market health
post advances[12]

Move now to "points," the numbers you see blinking on signs outside many brokerage offices. Points are not percentages, a common mistake of some reporters and copy editors who look at decreases in points and panic. Before you pass stories with sentences like "this is the worst decline in history . . . ," all based on percentages, be sure the drop approaches the figure of –12.82 percent of October 29, 1929, or the granddaddy of all crashes, the –22.61 percent of October 19, 1987.[13]

Points and percentages work off each other to describe the trading day.

Percentage ups and downs are based on those "points." Points involve how many stocks investors bought. If they buy many, the points increase. If they don't buy anything or if they sell a lot of stocks, the points decline (shown by a minus sign). For example, the 1929 "crash" had a point "decline" of –38.33; the 1987 crash, a point decline of –580.00.[14] Because you already know how to calculate percentage increases and decreases in budgets, computing them from points in Standard & Poor (S&P) or Dow indexes (or any others) should be fairly easy. The math procedure is the same.

Imagine that a wire service reporter is so unnerved by a Federal Reserve interest boost and the market reaction that the story omits the percentage of increase from the S&P index. Yet the copydesk policy, once again, is that percentages must also be shown. The S&P index yesterday was 1,360.22 points, but today it closed at 1,363.5 points. You can see the points went up, and the difference is contained in the story and in an infographic.

Circle the baseline points on which the percentage will be calculated (1,360.22). Subtract that number from today's points. You should have a difference of 3.28 points. To get the percentage, divide that difference by the circled baseline number. The sum should be 0.0024113, or, converted to a percentage, .0024 percent. That's a grain of sand on a big beach.

To determine if declines are a trend, check the percentage of gain reported on the Nasdaq index, heavy with high-technology stocks. Yesterday, it stood at 2,719.57 points; today, it's 2,752.37 points. Calculate the percentage. Is it significant? A trend indicator?

Then, check the Dow industrial index to see if the sky is falling on Wall Street and the nation. Remember that the Dow measures the stock activity of only 30 companies, compared with S&P's 500, Nasdaq's 1,500, Wilshire's 5,000, and others. Yesterday, the Dow stood at 11,299.76 points, but it closed today at 11,283.30 points. Calculate the percentage of "decline." Is it near –5 percent? Or those famed "crash" percentages of –12.82 percent and –22.61 percent?

The market fluctuates daily. To block overreactive copy about its ups and downs from the wire services or the staff reporter, it might be helpful to post the numbers that accompanied those two historic crashes.

"Times as Great" Is Not "Times Greater Than"

Reporters attempting to convey impact or enormity, especially in percentages or sizes, may confuse the two distinctly different comparative expressions of "times as great" and "times greater." Many copy editors probably have passed them as interchangeable expressions, even in other guises such as "as old as" and "older than," "as wide as" and "wider than," or "as large as" and "larger than." But they're not the same.

Professor Phil Meyer's *drôle* example points up the confusion:

> If you are 20 years old, and I am three times as old as you, I must be 60.
> But if I am three times older than you, then I am 80.[15]

In the first sentence, the age is 60. But in the second, the age is 80. One way to discern the difference begins with awareness that these comparisons appear in the giveaway term "as" for the first and the suffix "er" for the second. The second remedy to ensure the numbers' accuracy is to do the calculations. The first sentence ("as") states a basic multiplication exercise: Multiply the baseline number of 20 by 3 to see if the answer is 60.

The second sentence with the suffix "er" often is stated with other words such as greater, older, likelier, and so on. The answer is built atop the baseline number. The shortcut calculation requires focusing on the baseline age (20). Multiply it by 3 and top it off with that age. Put another way, because you're comparing the difference of the larger number to a smaller one, divide the difference into the baseline number.

Nautical Numbers

In stories about shipping or sailing, don't change nautical terms like "knots" to miles per hour or "long tons" to pounds. Instead, just use the unadorned terms. If an explanation is essential to the story's meaning, add a half sentence explaining the correlation to land life.

A knot is a nautical mile sailed per hour, so adding "per hour" is unnecessary. However, because millions know only land-based miles rather than those on the high seas, you could add that a knot is the equivalent of one and one-seventh land miles. Nautical numbers of any kind should be put in figures (5-knot winds) to avert any kind of confusion.

Size of vessels is measured by tonnage, the volume of space per ton, but their weight is not to be translated to pounds or plain tons, but in "long tons" (1 long ton = 2,240 pounds, however).

Betting Odds

This nation is awash with casinos, riverboats, dog and horse tracks, and athletic events, as well as odds predicted for such things as elections and medical outcomes—virtually any event of chance. To edit stories containing odds, you'll need to know more than the AP style mandate that odds are to be stated in figures and hyphens (e.g., "The odds were 3-2").[16]

Those numbers are calculated by oddsmakers who are like stockbrokers in that customers rely on them to predict results. Their expertise stems from knowledge about the event and the participants as well as statistical computations—and hunches. Oddsmakers can be salaried employees of a track or a casino whose predictions are contained in its program. Or they can be freelancers such as the famous Jimmy the Greek paid by gamblers who trust their judgment to amass fortunes.[17]

Odds generally are determined on the basis of points assigned to an event's participants and must fall within a certain range. For example, a dog track oddsmaker scans the list of nine greyhounds scheduled for the first race the next evening and assigns each points for prowess; the total points for all nine dogs must not be less than 114 or more than 125. The favorite might be assigned the greatest number of points, like 33, but, as a result, will also get the lowest odds of 2–1. That means for every dollar bet, the return might be $2. The more people who believe the dog will be the winner, the lower the payoff. The dog rating the least points (the most likely to come in last), say 6, could be assigned the highest odds of 15–1 ($15 per $1 bet).[18]

When the oddsmaker sets more complicated-looking odds (e.g., 6–5), the forecast is that the gambler might possibly win $6 for every $5 bet; odds of 8–3 mean possibly winning $8 for every $3 invested. However, the odds are only predictions of results. And even if the gambler does have a winner, the window payout might be totally different from the odds.[19]

The Writing Style Used for Numbers

You've probably learned from the AP stylebook that its form for numbers is to spell out one to nine, but to use figures for 10 and above. That rule is broken regularly when reporters must start sentences with numbers above nine. Most readers would be confused if faced with a sentence that started: "One million, nine-hundred and fifty-five thousand dollars and fifty cents . . ." or "135 students today . . ." The best solution is not necessarily to start off with "a total of," as some recommend, but to opt for readability and clarity by recasting the sentence so that the first word is not a figure.

The key in number style is clarity as well as economy of keystrokes.

For instance, nautical numbers of any kind are put in figures (5-knot winds), a rule that prevents confusion and reduces keystrokes. Some copydesks carry numerical clarity to ridiculous lengths, insisting that copy use expressions such as "the assessor plans to raise next year's rate from 2 percent to 3 percent" instead of "2 to 3 percent." But everything depends on the size of numbers in a range. With large numbers, the range should be stated fully: "The craft was expected to travel from 250,000 miles to 400,000 miles" instead of the misleading "from 250 to 400,000 miles." The same style applies to money. "The board expects costs of $3 million to $6 million" instead of a stopper such as "$3 to $6 million." Likewise, with significant numbers of people, make it "the population could reach 22 million to 47 million" instead of "22 to 47 million."

Fewer keystrokes are necessary also when numbers are rounded up or down, such as: "The cost overruns were expected to reach

$12.5 million" or "some 12.9 million people are expected to get flu shots." But if the newspaper has a rigid policy that the public has a right to an accounting of every budgetary penny or an accurate head count, be sure that the amount is stated as "$12,499,999.19" or "12,876,503 people."

In dealing with sizable quantities of commodities, it may be tempting to express amounts in tonnage, but that term is reserved for shipping stories. Keep the amounts in either bushels or barrels, whichever word is clearer to your particular readership.

Last, you may be totally accurate and follow the copydesk's style on numbers if you pass a reporter's sentence such as: "The Columbia river registered 37.9 feet, a little shy of the expected crest of 38 feet." But the paper will be the butt of local and national jokes if you do. Use some common sense on that kind of number.

18 | Attributions, Identifications, and Second References

Readers have a right to know what news source—person, organization, document, and so on—provides material for a paper's news and opinion columns. Police beat reporters usually are extraordinarily careful to "hang everything on the cops" for all details in a crime story. They've learned that attributions stave off subpoenas in a news section highly prone to libel suits. Too, recognition of law officers may enhance their cooperation with the paper.

But the same kind of attentiveness to attributions can be spotty elsewhere. Sometimes reporters' opinions ("in what looked like arson"; "E. Coli may have caused the fatalities," etc.) can set off an uproar. Careful copy editors never pass editorializing in a news story.

Attributions for *libelous* statements are something else again, especially if remarks are uttered against a private citizen. The copy editor who passes that kind of story can expect to involve the paper in litigation. Sources voicing opinions or leveling accusations at those in public life aren't usually providing facts but possible libel or slander actions. As late as 1999 in Oregon, a letter to the editor figured in litigation because it contained a phony signature.[1]

Another kind of nonattribution, the faceless "spokesperson," has helped chip away the credibility of newspaper and wire services for decades. True, presidents up to Harry Truman stipulated they would not talk to the press unless they were indirectly quoted,[2] scoops secured at a prohibitive price. That led to anonymous attributions such as that "government source" who talked to AP recently "on the condition of anonymity" about Amtrak trains, hardly a top-secret issue.[3] Watergate watchers in the 1970s had to trust that the source named "Deep Throat" leaking anti-Nixon data was real.

This practice has been so harmful over the decades that even when publishers of reputable papers such as *The Washington Post* insist on two sources for anonymous attributions, public distrust is still unlikely to be dispelled. Attribution deficiencies only support the claims of those aching to wipe out the First Amendment and that nothing in the newspapers can be believed.

It probably would take a national protest by publishers, editors, and copy editors to force news services to quit quoting "reliable sources" on noncritical stories. But that's not so on local and regional stories. Copy editors have the collective clout to demand support from publishers and editors to delete material that lacks adequate attributions—unless sources are police informants.

Attribution Form and the Venerable "Said"

Attributions come in an assortment of expressions tacked onto major statements and are fenced off by commas: (". . . , according to coroner Blaise Sonnier" or ". . . , says lifetime bowling expert Ernie Cooley"). Verbs come in an array of choices, but don't let writers use such bizarre stoppers as "he hazards" or "she externalized." Such verbs indicate they're so tired of "said" that they try to freshen up even hard-news stories with offbeat terms they've seen in alternative biweeklies, magazines, or books. One copy-editing expert recalls a time when reporters even used a "said" system. They started off with "said" and then moved through the paragraphs using a cycle of substitutes like "asserted, averred, declared, and stated" before returning to "said" and a second cycle. Avoid that system.[4]

The aim, especially in hard-news stories, is to reach readers—not experiment with trendy diction. Perhaps the only readers who balk at the honorable, fourteenth-century word "said" are reporters. Copy editors don't. And readers assuredly don't. "Said" is the first verb children learn in reading and, as adults, the verb they absorb quickest in newspaper stories and in all those other publications. In short, absolutely nothing is wrong with using "said" as an attribution verb *throughout* a story unless it's applied to an inanimate object such as, "the university administration says" or "the State Department was saying earlier this week . . ."

Reporters opting for variety need to choose reader-friendly verbs that truly depict either the source's tone or a physical description. If they don't, change the verb to "said."

For example, sources can't "smile" or "laugh" a quote. Also, did the sources truly "explain" something or did they just "state," "declare," "claim," or "assert" a belief? ("Aver" is a stopper today.) Equally, did the source really "point out" something that was unusual or unknown, or did she simply "note" or "say" something? Was a "replied" a response, or was "answered" an answer? Delete dramatic verbs ("bellowed," "shrieked," "barked," "cried").

When the reporter uses that tired filler "she was quick to say," or "he added," was the quote a snappy retort? Did the source really "add" something material to earlier statements? To avert legal action, never pass the verbs "admitted" and "confessed" unless they're tied to a crime or court stories; they have connotations that put sources in an unfavorable light. The verb "claimed" is another attribution word with negative connotations, chiefly of guilt or questionable position. Change it.

Some courthouse reporters try to impress judges and lawyers by using legalese and forget writing for newspaper readers. Some writers might avoid the verb "opined" for someone giving an opinion, because they know the copydesk would never pass it even in its proper environment, an appellate or supreme court. But many reporters use the equally confusing (to readers) verb "recuse" (a.k.a. excuse). Then there's the verb "depose." The verb "depose" has recently become popular in investigative and court reporting, causing negative connotations and high comedy. One of the secondary definitions of "depose" is that it means to testify under oath, generally in a "deposition." But the primary definition recognized by most readers is that it means to forcibly remove someone from a high position like a throne. Confusion can be expected when that verb is substituted for "testified" in an attribution such as, "'I had nothing to do with that bankruptcy action,' he deposed." And incredulous laughter when it becomes: "Cochran even deposed Fidel Castro."

In other words, when reporters use other verbs for "said," ensure they're among those considered the most reader-friendly (and fit their definitions) as listed below:

added	contended	pointed out
admitted	continued	proposed
announced	declared	remarked
answered	deplored	replied
asserted	insisted	reported
called	maintained	responded
cited	mentioned	retorted
claimed	noted	stated
commented	observed	vowed

Attribution Placement

Placement of attributions varies, but it should be next to the material used and should not impede the story's flow. That may explain why the prepositional phrase "according to" is such a popular and readable attribution. Copy editors concerned about polished attributions generally ensure that the verb is positioned after the source (". . . , Hebert claimed"). But when the source requires a lengthy identification, they'll place the verb in front of the source, or the story will have the kind of unclear awkwardness that's shown in boldface below:

> The difference between painted graffiti murals on the Broadway bridge pillars and vandalistic graffiti etched with glass cutters on Sellwood shop windows is that the first was done by an artist attempting to bring color and joy to a blighted

public sinkhole, the second was done by sadistic kids who get enjoyment out of making shoestring shopkeepers spend thousands to replace windows, **Edwin F. Maritain, owner of Antiques R Us and Sellwood business leader, said.**

In a lead, because the "what" of the 5W's is usually paramount, the attribution should follow, like this:

The search for emotional and spiritual development rather than eternal youth should be the focus of the senior citizen's leading magazine, **according to Lionel Fisher, the senior living columnist for** *The Daily Astorian.*

When "who" gets the emphasis, the attribution should start the lead:

Clanton's mayor yesterday denied the town's credit rating had been boosted from a B to an A by heavy expenditures in bond insurance.

Follow the same placement form in the rest of the story for smooth flow and clarity:

Students at Briscoe hall probably would vote to change its status to a silent dorm for next year, **Claybourne predicted.** But Briscoe residents have bucked the change by petitions ever since 1994 and voted it down, 114–23, last spring.

Attribution placement for stories containing quotations depends on the length of the remarks, but clarity still is the guideline. Don't let the reporter interrupt the quote's flow with an attribution in mid-sentence like this:

"We discovered mold," **Irwin testified,** "in every one of the 37 barrels of tobacco Dill delivered to the warehouse. I paid him $2,000 in cash. I telegraphed him that I wanted my money back because the tobacco couldn't be traded, but he wired me back to try. His widow refused to budge. To wait 20 years for justice and to only get 10¢ on the dollar is no justice."

In lengthy quotes, place the attribution at the start so that readers know who is speaking:

A tearful Irwin described the deal: "We discovered mold in every one of the 37 barrels of tobacco Dill delivered to the warehouse. I paid him $2,000 in cash. I telegraphed him that I wanted my money back because the tobacco couldn't be traded, but he wired me back to try. His widow refused to budge. To wait 20 years for justice and to only get 10¢ on the dollar is no justice."

How many attributions should a story have? Length and complexity generally determine the number. Obviously, a one-paragraph news brief may need none or just *one* if telephone calls for further information are expected.

Moviemakers will be reviewing snippets of their summer films Saturday, beginning at 8 p.m. at the Saturday Shooters meeting in Rm. 316 at Savannah high school, **according to president Nyellia Campara.** Instructions for the fall project are available by calling Campara at 478-3211.

By contrast, stories about crime, fires, and disasters are among those requiring *many* attributions because the copy usually involves *several* aspects of an event. A good rule of thumb is to echo the attribution for crime stories: every detail tagged to a source. If the reporter shies from sprinkling a source's name *repeatedly* throughout the story, especially in a feature story, add it as the events unfold. Names certainly can be repeated in some fashion ("says Martin"; "Martin points out that . . ."; "when Martin was a teenager . . ."), and nothing is wrong with repeating "Martin said" or "the police reported."

Beyond all this, attributions need identifications pertinent to the story or opinion piece. That duty also entails close monitoring about subsequent references (second, third, fourth, etc.) throughout lengthy pieces or a series of articles so that the reader is *never* in doubt about the source of the information.

Identifying Sources in Attributions

Identifying sources in attributions reveals their qualifications for making statements or furnishing material. You learned in reporting classes that every name in a story needs identification. But the source also needs credentials *pertinent* to the story. On high-profile levels, identification is easy because full names are not essential, and the flow of a sentence is undisturbed ("President Bush today assailed . . ."; "The Pope declared late last night that . . ."). It's the lesser beings who often present identification problems, particularly those wearing several hats.

For example, Dwight D. Eisenhower was a famous general in World War II, a president of Columbia University, and president of the United States. Common sense dictated that rather than encumbering Ike's identification with all three titles, only one was used and pertained to the subject matter. If the connection involved the military, the identifying appositive was: ". . . , who commanded D-day operations"; for education: ". . . , former president of Columbia University"; for government: ". . . , president from 1953 to 1961." Again, only one identification is needed and it should pertain to the story. So when a reporter rounds up quotes about a fire, the only identification needed is the tie to the fire: "Maureen Riley, a resident of a neighboring building, said . . ."

Titles such as Dr., Gen., Mrs./Ms., when paired with other identifications, clutter sentences and are confusing to readers. If Mayor

Dr. Leon Trousdale is never used as an identification, why permit *two* qualifiers such as Commissioner Mrs. Jane Norton or Toastmaster president Lt. Col. Jesse H. McMahon?

Where courtesy identifications like Mr., Mrs., Miss, and Ms. once were common usage for the second reference to someone in a story, they are largely relegated today to obituaries. In parts of the Deep South, however, the custom has been to deny first-name identifications for married women in the obituary headline ("Mrs. Wilbur F. Hutchinson"), secreting them instead in the text, discreetly surrounded with parentheses: "Mrs. Wilbur F. ("Jennie") Hutchinson, 82, died Friday. . . ." When a newspaper charges a fee for an obit, the family usually is permitted to use its own style—within reason.

Coping with Long Titles

Readers have no difficulty with the clarity and brevity of short qualifiers such as "Greek singer Nana Mouskouri said Tuesday . . ."; "Consumer advocate Ralph Nader now wants . . ."; or "Ned DuVol, a fraternity brother, denied they . . ." Long titles are a challenge because they block a story's flow and also cause readers to turn to other news. Consider leads with such lengthy qualifiers as "Former Assistant Secretary for the Department of Health, Education, Welfare, and Occupational Development Conyer W. T. Smith, Jr. yesterday warned . . ." Or "The House Subcommittee for Urban Renewal, Traffic Safety, Environmental Planning, and Maritime Projects voted 15–11 last night to . . ."

The solution for lengthy identifications in leads is to cut the sentence in two with only the pertinent identification carried in the second sentence, like this:

> A former cabinet member yesterday warned that public housing still was an improvement over forcing low-income families into the street. He was Conyer W. T. Smith, Jr., former assistant secretary for the Department of Health, Education, Welfare, and Occupational Development.

Long identifiers also impede text flow, as boldfacing in these two examples shows:

> In other business, Martin A. Thorpe, **who was** **elected to the House in 1992 and the Senate in 1996** **and has served as school superintendent in District** **No. 5 and is currently principal of Glenhaven** **Elementary school in Otis,** last night was named advisor to the Charter Schools Association.

> The new PC will outperform any Pentium machine, even of 700 Mhz, says Barry Humphrey, **regional project director for high-end technology** **for commercial and educational services of the** **Louisiana-Texas Systems Design Company.**

The first example exaggerates many real-world stories to make a point—but not by much. The identifying appositive contains 33 words before arriving at the verb, a clear case of a sentence with a "long-lost subject" (LLS). The second example's appositive contains 22 words, but fortunately doesn't depend on a verb. In both instances, perform the same kind of sentence surgery as is suggested with leads so that the identifications read like this:

> A local educator last night was named advisor to the Charter Schools Association. He was Martin A. Thorpe, **principal of Glenhaven Elementary school** **in Otis.**

> The new PC will outperform any Pentium machine, even of 700 Mhz, says Barry Humphrey, **a** **project director for the Louisiana-Texas Systems** **Design Company.**

The identification for officials who have retired or died is not "ex," but "Former president Jerry Ford yesterday . . ."; or "The late dean Clyde Wilkins was . . ."; or "Mayor James Broussard, who died four years ago, had . . ." No "ex-alcoholic," "former," or "recovered alcoholic" exists, by the way, for that incurable disease. Make it "Sandi Smith, a recovering alcoholic." Also, "ex-husband" has been changed today to "a former husband."

If the reporter is alluding to activities before an official died, delete confusing identifiers like "then state treasurer." Resurrect the dead like this:

> Communist witch-hunting in the government began when **President Harry Truman** signed an executive order that eventually unleashed the excesses of **Republican Senator Joe McCarthy**.

Second and Subsequent References to Sources in the News

Perhaps sportswriters wrestle the most with the "second references" to a subject. The initial reference to "the game" or "football" somehow cannot be repeated lest readers think sports reporters have limited vocabularies. Pride sometimes does go before a fall. On second and subsequent references, it's sometimes painfully obvious the thesaurus got heavy use because the reader finds that the word "game" used in the lead becomes "the contest" in the second reference, which becomes "the match" in the third reference, and so on. As for the word "football," subsequent references even confuse the players (globe, leather, orb, pellet, pigskin, pill, sphere, spheroid, etc.).

But non–sports types have their challenges too. Reporters with the news services and syndicates, for example, can't seem to allude to San Francisco twice or thrice with that city's honorable name. The second reference won't be "Frisco" or "SF," to be sure, but probably "the Bay city," or "Baghdad on the Bay," and, in Southern California papers, "the northern city." Local writers are no less guilty, especially on features. Spell it out.

You have a right to groan—and fix—second references, for example, when an elephant becomes a "pachyderm" rather than "the animal." Or when the second reference to a "dog" becomes "the canine"; a cat, "the feline"; judges, "jurists"; snow, "the white stuff"; senators, "solons," ad nauseam. Reporters today know better than to follow "wife" with second references from the last century like "the missus," "his frau," or "the better half." But subsequent references to all others can use a job title. The second references could be "the engineer," "a former CEO," "the onetime revivalist," "the quilter," "the veteran fireman," and the like.

Shifting identities on subsequent references *does* confuse readers, even when ships like the *Queen Elizabeth II* today are called "it" instead of "she." Never pass such terms as "the two" for partners or a couple, or permit those sickening musical analogies ("the trio," "the quartet," etc.) to stand in for the simple and clear pronoun "they." And don't let reporters switch from "women" to "females" within a story (or "males" to "men") or change "fat" to "obese" or "the poor" to "the disadvantaged" or that horror, "the economically challenged." Stick to the form used on the first reference.

If dollar signs can be repeated throughout a story, why not someone's last name? Obituaries repeat names. The writers of those fact-filled, compact stories are not uneasy about name repetition whether the obit contains five paragraphs or 50. Why, then, should a feature or a lengthy hard-news story require synonym gyrations for proper nouns?

About the inanimate nouns: Second references to organizations as "the firm," "the group," "the unit," and "the department" also jar readers attempting to follow activities of businesses, government offices, and professional groups, especially if the title is lengthy as is common in partnerships (McEwen, Hanna, Gisvold, Rankin & Van Koten). The same is true of equipment, medical devices, projects, and other inanimate entities.

One compromise that is effective in identifying inanimate entities has been the acronym, as was pointed out in an earlier chapter concerning the FBI and the IRS. The style is to give the full name on the first reference (e.g., American Telephone & Telegraph) and immediately follow it with the acronym set in parentheses (AT&T).

Having thus introduced an abbreviation to accompany the first mention of the noun, the copy can include it for subsequent references, like this:

> The Intrauterine Device (IUD) was considered an unqualified success when it was first marketed in 1965. But it wasn't long before users experienced excruciating pain from IUDs. And then came the discovery that bacteria climbed its string into tissue, often killing cells more rapidly than cancer.

> Sports utility vehicles (SUVs) continued to be the No. 1 seller among women in the nation, particularly in northern climes where sub-zero temperatures and blizzards equal hazardous roads. The leading dealer in SUVs in the state, Billy Navarre, said their popularity came partly from heavy promotion, but mostly from word of mouth from women stuck with chauffeur duties.

Nicknames work too, but only if recognized by most of a readership; that may take years, however. Readers no longer have much trouble with "the Mac" as a subsequent reference for Apple's Macintosh computer unless the allusion is to a fast-food company's larger-sized hamburger ("a Big Mac"), but would most know that a "Cat" is an earthmover? Be careful on such trademarks, by the way, because companies such as Coca-Cola not only will not permit its nickname in print, but its trademark department has been known to send "corrective" letters even to small-town high school newspapers making that gaffe.

One precaution about references involves trims in long stories. If several names are involved throughout the story, check the trim target to see whether it mentions someone or something for the first time that gets subsequent references in the remaining paragraphs. If so, substitute the second reference with the first.

Overall, remember that it is writers, not readers, who are uncomfortable with repetition on second and subsequent references. Clarity is better served if the first reference is retained.

Pronouns in Second References: When "He" and "She" Become "Their" and "They"

Because many reporters produce stories under tight deadlines, they rarely have time to read through their copy for grammatical howlers such as this one:

> He testified that they showed the women the guns
> and buried them under the shed.

A competent copy editor probably would have caught that error, but how about other bobbles on pronoun references, such as, "The hostess then invited everyone to sit on their chairs"? Or the sentence that begins with "The student" or "She" who then magically multiplies into a "they" or "their" by its ending? Or plural nouns such as "parents" at the front end of the sentence who shrivel to the singular status of "his" or "her" just before the period?

Most errors in agreement of numbers can be eliminated with a red-alert system for all pronouns, from "I" and "she/he/it" to "us" and "we" to the forms of "they." Reading aloud is still the best technique for picking off agreement errors. Only self-consciousness prevents copy editors from using this excellent tool. Most poets and fiction writers use this technique without an iota of shame. One copy editor says she's among the thousands who police pronouns in their heads while scrutinizing copy. But thousands of others mutter to themselves while editing. They (and you) could just as well include pronouns among the mutterings.

Another successful, and inaudible, technique is joining the pronoun police. That's the habit of checking *every* pronoun at the end of a sentence, especially for "it," "one," and that clumsy combination, "he and she." Also, look for tricksters like "anyone," "each," and the "bodies" (anybody/everybody/somebody/nobody, etc.). These singular pronouns perhaps are mistaken for plurals because they're longer words than "she" or "them." Another bugbear is the pronoun "it," which, when placed at the end of a sentence, can confuse readers about what "it" refers to. See if a proper noun can't be substituted so that a sentence doesn't resemble this puzzler: "Given a choice among a car, a trip to Ireland, and two years' tuition, Jacobi jumped at it."

Most agreement errors occur at the end of a sentence, usually because of "our forgetful authors." The choice then is among which subjects in the sentence should be fixed. Ease and clarity suggest that repairs be made to the subject at the front end. "A student," for example, that must match a "their" at the end, can be pluralized in a jiffy to "students." "Rear-end repairs" required to retain a singular subject such as "a student" often mean using that cumbersome and unsightly reference of "he or she."

Forget about pleasing the hairsplitting purists who "willfully misunderstand" potential ambiguities in omitted references, as one language expert once described such elitist carpings. Copy editors might ache to straighten out a dangling modifier in direct quotes such as, "After pointing out my bad behavior, I was booted out of the counselor's office." Their itchy fingers may be stayed by scruples about doctoring up direct quotes, but also because they know most readers would understand that statement. Yet many copy editors would paraphrase the remark.

Copy editors need to be on their toes about grammar, but sometimes perfectionism can cause them to trip over their own feet and truly confuse readers. For example, most readers *do* understand "elliptical" (omitted) words and would understand this sentence, once branded as ambiguous by a grammarian: "On her arrival, she was told the job was filled and offered $100 as expense money." This construction supposedly leaves the impression that the applicant is offering herself money. The verb "offered" must be chaperoned by "was," as in "was offered." Yet most readers know who's offering money to whom without the auxiliary verb.

Another side of "willful misunderstanding" of pronouns prompts many of the unsure to apply brackets unnecessarily for absolute clarity: "She told council member Reba Jones that she [Jones] should resign." Most readers would comprehend that sentence without brackets, but inclusion means a double take, followed by a rereading of the sentence and, possibly, another. Brackets generally are reserved for stellar occasions such as encasing facts directly following a paragraph of "facts" provided by successful headline seekers like Senator Joseph R. McCarthy back in the early 1950s.[5]

To paraphrase Sir Winston Churchill's famous remark about grammatical purists gumming up communication (in this case, his ending sentences with prepositions): This willful misunderstanding of ambiguities is the kind of nonsense up with which no newspaper copy editor should put.

19 | Catching Errors in Grammar and Usage
(That/Which, Who/Whom, Parallelism, Subjunctive Mood, and Other Pitfalls)

The headline section covered newspaper grammar: active voice, parts of speech, agreement of subjects and verbs, and the like. Much of it is applicable to text. Chapter 6, and especially the section on pronouns in second and subsequent references in Chapter 18, should shore up your knowledge about agreement between subject and verb.

As noted in the last chapter, grammatical wars are unending between language liberals and conservatives. Liberals insist that English is a "living language" for most Americans and newspapers must play to that "currency." Their equally vocal opponents are "linguistically disciplined" purists like John I. Simon, who in *Paradigms Lost* sounded the elitist battle cry to rouse writers, copy editors, and English faculties into action on the barricades: "Surely it behooves us to try to educate the ignorant up to our level rather than to stultify ourselves down to theirs."[1]

Copy editors usually lean toward the "linguistically disciplined," but they recognize the impossibility of satisfying critics so long as the goal is to make reporters' copy clear to 95 percent of the audience. Currently, that audience hovers close to a 12-year-old's reading level. Yet for newspapers to cater to liberal language would be to lose readership in any town. For example, copy editors know that the liberals' often-predicted demise of the pronoun "whom" has yet to happen. Conservative wits warn that such a death would mean renaming a Hemingway novel *For Who the Bell Tolls*. So you'll have to master the use of "whom" and other rules.

This chapter deals with the classic grammatical and usage dilemmas that turn up most often in reporters' copy, for example, the demons of "whom" and "lay" and "which" and other misused words, as well as problems ranging from parallelism to verb mood.

Because many of the paired dilemmas center around choosing word A or word B, an excellent technique for learning pairs of anything is to memorize everything about one part of that pair (or to "major" in the word), preferably one that receives less use. Introduced first at Oregon State University in 1984, the "majoring" system was found to cut memorization time in half.² Confusion about usage became minimal, and a correct choice was usually made instantly. For example, when confronted by the spelling of the "too/to" pairing, students have been taught to "major" in the word "too." "Too" has the advantage of having only one definition ("also") and is used far less frequently than "to." By elimination, students knew that if the word didn't mean "also," it was to be spelled "to."

The first section of this chapter will deal with the most misused and abused words confronting new copy editors. The entries in this section are alphabetized.

As and Like

The same memory system of "majoring in a word" can make you an expert on "as" and "like"—and in moments. Students confronted with this pairing generally "major" in "as" because it must be followed by a subject and verb (either actual or implied). In addition, they have been aided by an advertising slogan for a tobacco company that has outraged grammarians for decades: "Winston tastes good, *like* a cigarette should." Because a subject (cigarette) and a verb (should) followed, the correct choice should have been "as."

Although it's a convoluted memory device, that misbegotten slogan has taught thousands of students that "like" doesn't have a subject and verb, "as" the ad copy did.

If you decide to "major" in "like," remember that this term is used only to introduce words and phrases, not subjects and verbs, as is shown in the following examples:

> The plaintiff testified that the airline agent behaved **like** a lout.

> Some words are especially avoided by talk show guests, words **like** "I" and "me," because they don't want to look stupid before millions—and their English teachers.

One memory device for "like" involves a true story. A television anchor, more overwhelmed by the "like/as" choice than the disaster story he was reading off the teleprompter, ad-libbed: "It sounded *as* an atomic bomb." The profane growl from a *New York Times* luminary was that such errors from TV types "sound as hell."[3]

The moral of the foregoing is that if most slots and many readers know the correct usage of "as/like," you will need to know it too.

Because and Since

Reporters who believe the word "since" is a synonym for "because" seem to be as numerous as copy editors who pass this usage. The two words are *not* the same.

The recommendation for distinguishing one word from the other is to focus on "because" largely because, as the AP stylebook points out, "it involves a specific cause-effect relationship."[4] The cause must trigger the direct effect, not evolve through some circuitous route, as is the case with "since." Looking for a direct cause makes the choice easy. The pair of examples below show "direct cause":

> The woman explained she chained her 15-year-old daughter to the stair rail **because** it was the only

way she could go to work and prevent her from constantly running away from home.

Because he signed up largely for the perks offered by the Army reserves, he wound up on a transport headed for East Timor.

Lay, Lie, and Pay

The best way to differentiate between "lay" and "lie," among the most illogical and quirky verbs in the language, is to focus on "lay." The reason: "Lay" is a verb of high action and is far less complex to memorize than the lifeless, inert characteristic of "lie." "Lie" also has a puzzling past tense form and leads a double life as the noun for a falsehood. So concentrate instead on "lay."

In both present and future tense, "lay" is always involved with action. For instance, in the present tense: The police lay down spike strips in hot-pursuit cases, the assistant sports editor is laying out pages, a company lays off employees, or a talk show host is laying an egg with bad jokes.

In past tense, "lay" becomes "laid" (e.g., "The Panhellenic Council laid down an ultimatum to those two sorority houses about raising grades"). Add the auxiliary verb of "have" or "has" to the verb "lay" and the form is still "laid," as is shown below:

Today's tree-sitters are mainstreamers, the offspring of yesterday's tree-huggers who now claim to **have laid** the foundations for the Eagle Creek protests.

In other words, when copy suggests high action, the correct verb is a form of "lay." If no high action is taking place, use "lie" and its forms (lie, lay, lain, lying).

This is an appropriate way point to state that English is not a logical language and, unfortunately, has no such logical form as "layed" or "payed." Interns and cub reporters will use them, but remind them that illogical or not, the correct forms are "laid" and "paid."

Like and Such As

Years ago, when reporters led into lists or examples, formal composition habits mandated use of warning words like "follow" or "for example/instance" or a short sentence. All were followed by a colon, which many readers find difficult to see.

But those combinations warned readers that examples were forthcoming: "Schools closed include the following:" or "Officers elected Tuesday evening were as follows:" or "Bush's and Gore's statements on their Web sites are provided below for comparison:".

Because newspaper space is expensive, many copydesks began deleting such warnings, including the colon. Their slots assumed that readers had sense enough to understand a series was unfolding and the deletion trimmed composition costs. You may work on a copydesk that still forbids such prefaces. But where slots have decided that some kind of warning is essential for clarity before a sentence drops readers over a cliff into a series or an example, a quiet war has erupted over using either "like" or "such as." Either choice is correct.

The two-word warning of "such as" certainly provides plenty of notice to readers that a list or an example is to follow. But many slots like "like." A respected copy-editing expert has stated that "like . . . is correctly used . . . to introduce words or phrases." He points out that the 500-year-old word "like" has set off so many puristic skirmishes that many in the writing business avoid it altogether "even when it's right." So the rule about prefaces is: Use the slot's preference.[5]

On

The iron rule about the word "on" in leads is to delete it *before* days or dates because it's unnecessary clutter, particularly in one-paragraph briefs like this:

> Slides about the Litani River Project will be
> shown Wednesday, beginning at 7:30 p.m. at the
> Middle Eastern Institute, 1125 NE Wielder.

The exception to this rule in leads and the rest of text involves a
date or day placed *directly after* a proper noun. Omitting "on" could
cause momentary confusion if you were editing a sentence that said:
"Governor Jones said Tuesday that Tuesday Smith would be a guest
at the inaugural tea." The potential for awkwardness is present also
because ideally the "when" element of the 5W's should be located
close to the verb.

But clutter is just the iceberg's tip concerning the misuse of "on."
Problems with that word seem to have developed soon after someone coined it nearly nine centuries ago to be used only with references to location or direction. Indeed, an unabridged dictionary stipulates: "The primary signification of 'on' is a position of contact with
or against a supporting surface or motion into or toward such position."[6]

Back in 1983, a copy-editing expert ignored the abuse of "on" in
headlines because of the word's invaluable short count, but accused
reporters of going "berserk" in misusing it in text.

He warned that if such "Far-Western barbarisms" were not expunged by copy editors, the steady oozing of "on" into newspapers
could "knock all prepositions out of the language."[7]

A decade later, the ooze was much thicker and was threatening
other prepositions, especially in idiomatic expressions ("The social
worker said Laura was on drugs"). An abridged dictionary in the
early 1990s listed 23 definitions for "on" as a preposition alone. "On"
is also used as an adverb and adjective (e.g., "The game is on") with
five definitions apiece.

Despite all the loose use, be warned that a legion of crusty slots
still insist that the word "on" must pertain to location or direction.
Trying to turn the tide back to twelfth-century usage—or scrapping
popular Christmas poetry or fight songs ("On Donder, on Blitzen"
and "On, Wisconsin")—may seem an impossible task in the race

against the newsroom clock. But at least you can change "on" when it's mistakenly used instead of these prepositions:

about	from	of
at	in	to
for	into	toward

Should and Shall

Most students have little difficulty knowing how "would" and "will" are used, but they are unsure about the use of "should" and that antique and elegant term "shall." The activist song of the 1960s, "We Shall Overcome" indicates that "shall" is a word of great determination—but aimed at the future. And a psalmist chronicling the Babylonian captivity nearly 2,600 years ago lamented what looked like a bleak future: "How shall we sing the Lord's song in a strange land?"[8] Another distinguishing characteristic of "shall" is that it's confined to first-person usage only ("I" and "we"). The word "will" is used with the second- and third-person pronouns. Fortunately, the newspaper use of "shall" is infrequent and usually found in quotations. However, those stirring songs of future action furnish an excellent pair of memory devices to know that "I" and "we" "shall" overcome.

"Should" has gained singular notoriety in the last two decades as a dictatorial command like "ought." Both terms are steeped in obligations laid down by those applying the lash of guilt, fear, or taxes, as shown in this example:

> Stein argues that if only 45% of pet owners buy a license, they **should** pay the bills of the animal shelter through a tax on cat and dog food.

"Should" also is considered a verb of regret used to second-guess past actions (e.g., "Judge Brack said that the plaintiff *should* have known he could not get away with tax evasion"). Years ago, purists demanded that "should" be used only in the formal and prospective sense. Like the word "shall," the pronouns accompanying this verb were the first persons of "I/we." But modern usage has substituted the word "could," as in: "Melonkampf admitted he could not have passed calculus without four tutors and four tries."

Where

If you find the nervous expression "you know" irritating when it punctuates almost everything someone says, editing copy that misuses "where" for "that" will become equally irritating. "Where," like "farther," involves geographical distance. Veteran copy editors are brutal in substituting "that" for "where" in sentences like this example:

> He admitted to FAA officials he could see **where** excessive bumping practices could drive customers to Southwest Airlines.

While

The word "while" is not a substitute for words like "and," "but," or "although," as in: "While Reagan might have been a movie star too, actor Warren Beatty has never held public office." The word "while" requires that two actions be going on simultaneously— hardly the case in comparing two politicians over a span of two decades.

Who and Whom

The suggestion for sorting out the who/whom pairing is to memo- rize the use of "whom" chiefly because it's used far less frequently than "who." By the process of elimination, if the pronoun isn't the object of the action in a sentence or clause, the correct choice has to be "who." By the way, "who" is more difficult to memorize because it has two full-time jobs: as a subject in main clauses and a subject in both essential and nonessential dependent clauses.

By contrast, "whom" has never been as busy as "who." It has only one function to memorize: to be the object of all action flung at it by a subject. In other words, "whom" is always the receiver of something, not the doer. The following examples show "whom" as the object of action:

> South Dakota authorities refused comment about the Oglala Sioux council to **whom** the three defendants looked for support.

> The big question at Tektronix all day Thursday was **whom** did the company plan to downsize next?

In addition, "whom" is never accompanied by a verb, but often goes armed only with the preposition "to" standing before it. In other instances, "to" is like a concealed weapon, but is still understood to be present. The second example above has the concealed "to" that is present even if it's not visible. Match up the two subjects ("question" and "company") with their verbs ("was" and "[did] plan") and "whom" stands revealed as the object of the downsizing.

Above all, forget about making the correct choice by the sound of whom/who in a sentence. When copy presents a who/whom dilemma, determine whether the pronoun is an object. If it *isn't*, use "who."

Who's/Whose and It's/Its

The expression "who's" is the contraction for "who is," just as "it's" is a contraction for "it is." Neither contraction is a possessive like "Frank's hat" or "its cycle" because pronouns don't have apostrophes to indicate that they possess something. The possessive form is "whose" and "its." For example, "The dead woman, whose car was stripped of its stereo, lived with a sister."

Again, memorize or major in one choice in each pair of words. Most students facing this choice have selected "who's" and "it's." Perhaps that's because these contractions are more interesting than "whose" and "its," but they also have the decorative touch of apostrophes, the tip that "is" follows the pronouns.

The last section of this chapter focuses on the most common and most visible grammatical pitfalls noticed by copy editors and teachers of composition.

Parallelism

Journalism's emphasis on tight writing may be responsible for the demise of using identical patterns in setting out strings of verbs, of phrases, or of clauses to make stories "reader-friendly." In both the spoken and written word, the technique of repetition always has held audience attention. Classes in beginning reporting teach students to set out nouns equally in a series, like this: "She also won awards for **a** science project, **an** English paper, **a** television script, and an advertising campaign." Grammarians call such a structure of sets "parallelism." Note that each phrase in the example includes a single adjective and a single noun. Boldfacing marks the single article (a or an) that leads into each phrase.

However, copy-editing deletes unnecessary words. That means after the first use of the article (a, an, the) in a series, the rest of the articles are "understood" and deleted like this: "He served with the Seabees, Seals, Green Berets, and Hornets."

Parallelism can also be used with pronouns, phrases, clauses, prepositions, tenses, weights, and measures, as is shown in this example (parallelism indicated by boldface):

> Two of the terms the union sought were **to add** the unemployment payment period from 26 weeks to 36 weeks and **to change** the dental deductible from $500 off the present 100% coverage to a $100 deductible to a future 80% coverage.

> The patient had asked for only 80 **mg** of medication for pain but had been given 550 **mg** for perceived medical distress.

Parallelism is also used in longer and more complex combinations. Many authors employ it for special effects in fiction and poetry. In the example below, the writer has used a repetition of infinitives (in boldface) to establish a cadence reflecting a chaotic lifestyle:

> She likes **to go** to the movies, **to visit** foreign countries, **to leave** the cooking to chefs, and **to flirt** outrageously with death by climbing Smith Rocks.

Errors occur when reporters break the pattern of parallelism in a set. Readers have difficulty following sentences with a mishmash of verb uses like *playing*, *sings*, *recorded*, and *might make*. So watch out for a mix of apples, oranges, and peaches.

Relative Pronouns: That, Which, and Who

The term "relative pronoun" is one of those "grammar terms" like "gerund" and "antecedent" that have triggered fear and loathing in many students since grade school. To avoid repugnance, relative pronouns will be referred to as "RPs" throughout this section.

Because the subjects of clauses at the end of a sentence are directly "related" to the clause subjects at the start of the sentence, they are called "relat-ive" pronouns. RPs are important to copy editors because too many reporters and even novelists misuse "that," "which," and sometimes "who" in long sentences. Many also forget that when the clause with the RP nestles inside a long sentence, it may need to be fenced off with commas. The clauses set in boldface type below contain the RPs:

> Attorney General Janet Reno asked to see the aerial infrared tapes **that purportedly show the use of combustible tear gas on the Waco compound.**

> Measles, **which used to average more than 50,000 cases per year,** now joins other highly contagious diseases nearly eradicated in the United States.

The determining factor about which RP to use is whether the sentence will make sense if the clause is deleted. If the clause is vital to the sentence's meaning, the correct RP is "that."[9] For instance, the clause can't be deleted in the following sentence:

> The apartment **that has the best balcony plant display** will win its tenants a month's free rent.

If people are involved, they should be dignified with the RP "who." (Animals have yet to qualify for "who.") By the way, "who" can lead dependent clauses that are either essential or nonessential to a sentence's meaning. In these examples, the correct RP would be:

> The apartment tenant **who has the best balcony plant display** will win a month's free rent.

> The tenant, **who was born in Dallas,** won the landlord's prize for the best balcony plant display.

Long clauses and prepositional phrases can keep a reporter from spotting the sentence's subject and ensuring that the verb matches. But they also can obscure the match between subject and an RP if that subject is a collective entity like "the university" or "the committee." Should the RP be "they" or "it"? The answer is that organizations or companies—IBM or the army, a school board or a football team—are never "humanized" by the second reference of "they." Use "it." That situation is shown in the examples below:

> The board told the administrative staff that because the Wye Accord did not specify which kind of prisoners to release out of the 750 stipulated, it had voted to start with 250, mostly hardened criminals, rather than those jailed for political militancy.

> The Interfraternity Council's ad hoc committee of representatives from 23 houses pointed out that it was unable to guarantee rent for the annual Greek-Week sing.

"Which" is used only when its clause can be deleted without harming the sentence's meaning.[10] An additional signal that the clause is not essential to the sentence is that it's set off from the main clause by commas, like this:

> The apartment with the best balcony plant display, **which includes mine,** will win its tenants a month's free rent.

If "which" leads a clause ending the sentence, only *one* comma is needed:

> The squirrels at Garden Park apartments love the aspen branches, which generally can't hold a lot of weight.

Verb-Agreement Dilemmas

Headline writing taught you that if a story had one subject, its verb had to be in the singular form. If the story had two subjects (e.g., Bush and the pope in a headline below), the verb had to be plural. Even if the subject had one proper noun paired with a collective proper noun, as shown in one of the headlines below, the verb had to be plural too:

Bush, Pope   **Bush, Palestinians**
agree on   **spar on W. Bank plan**
E. Bank plan

In text, the rule for agreement is largely the same.[11] But some text has more complex subject-verb arrangements that present troublesome agreement situations.

Most agreement dilemmas that concern "mixed" subjects involve more than proper nouns. Nouns that follow paired conjunctions like "either/or" and "neither/nor" are not considered compound subjects. One language expert calls them "alternate subjects."[12] In a sentence with "alternate subjects," the noun nearest the verb determines the plural or singular form of the verb: so a singular noun takes a singular verb; a plural noun, a plural verb. Correct agreement for these two pairings is shown below. The alternate subject and its verb are set in boldface:

> Neither Roy Cohn nor McCarthy's other **sycophants were** aware that their support was eroding.

> In the skirmishing around Capitol Hill, either the Republicans or the majority **whip,** another party member, **had** a clear view of Johnson's machinations.

Another kind of "alternate" mix is also complex, but employs the same kind of agreement form used with either/or and neither/nor situations. For example, take single and plural noun phrases: if the noun *nearest* the verb is singular, the sentence's verb must be singular. An example of such agreement is shown below. The nearest noun and the sentence's verb are set in boldface:

> Movie hits from his books and a **secure desk job** at Freightliner is what Chuck Palahniuk will be talking about in his lecture titled "Tough Tradeoffs" slated Wednesday, starting at 7:30 p.m. in Marsh Hall.

Long sentences usually cause agreement dilemmas, as has been noted. One classic problem concerns the sentence containing that long-lost subject (LLS) separated from its verb by lengthy interrupters like 24-word clauses or parenthetical material. That's the primary problem. Reporters notorious for long, information-packed sentences finally arrive at a period, but have forgotten whether the subject was singular or plural. Examples from university newspapers demonstrate that copy editors failed to notice how difficult the following paragraphs were to read. The interrupting verbiage is in boldface:

> Students, **along with faculties of the colleges of agriculture, science, business administration, law, health and physical sciences, nursing, medicine,** will be invited to an afternoon tea at President's home, 12 Franklin Lane, Sunday from 2 to 4.

> The players **permitted on the team plane, which has been grounded by FAA examiners four times in the last year—Nov. 8, Dec. 9, Jan. 3, March 22—and finally retrofitted as required,** are expected to follow behavior rules stipulated by the NCAA.

The separation between subject and verb may not be as extreme as in the above examples, and the reporter may have correct agreement. But just to be sure, when you encounter a "monster" sentence, jot down the subject and track through the jungle of clauses or phrases to ensure agreement between subject and verb.

Copy editors recognize that certain reporters have patterns of errors in spelling and grammar. You'll see those patterns on a university paper and as a copydesk intern. Making them aware of such mistakes usually starts corrections. One quick remedy for agreement errors and the LLS habit has been to show them a hard-copy markup. To show the long stretch between subject and verb, circle both with a felt-tip pen and link them with an arrow. Circling gets attention and sometimes even an immediate change, and often a "thank-you."

Split Infinitives

When the word "to" accompanies a verb ("to go," "to think," "to have," etc.), the combination is called an "infinitive." The "to-be" infinitive forms range from "will be" to "might be." Writers or speakers who "split" the infinitive insert a word—usually an adverb—between the "to" and the verb like this: "to greatly enlarge" or " to possibly feel forgiveness toward." Even veteran speechwriters will slip sometimes and send high officials to face the media with a split infinitive like: "'The United States and Vietnam will forever be linked by history,' Albright said."[13]

To some purists and slots, splitting an infinitive is a high crime against good writing. Instead of strengthening a sentence, a split often weakens it to the point of awkwardness. Or it may damage the rhythm of the sentence. But the jury has yet to return. A pair of famous writing experts argue that writers have been splitting infinitives since the fourteenth century, but they do admit that such "construction is for the most part avoided by the careful writer."[14]

The "nonsplit fanatics," as a more flexible expert calls them, may be so insistent about recasting *all* such sentences to avoid this "crime against the English language" that the result is even greater damage. Essential adverbs just have no other home, he believes. To prove his point, he once challenged purists to try improving these two examples by repositioning the adverbs on either side of the infinitive—or by rewriting the sentence:

> Production of food fats is expected to **moderately** exceed domestic use and commercial exports.

> This will permit the nation to **quietly** drop her [sic] violent opposition to the treaty.[15]

Ultimately, the copy editor's decision about passing a split infinitive seems to rest on whether readers will understand the sentence.

So when you encounter a "split," try positioning the adverb either before or after the infinitive. Does the switch change the sentence's meaning? Does it harm clarity or readability? Is it cumbersome? If the original split infinitive passes all these hurdles, make no change. If the slot objects, you're free to argue clarity, common sense, and the writing customs of the fourteenth century.

Subjunctive Mood: "If I (*Were/Was*) a Rich Man"

Perhaps the best way to explain the "subjunctive mood" and to provide a memory device for its correct application is to consider the lyrics of that bouncy old song "If I Were a Rich Man" from the Broadway musical *Fiddler on the Roof.* The impoverished peasant who sings it has an abundance of wishful thinking but, short of emigrating from old Russia to the New World, has no likelihood of ever becoming a rich man. He's in the "subjunctive mood" because his wishes are contrary to reality.[16]

When such wishes are expressed, the past tense of the infinitive "to be" (was/were) takes a curious shift. Instead of coupling the usual singular form of "was" to whoever is in fantasyland, the reporter must shift to the verb's past plural form, "were." That expresses the subjunctive mood—a condition contrary to fact or a situation unlikely to change. In news stories, the subjunctive mood turns up most often in comparisons, in projections, and especially in interviews, features, and columns. Be sure the verb is "were," as in these examples:

> If Mayor Barry **were** governing another city, he'd probably turn on his tormentors, but not when he needs every possible vote in Wards 8 and 15.

> If a medical researcher **were** to cure the common cold, Mehan said, s/he might free up trillions in future grant monies.

In sum, if you have begun to master most of the areas covered in this chapter, you'll never again have to use the subjunctive mood and lament: "If only I *weren't* so dense about English, I could ace any writing course" (or avoid the slot's snide remarks). You'll be sure of your command of the magnificent language of Milton and Shakespeare—as well as protecting it in newspaper copy.

20 | Transition Words and Forbidden Terms in Text

The two most popular words with readers may well be "for example" or their cousins "for instance." These are transition words, connectives tipping off the reader that the writer is about to provide an anecdote or a simplification to explain a complex point. They're akin to other crossroad signposts like "however" or "in other council action," indicating that the writer is detouring slightly (as in the case of providing examples) or shifting directions or presenting a contrary viewpoint.

If readers are to follow a story to the end, particularly long pieces, transitions are vital hints or outright statements that the writer is shifting gears. Used mostly on lengthy pieces, transition words or phrases need not be numerous, but they must appear at crucial points. Overuse of transitions—say, every second paragraph—is distractive and clutters writing.

Like freeway directional signs, transitions serve the reader best when placed at the *start*, not at the end, of the first sentence of a paragraph. Changes in midparagraph need the same positioning. If reporters fail to provide transitions or bungle the "lane changes," the copy editor must do the tagging.

Hard-News Transitions

In hard news, writers may get just as bored with simple transitions like "the mayor *also*" and "elsewhere in the state" as they do with common verbs like "said" and "reported." But the taut style, tight space, and deadlines of hard news dictate simplicity. In stories containing long lists of names—usually six per paragraph—instead of starting a paragraph with a name or another kind of noun (e.g., Standard Insurance Company), the longtime, sensible custom has been to use the word "also":

> Carole Rothmore, E.J. Thompson, Merri Wadsworth.
> Also, Sharron Wauword, John Wausau, Marilyn Wavers, Terri Wavers, Henry Wawthorne, and Dorothy Young.

Gifted writers work at creating transitions from the cloth of story events, trying for seamless stitchery in adding information so that readers easily absorb the change, like this:

> Two other hurricanes forming off Bermuda, . . .

> Although Kingsale isn't showing anxiety, . . .[1]

> Another political/religious site is the Hebraic Roots of Christianity Global Network (www.hebroots.org), . . .[2]

Don't touch that kind of transition, but *do* curb those with trendy expressions, especially those obviously lifted from best-selling books or avant-garde alternative weeklies and magazines. They'll be dated within a few months. Besides, most newspaper readers are plodders, unfamiliar with those publications and light-years behind current buzzwords. Because copy editors are the guardians for readability and the guarantors of high circulation figures, they need to substitute familiar transitions for recent stoppers like "absent" (a.k.a. "without") as in "absent new data, . . ." Until such words become commonplace in hard news, replace them with those found in the last part of this section.

Not all "oldies" are "goodies." Some need substitutions because they add absolutely nothing but wordiness. One copy editor despises "basically" in quotations as an "omnipresent introduction," a word he delights in axing. Stoppers like "obversely," "contrariwise," and those banes of the copydesk, *very*, *in order*, and *ergo*, deserve a similar fate.

Feature-Story Transitions

Feature story transitions often present the greatest challenge to copy editors because the writers have space and time to display their creative wares. If a section requires a transition, you may be tempted to take liberties and add a transitional phrase ("Borneo has many other sights . . ."; "Another landmark for the doctor was . . ."). Before putting energy into "smoothing up" a story with your own artistry, know that venturing beyond substituting one or two words means you've strayed far beyond copy editing. Instead, ask the writer to add a transition because readers will need a guidepost at this or that junction.

Most good writers *do* listen to copy editors' suggestions, no matter what you may perceive, and they will try them out (especially on features) giving you an opportunity to do some coaching about what's stale and what's still hale in transitions. For example, most writers would never dream of using that comedic old phrase "meanwhile, back at the ranch," but they see nothing wrong with using the fast-tiring phrase "fast-forward to . . . ," drawn from electronic devices like tape recorders.

However, if howls of artistic temperament follow your deleting the latest jargon, point out that for years, travel writers have set the pace for those midstream changes. Circle the evidence with a felt-tip pen from any Sunday travel section to show how these journalists have mastered the effortless glide into new pathways, as is shown below:

> Windstar Cruises is another line that runs under
> sail, . . .[3]

> River cruising is not limited to Europe.[4]

> Some cruise lines have changed their shore excursions to accommodate kids, . . .[5]

Tell them also that the transitions for features don't have to be fancy. Straight-shot, unadorned expressions containing new data will do, like:

> The west side segment's safety record is much worse than that of the east side.[6]

That transition not only marked a directional shift, but served to introduce subsequent paragraphs detailing fatalities, accidents, and preventive measures.

Another transition device, if space is available, is the "breather," a one-sentence paragraph serving as a major stop sign between two different aspects of a story. You've probably encountered "breathers" similar to these examples:

> Under-prescribing was not the only charge brought against him by the medical board.

> Three explanations were offered for Bradley's surprising showing.

> The next step involves welding.

Readers appreciate such obvious markers because they signal the completion of one part of a feature and the start of another. Breathers also offer readers an opportunity to digest and mull the previous material before continuing into the new material. Another advantage is that if they're well done, they lure readers into subsequent paragraphs.

Moreover, breathers are an attractive typographic device that break up long columns of grayish type, especially in a serious story. Two breathers are perhaps the maximum for one story. Don't spoil their beneficial effect by merging them into the next paragraph unless a trim is ordered. In that case, merge the breather's content carefully into the next paragraph to avoid confronting readers with an abrupt shift.

Some precautionary checkpoints about *all* transition words or expressions should be noted.

Forgetful or distracted writers often overlook one of the "count-offs" when they are setting out paragraphs or sentences beginning with "first" to "fifth." Check for omissions. Don't pass count-off forms such as "firstly," mistakenly used to match "secondly," and so on. Change them to "first," "second," "third," and the like. Ensure that "further," "also," "too," "moreover," and forms of "in addition" do add information. Be literal. Is "finally" or "last" truly the prelude into a final point?

Another common lapse occurs when a writer begins with "on one hand" and fails to follow up with "on the other hand." Make sure that both hands are accounted for. Other usage reminders are: Is "in fact" followed by a fact? Does "by contrast" or "likewise" or "similarly" lack previous paragraphs as counterpoints? Are they genuine contrasts or likenesses? Does the material following "but" show an opposite point from a previous one? Does "in sum" or "thus" lead into summation of all previous material in the story? Is "in short" truly short or is "equally important" followed by important factors that are equal? Are the sentences following "consequently" or is "as a result" a consequence or a result? And as for that new buzzword "arguably," is it applied to something disputed or being successfully argued?

Watch out also for repetitive transitions in lengthy stories, a trait that one copy editor calls the "howevers." Some writers have serious cases of literary "conjunctivitis" because they start too many sentences or paragraphs with *and, or, nor, yet,* and *but.* One cure is awareness, so overuse of a pet transition becomes a red flag. You can help writers by circling hard copy with all the repetitions and by advising them that when they finish a piece, to use the computer's Find tool to hunt the overused transition.

Many transitions most familiar to you and readers are those all-purpose and brief expressions that may be inserted as substitutions in many types of stories. Sorted by two main categories—and some are interchangeable—the most common transitions are:

For Descriptive Passages

above	before/behind	nearby
across from	below	next to
adjacent to	beyond	on the left/right
also	farther	opposite to
at the rear	in the distance	

For Hard-News Stories and Features

accordingly	but	further/furthermore
after/afterward	by contrast/	granted
after all	in contrast to	however
again	certainly	in addition/
alas	clearly	additionally
all things considered/	consequently	in conclusion
being equal	despite	in fact
also	during	in short
although/though	earlier	in sum
and	equally	in the first (second,
another	equally important	etc.) place
as a result/	essentially	indeed
consequence	even though	it follows that
at last	finally	last
at the same time	first/second, etc.	later
because	for example/	like/likewise
before	instance	moreover
besides	for this purpose	nevertheless

next	simultaneously	too
now	since	truly
on one hand/the other	still	undoubtedly
hand	surely	unlike
on the contrary	then	whereas
otherwise	thus	while
overall	to be sure	without a doubt
similarly	to sum up	yet

The Master List of Forbidden Words and Expressions in Copy

A master list of forbidden words in headlines was provided in Chapter 5, and the copy you'll be editing requires even a greater effort to root out forbidden words or expressions. That's because you usually don't write compositions just with headlines. Killing forbidden words in copy will be painful because some probably have been your favorite crutches or have appeared in poorly edited publications. Reporters' copy will contain plenty of old (and new) favorites that were once fresh. And buzzwords and coined words whiz around the English-speaking world with the speed of a comet, and often take longer to die than a dwarf star. If you feel trepidation about cleaning up language usage, remember that your job title is "copy *editor.*"

One of the most ferocious enemies of coined words has been James J. Kilpatrick, author of *The Writer's Art*[7] and a tart-tongued protector of standard English. His syndicated column on usage has amused, educated, and updated thousands of copy editors about the sensible rules of newspaper English. Thousands of other language lovers have sent him grammatical and mechanical bloopers as grist for his column. These errors are on a thousand bulletin boards.

Among those submissions were hundreds of what he called "wantonly coined" words. No reporter in your future newsrooms may ever dare to use any of the following 20 words that Kilpatrick branded the worst offenders. But these will at least alert you about homegrown variations with the giveaway suffixes of "ed," "ing," and "ized"—especially in sports and education copy:[8]

ad hocking	deaccession	[is] officed
administrated	decisioned	outstatisticked
audibilize	defensed	outyardaged
authored	eternalized	strategizing
biographizing	mediocracy	sunsetting
Christmas-treed	[will] obsolete	uptempoes
cowboying	obtention	

When you're ready to act, tell reporters who use jargon or gobbledygook to impress sources that they need to impress their *readers,* who want simple terms and clarity. You might set Kilpatrick's famous line in type and place it over your work area:

> When we let our prose go gobble-gobble-gobble,
> we turn out sentences that are turkeys. . . . Let us not
> inflate a simple thought with gassy prose.[9]

You need to give fair warning to reporters about "hard-editing" and that you are about to prune out such tired terms as "very" and "in order" and give early retirement to new slang like "fast-forward" and "pushing the envelope." It's wise to warn courthouse reporters, for instance, that "evidentiary hearing" will be boiled to "hearing," and "recuse" (still a stopper to most readers) will be changed to "excuse"; that "depose" won't survive unless someone actually has toppled the high and mighty because the dictionary's first definition is what readers understand. Overall, make it clear to *all* reporters that because only sources understand terms such as "conditional-use permit" and "near-term question marks," these words will be translated into reader-friendly expressions. The change from "informational seminar" to "seminar" may take a few weeks, but as "value judgment" becomes "judgment" and "try and" is pruned to "try," you will find unpopularity in a newsroom is in direct proportion to improving reporters' work.

Forbidden Terms in Text

This section of the chapter contains a helpful reference list of the most forbidden words seen in copy and provides substitute terms for "inflated" words. The terms are drawn from the collections of a multitude of copy editors as well as from books and publications on usage.[10]

These terms are sorted into three general categories: (1) clichés and bromides, (2) inflated words with boldfaced substitutes in parentheses, and (3) abused and misused words either to be deleted or to be replaced by accurate terms. Keep this section open while you first-edit copy for a ready reference of forbidden terms.

Clichés and Bromides to Delete

a country mile

a New York minute

all hat and no cattle

at the helm

beat a retreat

bet your bottom dollar

bird in hand

bites the dust

bitter end

bottom line

bound and determined

catbird seat

chickens coming home to roost

chip off the old block

cold shoulder

cut a wide swath/path

cutting edge

die is cast

don't look a gift horse in the mouth

doomed to disappointment

drop a bomb/bombshell

ducks in a row

fast-forward

feathering her nest

find a few nuggets

finely etched

fine-tuned

fire a barrage/broadside

firing a shot over the bow

flies in the face of reason

get in a rut/lick

getting up steam
grist for the mill
harp on a theme
hit a sour note/pay dirt
holding pattern/the bag
in high/tall cotton
ink-stained wretches of the press
it all began
it's in the bag
kith and kin
land-office business
launch a campaign/thousand
    ships
launching pads
leave no stone unturned
lion's share
little did they know
living on the edge
lock, stock and barrel
loose cannon
make hay while the sun shines
making silk purses from
    sows' ears
making whoopee
[a] man after his own heart
man the barricades
moment of truth/madness
no quarter
no respecter of persons
not playing with a full deck
old soldiers never die
paint on a broad canvas/with a
    broad brush
piece of cake
play second fiddle

primrose path
psychological moment
push the envelope
put out to pasture
quantum leap
quiet as a mouse
rattling the saber
remains to be seen
road to ruin is paved with good
    intentions
roll out the big guns
safe harbor
safe port in a storm
safely to port
salt of the earth
sea of red ink/troubles
seeing is believing
selling/going like hotcakes
seventh heaven
ship of state/fools
shot in the arm/dark
showing the flag
sing/singing the blues
slim pickings
smell a rat
smooth as silk
something's rotten in Denmark
sour grapes
still water runs deep
stood the test of time
straight and narrow
strangleholds
struck a responsive chord/blow
    for humanity
sweet as pie/potato pie

swing of the pendulum

take a new tack

take hostages/no prisoners

tall, dark and handsome

[the] team exploded

throwing caution to the wind

timely exit

tip of the iceberg

toe the line

Tom, Dick and Harry

tongue in cheek

tough as nails

tough row to hoe

vicious circle

walk the plank/in the park

what's sauce for the goose is
sauce for the gander

white elephant

win in a walk

wouldn't know him from Adam

Words to Deflate or Simplify and Some Suggested Substitutions

access **(obtain)**

accompanied by **(with)**

actress **(actor)**

acts of a hostile character/
nature **(hostile acts)**

acute emergency **(emergency)**

additionally **(in addition)**

adequate enough **(adequate)**

administrative assistant
(secretary, clerk)

advance planning **(planning)**

advance reservations
(reservations)

affiliated with **(with)**

after very careful consideration
(after considering)

aggravated/nonconsensual/
forcible rape **(rape)**

alcoholic liquor **(liquor)**

alot **(a lot)**

and/or **(or)**

answered in the negative
(said no)

appears to be suggestive of the
possibility that **(suggests)**

as in the case of **(like)**

as of now/that date **(now)**

at 4 a.m. this morning **(4 a.m.)**

at 5 p.m. last night **(5 p.m.)**

at an early date **(soon)**

at that time **(then)**

at the intersection of Market and
Main **(at Market and Main
Streets)**

at the present time **(now)**

at this point in time **(now)**

at which time **(when, during)**

attempted holdup **(holdup)**

authored **(wrote)**

avenues to explore **(ways)**

avid readers/sports fan
(readers/fan)

be cognizant of **(know)**

be in receipt of **(get)**

bitter quarrel **(quarrel)**

born out of wedlock

   (illegitimate)

brand new **(new)**

brutal slaying/murder

   (slaying/murder)

by a score of **(by)**

by the same token **(equally)**

by virtue of the fact that

   (because)

Byzantine **(elaborate/confusing)**

call for **(propose, demand,**

   urge, ask)

called her attention to the fact

   that **(reminded, notified)**

came to a decision as to

   (decided)

cancel out **(cancel)**

carnal knowledge **(sexual act**

   with a minor)

caseloads **(cases)**

center around **(center on)**

church services **(church service)**

cirrhosis of the liver

   (cirrhosis)

claim v. **(assert)**

class I (II, III) assault **(assault)**

close proximity **(near)**

close/personal contact **(contact)**

cognitive **(to learn)**

cognitive learning **(learning)**

collateralized **(secured)**

come in contact with **(meet)**

completely decapitated

   (decapitated)

completely eliminated/naked/

   nude **(eliminated, naked/**

   nude)

completely surrounded

   (surrounded)

component parts **(parts)**

concept **(idea, notion)**

conceptualize **(think)**

conditional-use permit

   (use permit)

consensus of opinion **(consensus)**

contend **(disagree)**

continuum **(link)**

contributing factor **(factor)**

controversial issue **(issue)**

contusion **(bruise)**

convolutions/convoluted

   (complex)

cooperate together **(cooperate)**

cost-effective **(profitable,**

   money-saving)

counterproductive **(futile)**

court litigation **(lawsuit)**

currently **(now)**

dedication ceremonies

   (dedication)

definite decision **(decision)**

definitizing **(stipulated)**

deplaned **(left)**

depose **(dethrone)**

deputy sheriffs

   (sheriff's deputies)

despite the fact that **(although)**

disassociate (**dissociate**)

disposable income (**income**)

downsizings (**layoffs**)

due to the fact that (**because**)

during the course/time of
(**during, when, while**)

during the period from (**from**)

each and every (**each**)

economically disadvantaged
(**poor**)

effectuate (**bring about, start**)

efficacious (**efficient/effective**)

emitted (**gave**)

end result (**result**)

entire monopoly (**monopoly**)

entirely destroyed (**destroyed**)

equally as (**delete one or the
other**)

evidentiary hearing (**hearing**)

exact replica (**replica**)

exhibit a tendency to
(**tend to**)

exit (**leave/quit**)

facility (**office, building,
headquarters, etc.**)

feasibility study (**study**)

featured speaker (**speaker**)

federal mandate (**federal law**)

feedback (**response**)

final climax (**climax**)

fireman (**firefighter**)

first formed (**formed**)

first of all (**first**)

firstly/first ever (**first**)

focal point (**focus**)

for recreational purposes
(**for recreation**)

for the purpose of (**for, to**)

foreseeable future (**future**)

fragmentation (**chaos**)

free gift/pass (**gift/pass**)

frigid weather (**cold weather**)

from whence (**from**)

full feasibility determination
(**approved**)

gavel a meeting (**chair/lead**)

general consensus (**consensus**)

general rule (**rule**)

give consideration to (**consider**)

has the capability of (**can**)

he is a man who (**he**)

help to (**help**)

high rate of speed (**speeding**)

hosted (**was the host**)

housed/domiciled (**lived**)

human resources (**personnel
department**)

if and when (**when**)

if that were the case (**if so**)

impact negatively (**worsen,
wreck, destroy**)

important essentials (**essentials**)

imposition (**to levy, to pass**)

in a hasty manner (**hastily**)

in back of (**behind**)

in case of (**if**)

in close proximity (**near**)

in excess of (**more than**)

in most cases (**usually**)

in regard to (**about, concerning**)

in short supply **(scarce)**

in spite of the fact that **(despite, though, although)**

in the case of **(concerning)**

in the event that **(if)**

in the immediate vicinity **(near)**

in the last/final analysis **(finally)**

in the majority of cases **(usually, most)**

incumbent officeholder **(incumbent)**

inflammable **(flammable)**

informational seminar **(seminar)**

infrastructure **(bridges, highways, buildings, etc.)**

innovative **(new)**

inoperative **(doesn't work)**

insist **(use only for someone insisting upon something)**

insurmountable differences/ difficulties **(differences/ difficulties)**

interaction **(contact, talks, meetings)**

interface **(meet/work with)**

intermunicipal agreement **(city-to-city pact)**

invited guest **(guest)**

irregardless **(regardless)**

is of the opinion **(believes)**

it is the opinion of this author **(I believe)**

it's often the case that **(often)**

Jewish rabbi **(rabbi)**

joined together **(joined, linked)**

journeyed **(traveled)**

juvenile youth **(juvenile)**

kind/sort of **(somewhat, quite)**

labor-intensive **(high labor costs)**

lawman **(bailiff, judge, FBI agent, police officer)**

legal right **(right)**

lengthy **(long)**

little baby **(baby)**

mainstreaming **(rejoining/joining)**

maintenance dollars **(repair costs)**

make an examination of **(examine)**

make inquiry regarding **(inquire)**

make mention of **(mention)**

make use of **(use)**

marriage dissolution **(divorce)**

massive **(use only with physical mass)**

maximize **(to get the most)**

medication **(medicine)**

mega-anything **(big, going beyond the ordinary, vague)**

methodology **(methods, rules)**

micro-anything **(small)**

mining operations **(mining)**

misdemeanor/felony assaults **(assaults)**

modality **(style, method)**

module **(part, unit)**

more importantly (more
   important)
more universally accepted
   (universal)
most (is not "almost")
most equal/perfect
   (equal, perfect)
motivations (motives)
near future (soon)
networking (linking, meeting)
new initiatives (initiatives)
new recruit (recruit)
nexus (link, center)
noon luncheon (luncheon)
normalize (stabilize)
not the case (not so)
not too distant future
   (eventually, finally, next year,
   sometime, ultimately)
off of (off)
official business (business)
offshore (foreign)
oftentimes/oft-times (often)
old adage (adage)
old veteran (veteran)
on account of (because)
on the occasion of
   (when, during)
once again (again)
one of the only (one of)
ongoing process (process)
only a fraction of (a fraction)
operational (working)
optimal (ideal)
optimize (to get the most)

option (choice)
oral conversations (talks)
orchestrate (run, direct)
orient (explain)
orientate (orientation)
originate (start)
origination (origin, start)
outer space (space)
outplacement (layoffs, firings)
outreach coordinator
   (clerk, secretary)
overriding (major)
owing to the fact that (because)
own autobiography
   (autobiography)
parameter (use only for statistics,
   math, astronomy,
   crystallographics)
parity (equality)
partly nude/clad (nude, clad)
past experiences/record
   (experiences, record)
period of time (period)
personal aides (aides)
personal friendship (friendship)
personally attest/testify
   (attest, testify)
pertaining to (about)
pilot program (pilot)
plans originally veiled in secrecy
   (plans are unveiled)
policeman (police officer)
positive attribute (attribute)
pragmatic (practical, feasible,
   workable, flexible)

preemptive strike **(attack)**

preplanned **(planned)**

present a picture similar to **(resemble)**

presently **(now)**

preventative **(preventive)**

primatize **(improve)**

prior approval **(approval)**

prior to **(before)**

prioritize **(rank)**

produce an inhibitory effect on **(inhibit)**

prospective plans/developments **(plans/developments)**

protest against **(protest)**

proverbial **(use only if it *is* from the Book of Proverbs)**

pursuant to **(according to)**

qualified expert **(expert)**

quality control standards **(quality)**

ramifications **(results)**

razed to the ground **(razed)**

reach a truce **(agree)**

reached a conclusion as to **(decided)**

reactivate **(activate)**

reason why **(why)**

rebellion in the ranks **(rebellion)**

recovered alcoholic/addict **(recovering alcoholic, addict)**

recuse **(excuse)**

red hot **(hot)**

refer back **(refer)**

regulatory mechanism **(law, ordinance)**

relate to **(understand)**

remanded back to the lower court **(sent)**

reoccurrence **(recurrence)**

repeat again **(repeat)**

residential housing **(housing)**

rose to his feet **(rose)**

rushed to the hospital **(taken to the hospital)**

scenario **(sequence of events, the picture)**

schizophrenic **(two-faced, conflicting)**

secondly **(second)**

seeing as how **(because)**

self-conceit **(conceit)**

self-confessed **(confessed)**

self-image **(image)**

senseless murders **(murders)**

serious crisis **(crisis)**

serves the function of being **(is)**

shortfall **(lost revenue/debt)**

shower/thunderstorm activity **(showers/thunderstorms)**

single most **(most)**

small child **(child)**

sob audibly **(sob)**

special guests **(guests)**

specific deadline **(deadline)**

state-of-the-art **(newest, new, latest, modern)**

statutory decree/grounds **(decree/grounds)**

statutory parameter **(boundary)**

statutory rape **(rape)**

stimulation **(stimulus)**

stonewalling **(defiant, obstinate, silent)**

strangled to death **(strangled)**

student body **(students)**

subsequent to **(after)**

sufficient number **(enough)**

sustainability-driven measures **(long-term effort)**

sworn affidavit **(affidavit)**

systematize **(organize)**

target **(plan, schedule, focus)**

tax increment **(tax increase, raising taxes)**

terminated **(fired)**

the question as to whether **(whether)**

the reason is because **(because)**

the reason why **(reason is)**

there is no doubt but that **(no doubt, doubtless)**

this is a subject that **(this subject)**

thorough investigation **(investigation)**

thoroughly enjoyed **(enjoyed)**

time frame **(schedule, timetable)**

total abstinence **(abstinence)**

totally fabricated **(fabricated)**

track record **(record)**

transpire **(happen)**

true facts **(facts)**

truth and veracity **(truth)**

try and …

turned up missing **(missing)**

ugly scar **(scar)**

unconfirmed rumor **(rumor)**

uneasy truce **(truce)**

unless and until **(until)**

unproved suspicion **(suspicion)**

unvarnished ardor/truth **(ardor, truth)**

up **(omit when used with: saddle, free, type, close, clutter, fold, make, wash, warm, finish, hunt, muss, lock, start, burn, fatten)**

uptick **(increase, rise)**

upwardly mobile **(ambitious, rich, successful)**

value judgment **(judgment)**

vast difference **(difference)**

verbal **(talkative)**

verbal statement **(oral, written)**

very unique **(unique)**

viable **(workable)**

violent explosion **(explosion)**

visual observation **(see, saw)**

voted unanimously **(passed)**

water resources **(water)**

watershed **(key, major moment)**

weather conditions **(weather)**

were as follows **(were)**

who is a member **(a member)**

widow woman **(widow)**

with reference to **(about)**

work session **(session)**

would-be killer **(the accused/suspect)**

yellow jaundice **(jaundice)**

young girl **(girl)**

Abused and Misused Words to Delete or Replace

absent of	in order	really
accessorized	in which	red-faced/handed
arguably	is the fact that	refreshments will
back burner	ladies	be served
basically	logjams	the fact that
bottom line	mixed bag	there is/are
contexting	nice	torrid
cute/cutesy	nuancing	transpire
cutting edge	off-color	uptick
dazzling	off course	vaunted
desperation	parameterize	very
fenced in	poised	when asked
heave	poly-anything	wily
high wires	pretty	

21 | Writing and Editing Captions

Whether the copy under an illustration—photograph, infographic, line drawing, and so on—is called a "caption," "cutline," or "legend,"[1] ultimately it will be edited or written by a copy editor.

Illustrations and headlines may empty the newsstands, yet it's usually the captions that determine whether related stories will be read. Even if the picture is one of those break-page features that get high interest from readers and low opinions from world-class designers like Tim Harrower ("squirrel-in-the-park stuff"),[2] the caption might be read many times and accompany the illustration on bulletin boards and refrigerators, or be sent to family and friends.

A caption's popularity can be demonstrated even in a left-handed way: some papers have been starting pressruns with missing captions—usually in sports because they are often the last pages to close—for the first hundred copies of a first edition until a remade plate of the page fills the "holes," on the press.[3] At least one daily has almost completed a run with captions containing only "space-holders" of bogus type ("This is a credit/cutline combination. It is made of two text boxes that have been grouped together"). Readers certainly noticed those gaffes. Because delivery deadlines are deemed more important than catching glitches that can be repaired early in the run, it is the last text that's set—often sports captions—that suffers. However, a dozen complaints, measured at a ratio of 1:100, indicates that though a picture may be worth a thousand words, 1,200 readers will be annoyed about a missing caption.

Making Captions Fit

The first consideration in caption writing is to check the specifications for the column size. To have to rewrite a caption because you misread a "2 column" instruction as "3 columns" is time-consuming, reveals inattention, and can rattle you into making additional errors.

Page format and page placement affect caption writing, but scarcely to the degree of typography. Layout varies from paper to paper: A one-line caption doesn't mean a short line. It may extend for five columns. Another paper may justify all lines. Some may use as many as eight lines boxed with an overline and the photo (a.k.a. "caps-carry"; the caption "carries" the entire story). Still others have a penchant for boxed "sidesaddles" whereby captions can be placed on either side of pictures in line widths ranging from the 6-pica minimum for readability to a maximum of 12 picas.

Type *does* govern caption space. Some captions are set in eight-point boldface serif fonts, requiring more space than a seven-point sans serif font set in regular type. Italic captions are not too common these days because of readability, but their slant to the right, especially in boldface, will consume significant space. Wide and narrow fonts also affect fit.

Before computers, copy editors either had an instinctive sense about fit or used a homemade caption-count sheet with samples for various column sizes. Instincts rarely work with justified captions or on newspapers that ban "widows." Today, the computer "tracking" feature can expand and contract type automatically for that style, but "holes" will show if the last line is short by a dozen characters. Papers like *The New York Times* still justify most caption lines, a skill that is recognized on the nation's copydesks as high art, but is unobtainable for shorthanded staffs without long lead times to deadlines. That no-widow tradition, carried on at the Seattle *Post-Intelligencer*, looks like this:

> Jimin Kang works on chipping with her coach, Dan Smith, who says he wasn't surprised by Kang's breakthrough at the U.S. Women's Amateur.[4]

Practice will make you versatile in fitting captions to several typographical styles, including those using boldface lead-in words.

Writing the Caption

The fundamental rule of writing hard-news captions is that, like a hard-news story, the 5W essentials must be in the first sentence. Less important details follow in subsequent sentences. In other words, it's the same inverted-pyramid structure used in a hard-news story. Samples are as close as wire service captions in your daily paper, like this one:

> Kay and Buddy Allen look over their dead livestock Thursday as they tour their flooded farm near Greenville, N.C., by boat. A few of their 300 head of cattle managed to survive in a trailer.[5]

Just as caption writers use a serious vein on photos of foreign uprisings, natural disasters, and statehouse activities—well larded with facts and statistics—you need to do the same for scenes of local fires, crimes, and accidents as well as upgradings of schools and downsizings. Feature captions still require the 5W's, but the word choices may have far more life, like this:

> Rick Neuheisel said he wants his players to smile— something a college football coach isn't always able to do.[6]

In hard news, tight space will force you to use short words and unadorned facts in sentences structured in active voice (subject, verb, object). If sentences are so lengthy and packed with facts that clarity is sacrificed, cut them in two. AP instructions to member papers bar adjectives in hard news; however, in suggesting captions should be written "in a sprightly lively vein," a caveat adds, "whenever appropriate."[7]

Verbs bear the largest burden in any sentence. That's why the variations of "to be" and "to have" are so prevalent. The English language is rich in other verbs, but when you make your choice, be sure it's not on the forbidden-word lists in this textbook and that it's recognizable by most readers. The AP guidelines have banned adjectives because they are subjective and consume space. So do adverbs.[8]

The best role model for captions is still the AP, the font of excellence despite the greatest workload in journalism. Nearly 800 illustrations per day are scrutinized at its Washington, D.C., photo center.[9] Its photo editors have been at it since January 1, 1935, when their captions—dependent on the accuracy of client papers—first accompanied illustrations on the wirephoto machines placed in subscribers' newsrooms.[10] Their flair for moving interesting, fact-packed captions within "two concise sentences" still seems composed in nanoseconds, even on late-breaking news.[11] So trusted is their credibility for captions that few copy editors tinker with AP data. To bring newspaper submissions up to their high standards, most of the AP stylebook editions have included an 11-point set of timeless guidelines.[12]

Heed AP instructions, particularly two red flags: (1) Don't use descriptive overlines unless you are 100 percent certain that you're accurate and you don't offend anyone, and (2) look for late warnings from AP such as "CORRECTIONS" (nonlibelous errors of scores, misspellings, etc.), "ADDITIONS" (misleading, poor taste), "KILLS" (libelous, copyright infringement), and "ELIMINATIONS" (errors, poor taste, inaccuracies).[13]

Traditionally, all other captions were written at the copydesk because too many photographers were unschooled and reporters were busy with new assignments. Copy editors had already processed the accompanying stories and were familiar with their details.

They also were the most aware of libel and privacy laws and the latest rulings, vital for captions of crime shots or seemingly innocent-looking feature pictures. Who else could put the 5W's on a hard-news photo or write spare yet lively lines for a feature illustration under tight deadlines? Only those able to do headline counts could make captions fit, no matter what the column size. An added plum was that if AP picked up the photo, a copy editor's caption might well appear in papers all over the country.

Caption writers at prestigious publications like the *Times* and great "photo books" like LIFE magazine have always worked at adding extra dimension to a story's text and a photographer's artistry. At LIFE, as well as at the Associated Press and the *Times*, caption writers have been trained never to waste words on the obvious overall scene or to repeat anything from the text. They add important information excluded from that text because of space limitations. Or explain some sidelight concerning the photo, some extra fact.[14]

That's a policy followed by papers like the *Atlanta Journal-Constitution* on this local story:

> The tubular bamboo instrument is played by banging it on the ground and hitting different parts of it with a drumstick.[15]

An AP staff photo of windmills carried a caption reporting that 105 of them were on the site. The writer gave the exact geographical location in Wyoming and noted that one place (Arlington) is "possibly the nation's windiest town."[16] As the AP caption team in Washington, D.C., processed thousands of pictures from Hurricane Floyd in 1999, neither tight deadlines nor incoming photos from earthquakes in Turkey or Taiwan could shake them from following caption guidelines in detail-filled captions, such as this one:

> Scott Hoelz of the Newport News, Va., Fire Department's dive team swims out of a U.S. Navy housing community Thursday after helping rescue residents.[17]

The State of the Caption Elsewhere

Unfortunately, because of added duties assigned to shorthanded copydesk staffs today, caption standards have slipped. At all too many papers, large and small, captions have been relegated to sharing the lowly status of "pullout" quotes used to break a sea of gray type.

A story's text is combed for a sentence to be copied and then slapped under a picture, often with little relevance to what's depicted. Cost-effective though the practice may seem to be, expeditious sloppiness, in terms of potential litigation, is considered highly dangerous by photo services such as AP.[18] But the long-term effect of this cost-cutting practice could be readers deciding that with a headline, a deck, a pullout quote, *and* a caption, why bother reading the story?[19]

Worse, the AP depends heavily on pictures and captions from client papers, but today nearly two dozen staffers have to *rewrite* most captions because submissions don't meet the guidelines for captions or for archival "headers" (computer-search data).[20] One of its operational philosophies has become: "If you find a dozen errors, look for the 13th."[21]

Because AP's survival rests on meeting deadlines tighter than any publication's press and delivery systems, its editors take a dim view of newspaper time constraints as an excuse for failure to follow the basics rules, particularly as it concerns *all* spelling.

For the emergence of such problems, it's difficult not to fault newspaper management's decision to shift caption writing from overworked copy editors to overworked photographers, many of whom resent and resist the extra burden. Veteran "shooters" liken it to asking a Pablo Picasso, an Alfred Eisenstadt, or a *National Geographic* photographer to write captions. Prior to Polaroid or Instamatic cameras, many newspaper photographers had to juggle 4x5 cameras, sleeves of flashbulbs, film packs, tripods, and light meters. They had to know composition and the physics of light as it changed every five seconds in relation to shutter speeds and then process and print the results. Notes might be scribbled inside empty film boxes or information given orally to copy editors who grilled exhausted shooters for facts.

No more. Photographers are now required to write the captions at many papers. Cost cutting and an abundance of shooters applying even at small dailies have forced photographers to wear two hats.

Many who hold photojournalism degrees never expected to have to put newswriting training into practice, either to write captions or to provide accurate 5W data for those who do. As a copy editor, you probably will be editing or rewriting a photographer's copy. At least one major daily has coped with this industry-wide change by having such captions edited three times: by the photo desk, a team leader, and the copydesk.[22]

One paper that accepted this reality has become a national pace-setter for photographers teaming with copy editors to write captions: the Pulitzer Prize–winning *St. Petersburg Times*, an industry leader since the days when owner Nelson Poynter (1947–1978) set up its 15 standards of excellence.[23] The paper's stable of nearly three dozen photographers have to be good shooters, good reporters, and good partners of copy editors.

Poor spellers or fact gatherers are neither hired nor given internships. "If they have misspellings in their *resumés*, what would they do on deadline?" says Sonya Doctorian, its former photo director. She set the policy for photo captions.[24] Strenuous efforts to provide accurate caption data and to zero in on misspellings under a motto of "CQ's as Good as Gold" (CQ is wire service code for "correct") have created a caption-writing corps that even the nation's grumpiest copydesk would regard as stellar for credible material.[25] The teamwork between photographers and copy editors who apply a little shine to their captions produces work like this:

> A 3- to 4-foot alligator swims in the pool Tuesday night at the Chateau Versailles condominiums at 2255 66th Ave. N. in St. Petersburg. "If he stays in any longer, I'm going to charge him a maintenance fee," resident Shirley Griffin said. Griffin first noticed the reptile relaxing in the pool early in the afternoon. "There's not enough gator there to make a purse for my wife," resident Robert Puffer added. The neighbors watched the gator from outside of the fenced-in area of the pool while trying to call trappers to have it removed. Among the rules the

gator violated were No. 3, requiring a pool pass, and
No. 8, requiring proper swimming attire.[26]

An overabundance of the supply of photographers means that
other papers probably will follow the *St. Petersburg* example and that
you will be handling captions in the same kind of joint-operating
arrangement. But you may be teamed with a more trustworthy
source of caption material than some reporters. The day could come
when AP uses your caption—with no changes. To attain such skill,
the next part of this chapter provides you with a training acronym,
LOMISA, which stands for:

  L = look at the illustration carefully
  O = omit the obvious, and add meat
  M = reflect the mood of the picture
  I = get the identifications right
  S = use correct spelling and grammar
  A = ensure accuracy and prevent litigation

L = Look Before You Leap

The AP's cardinal rule, one "never, never to be violated," a rule so
important that it's set in caps in its stylebook is: Never write a caption without seeing the picture.[27]

Even if you're writing a deadline caption as the illustration is
being scanned or poured into a page from a digital camera, the
words should reflect the picture's *overall* content.[28]

Study the illustration carefully before you write or edit any caption. Look at facial expressions. Should you use a verb such as
"laughs," "cries," or "challenged" or a description about "rapt attention" or "disinterest"? Is that what was going on—for everyone?
Ask yourself some of these questions, which readers assuredly will
be pondering when they see the illustrations: Do those near–tidal
wave descriptives fit such a placid scene? Are those *regular* army

troops or insurgents in uniforms stripped from victims? Is the semi-trailer truck "jackknifed" or on its side? Is it a 16- or an 18-wheeler? Are four people identified when there are only three in the photo? In that art feature, are you certain the medium was charcoal or might it be crayon? Are you confusing Michael Jordan with Michael Jackson? Don't those coat lapels or the backward numbers indicate the photo has been "flipped"?

Double-check all mug shots. Many embarrassing "corrections" involve mistaken identities in thumbnail portraits. File photos also present high-risk situations, particularly if the attached data or notes on the print's backside are ignored. No matter how flattering the 1962 portrait of the deceased is, objectivity and ethics demand the date be included (e.g., 1959 file photo), especially for obituaries.

O = Subtract the Obvious
by Adding Substance

Whether the illustration is a feature shot or shows earthquake rescuers lifting people from debris, don't waste caption space on overall factors obvious to the reader. A sports picture of one person in a sea of 15 rows of empty seats shouldn't start off with: "A man watches the Cardinals' batting practice . . ." Readers *do* notice that players are leaping and being tackled, that mobs are throwing bottles, and that children are being hugged, dogs pant, and mall rats hang out. Instead of "An earthquake victim is lifted by a soldier . . ." broaden the copy either by saying that "Taiwan soldiers, working in hotel rubble . . ." or "This woman was among the 46 hotel residents rescued Saturday by Taiwan army teams as . . ." Even "squirrel-in-the-park" pictures can contain captions of substance. For example, a caption writer for the Seattle *Post-Intelligencer* glanced at the photo of a pair of canoeists and wrote:

> Kaori Kojima, left, and Song-Mi Ryo, both language
> students at Seattle Pacific University, take advantage

of a sunny afternoon as they paddle through the waters at the Washington Park Arboretum. Yesterday's summery weather and temperatures are predicted to last throughout the week, with today's high expected to be near 85.[29]

Scrutinize illustrations *as if you were a reader* for details, interesting sidelights—or something that might be misunderstood. Readers are interested in extra details that might even go beyond the shot. Busy as the *St. Petersburg Times* photographers were in shooting a spread for yet another oncoming hurricane, one fact-packed caption also satisfied reader curiosity about what would happen next, like this:

A Clearwater police officer tells Brett Austin, who recently moved to Oldsmar from Hawaii, that he can't use a surfboard off Clearwater Beach on Tuesday. After Austin put his board in his truck, he went bodysurfing.[30]

Readers can misunderstand some minor elements too, unless captions head off their rush to the telephone, to the letters column, or to the streets with placards. For example, why are all those men suited up for a women's Race for the Cure run? What's that white powder on the governor's desk? Is that a swastika in the lower left corner of that woodcut? Many times it's nothing major. A caption writer for the Cleveland *Plain Dealer* knew that readers would wonder about a dirt pile in one shot of a feature on school bands. The caption explained it:

At left, Medina High School Band members can't miss director Gary Ciulla during practice. His 20-foot-high podium—a pile of dirt—is a fringe benefit of recent construction at the school.[31]

Using facts *beyond* the text or the illustration can offer invaluable additions to a story's scope and depth. Talk to the photographer or the reporter for material that either was squeezed out of the story or is in unused notes. Other factors can be pulled from references or the Internet (provided it's from a "red-check" source)—and on deadline. That's what one writer did in a few minutes spent with an almanac and the microfilm files of *The New York Times:*

> Earl Wu, at left, distributes union pamphlets in Chinese today in mid-town Manhattan that detail the Triangle Waist fire of March 25, 1911. That fire killed 146 workers who either jumped from windows and down elevator shafts or were trapped in the 10-story loft building in downtown Manhattan in sweat-shop work surroundings seen by the union as less hazardous than today's conditions. In the noon-hour rally, Wu quoted Rose Schneiderman, a union spokesperson, who admonished workers to join because the only way to "save themselves . . . is through a strong working class movement."

Instead of the lazy and widespread practice of lifting story quotes for mug shot identifications, caption writers for *USA Today* use additional data. The boldface lead-ins focus on the "who," followed by a few words explaining the subject's news significance:

> **Founder, CEO:** Bruce Merrell says his Laptop Lanes get up to 100 customers a day.

> **Working toward a deal:** White House economic adviser Gene Sperling calls talks 'positive.'

> **Ex-Seattle police officer** Sonny Davis examines some documents before his trial starts. He is accused of taking $10,000 from a crime scene.[32]

M = Reflect the Mood of the Illustration

Outside of hard-news areas, captions should reflect the mood of the illustration—somber or light, serene or frightened—whether it involves sports or lifestyle, real estate or arts and entertainment. Verbs still bear the burden of carrying a caption's tone and color, but the shorter and more familiar they are, the better. Pick adjectives and adverbs as carefully as a good poet would.

Considering that copy editors see thousands of bloody and heart-rending illustrations—along with the sappy and the superb—it's easy to understand the cynical and gallows repartee sometimes over-heard in their corner of the newsroom. Shakespeare, after all, knew that a comic line released built-up tension and restored sanity. Yet readers rarely understand "dry humor" in captions and as for satire, almost never. Forgo such impulses and stick to captions that reflect the moods accepted by most of the paper's readers.

In local hard news, captions usually follow the pattern used by the A section so that enough latitude exists to include tinges of sadness or touches of fun among the 5Ws. But don't get maudlin or too merry. For example, sports scandals are common, but this caption captured the fears of an athlete in deep trouble:

> Jason Stanford, a University of Minnesota senior majoring in electrical engineering, reflected Wednesday on the nightmare that unfolded for him and three of his Gophers basketball teammates, who were suspended from a tournament game when it was alleged they participated in academic fraud.[33]

A stunning travel spread on the gardens in Suzhou, China's canal city, had its tranquil pictures and text enhanced by captions match-ing their mood with the use of simple and euphonic words. One cap-tion said:

> Surging Wave Garden is small, intimate and peaceful with fewer visitors than other Suzhou gardens.[34]

Business captions tend to mirror the serious mood *Fortune* maga-zine set at its debut in the Great Depression (1930). Facts, figures, and exactitude on corporate names do reflect a bloodless environment. But features permit brighter tones and even slang, as in this one:

> **IN THE SWITCH ROOM:** Mike Gallagher, CEO of Florida Digital Network, wants a piece of the state's $11 billion local phone market.[35]

I = Check Identifications

Every person, place, or object appearing in an illustration must be identified. Some of the best identification practices are found in sports captions because the writers identify the teams and players, and, to prevent confusion, may even include the jersey number, like this:

> Michigan's Bob Renes (58) pressures quarterback Chad Richardson.[36]

Even if the subjects are identified in the text or are so famous you believe every reader should recognize them, identification still bears repeating in the caption because some readers may never get to the story. For photos of celebrities or prominent residents, identifications generally follow the same rule as for text: only one title, and that must be related to the story's thrust. As previously noted, a civic leader may serve on several boards of directors or hold membership in many organizations, but in the tight space of a caption, that person needs only one identification.

Small-town papers always print photographs of large organizations because they build circulation and a reputation for community interest. That needs to be kept in mind as you write perhaps the most difficult and dangerous captions of your life, considering the sins of omission and misspellings that can occur—and the ability of the victims to contact the publisher. The faces may be barely recognizable, even to the leaders of such groups. And after age 35, most people are displeased with their photos, but *do* want to see their names in the caption. If your newspaper's policy doesn't list names when the group is larger than 30, at least include the correct name of the group and identify its key people.

Paragraphing the identifications for large groups ideally is done by rows with the word "also" leading into subsequent paragraphs, as was shown in the last chapter.

Photographers experienced in shooting groups often pass out forms so that subjects can write their names in row-by-row sequence, ensuring that nobody goes unidentified or has a misspelled name (providing the handwriting is legible), and that genderless names like Leslie, Lynn, and Kim are not open to question. Such a sheet is an excellent backup document for any later complaints. If your paper prints a lot of group photographs and lacks such a system, suggest one.

The greatest peril of all in group photos involves writing captions of children because their families call on misidentifications. In shots of teams, classes, organizations, churches, and so on, match the names with the faces in each row—*three times.* If someone is unidentified, either ask the photographer or the studio to check its notes or call a group adviser for help. Only if such efforts fail should you resort to using "unidentified" in a caption. That process takes time and effort, but on small-town newspapers, each child's name probably will sell at least two copies over the counter to families; photocopies are unsatisfactory. As for the kids, those "five-up-and-ten-across" pictures are treasures most will keep for a lifetime. If you doubt it, check *your* scrapbooks.

Last, never waste caption space on warm-up phrases such as "posing for," "shown above," "pictured," or any other allusion to photography. Depending on the size of a group or their configuration, the easiest systems for readers to follow are still phrases like "from left," "clockwise from top," "Row 1, Row 2" or "standing" and "seated." If only two people are depicted, use that classic parenthesis identifier "(at left)."

S = Spelling and Grammar

As indicated above, perhaps the most important rule in a caption is that people's names—especially local residents—be spelled correctly. As with the story's text, readers will forgive a multitude of sins, from wrong scores to misidentifications, but rarely the misspelling of their names. Once you have the print and the raw list of names, use both index fingers (one on the photograph, one on the list) and read the "matches" aloud. In the first round, match the name with the face. In the second round, either find someone who'll listen to you spell the names or just read them aloud.[37]

Know that it's in the typing of those names that the door is flung wide to errors. But many safeguards exist. The main one is never to trust *any* retyped list of names, least of all the one *you've* keyboarded. You're likely either to miss someone or to misspell names.

Check the spelling and official titles or any other proper nouns connected to organizations and companies. Is it Center for Disease Controls or Centers for Disease Control and Prevention? The Confederate Veterans Sons or Sons of Confederate Veterans? Batton, Barton, Morris, and Durstein Inc.? or Barton, Morris, Durstein, Batton & Sons?

The *Columbia Gazetteer* is the red-check source for geographical places, and the city map usually will indicate whether "Broadway" is an Ave., St., Dr., Blvd., or Pl. Use the copydesk's reference tools like telephone books and the city directory.

Then, check the caption's remaining words. The AP writers' main complaint about submitted captions is poor spelling, something scarcely confined to proper nouns. If the newsroom lacks an equivalent to *The St. Petersburg Times*'s operating rule of "CQ's as Good as Gold," your work will be cut out for you because of the resistance to use the computer's spell-checker feature or a dictionary. Considering that the copydesk exists to catch errors, your attitude should be one of gratitude rather than resentment that others are not equipped to be copy editors.

Readers might overlook grammatical errors in text, but mistakes loom large in captions. Because the only writing most copy editors do involves captions, they are far more prone to commit as many grammatical errors as reporters and photographers. Grammatical excellence demands regular practice and at far more than writing captions. That means you must take great pains to meet grammar standards demanded of photographers.

So check for complete sentences. When a caption is fact heavy and comma filled, it's easy to omit a verb, the prime culprit in incomplete sentences. In headline writing, you learned to label the subject and verb with a large *s* and *v* so you could detect the actor in active voice. Use that same technique in captions to monitor agreement.

The other challenge with subjects and verbs is ensuring agreement despite a caption's usual length. Long captions all but guarantee grammatical errors. To practice, label the subject and verb in the caption below. Then circle the incorrect *pronoun* reference—pronouns are near the end of a sentence:

> Jennie and Flint W. Norton, whose production company Poolesville, Rockville, and Bethesda Film-Making Institute of Maryland, a perennial Sundance Film Festival finalist whose most recent entry is *Dawn Strikes and Other Fables From the Molly McGuires*, have teamed with the owners of the Holladay Bank, Ltd. of Greater Winnipeg to finance his next production *Luddites, the Ludlow Massacre and Mr. Rockefeller*.

So far as tense is concerned, stick to the present form for verbs in the caption's opening sentence. The example below contains three sentences, all using present-tense verbs. The verbs are singled out in boldface type:

> Eritrean soldiers **watch** Ethiopian troops from a trench at the Badme front line. Most days **are spent** waiting and hiding. But sometimes the combatants **launch** infantry assaults, causing tens of thousands of deaths.[38]

If historical data are used in a second sentence, shift to a *past*-tense verb.

The next example shows that kind of shift in two sentences (verbs are set in boldface):

Taketo Yamakawa of GE Capital **meeting** with some managers at the company's headquarters in Tokyo recently. Mr. Yamakawa **has turned** a one-man operation into a thriving business, expanding total assets to about $20 billion in the region.[39]

A = Accuracy and Preventing Litigation

Again, remember that the first step *before* writing any caption is to do a head count to ensure that everyone in the illustration is accounted for, particularly in pictures using the "clockwise from left" directive. Time was when copy editors also checked the crop marks to see if people identified in captions had been trimmed from the picture ("You got eight names but only four people"). They also hounded the photographers or reporters to supply missing names, a practice that is not dead. Use it.

Accuracy also involves getting the right city, the right street address, the right dates, the right numbers, and the like. Don't pass zip code abbreviations for states instead of those listed in the stylebook. And is it Bismark, S.D., or Bismarck, N.D.? Is it the Eastmoreland Recreation Center or the East Moreland Recreation and Outdoors Centers? Has a typing bobble turned 4th District Court into 14th District Court? Many copy editors save time by making their own lists of "pesky" titles. Study every word in the caption before you close it because readers assuredly will and love to tell your bosses about such gaffes.

Call the morgue about captions citing previous stories. Between the desk's reference tools, the morgue, and the Internet, you have the largest library in the world at your fingertips. Use it regularly and it will take only a few minutes to find reliable sources for facts like the discovery date of the Heidelberg Man, the average life expectancy of those over 60 stricken with lymphoma, and how much money was raised for the local 1984 United Way drive.

The final warning about captions involves preventing lawsuits, particularly concerning photographs about crime or courtroom actions.

The word "murder" used in captions sent to the AP is one that its staff regards as a major hot button for danger.[40] Use "killing" or "slaying." A pretrial story on criminal activities may contain safeguards ranging from attributions to the charges, and the story's precautions must be included in the caption.

Also, a story might list the 4500 block as the suspect's address, but it doesn't "show" the suspect. A photograph does, making that individual recognizable at work, in the supermarket, and in society. If an arrest does not lead to charges, as is often the case, that photograph and caption can ruin many lives—to say nothing of giving a paper a bad image and possibly a defamation lawsuit. The Atlanta Olympics bombing case demonstrates that suspects *do* sue and can win millions from copy editors failing to distinguish between being arrested and being charged. Because lawyers work on contingency fees, ordinary people now have champions who *do* know the difference. They have nothing to lose by suing a newspaper, whether it's a weekly or big daily or an alternative paper. So before you pass a caption involving crime, know your ground.

The same care needs to be exercised on civil suits because a caption about a defendant, even in a spectacular case that the desk considers "hot news," may not be viewed in that same light by a jury or an appeals court. The landmark *Firestone* case detailed in the AP stylebook[41] should furnish sufficient evidence to support care on captions in civil actions. Again, as in all editing, follow the copydesk's motto emphasized repeatedly in this book: "When in Doubt, Leave It Out."

PART III

ACCURACY
AND LIBEL

22 | Two Safeguards for Headlines and Copy: Pursuing Accuracy and Avoiding Lawsuits

Whether you're writing headlines or processing copy, it's essential that you be prepared for a relentless pursuit of accuracy and learn eternal vigilance methods to prevent lawsuits. The classic and seminal newsroom resource on libel, slander, and invasion of privacy is still the *Associated Press Stylebook and Libel Manual*. That inexpensive, invaluable paperback contains its definitions and applications as well as landmark rulings by the U.S. Supreme Court that seem to have been the most frequent causes of litigation.

This chapter is designed as a companion piece for the *Associated Press Stylebook* to show you how to pursue accuracy with avidity and how to avoid ever hearing that most dreaded of summons: "The company lawyer wants to talk to you about a story you handled in Monday's paper."

Part of the problem seems to be nearly 30 years of reporters following the "new journalism" and "literary journalism" writing styles of novelists such as Norman Mailer and Truman Capote or columnist Jimmy Breslin—and, yes, the fiction of Pulitzer Prize–loser Janet Cooke. Their rationale was that news had become so complex that readers needed them to *interpret* rather than just report the stark 5W's for hard-news stories.[1] To the shock of copy editors and "old-fashioned" reporters, many editors, publishers, and focus groups agreed with them.

That would have been a positive way point for journalism if every reporter had the investigative depth to produce, say, the authoritative series on the Ford Pinto that appeared in the advocacy magazine *Mother Jones*. But the upshot has been that even small-town council meetings have been covered by those copying the "anamorphic prose"[2] of writer Tom Wolfe or the "gonzo" journalism of novelist Hunter Thompson. Literary varnish has been applied thickly on downtown topics, and posturing quotes from local showboaters devour valuable newshole space that would be better spent on a county commission's *full* agenda.

Specialty reporting, especially in high-tech, science, and business areas, too often spawns "groupies" who accept what experts in those fields tell them without question. Too many of such "specialty" reporters lack both the investigative training and grueling peer reviews required for research, but spout what their idols espouse as gospel. Nevertheless, they pose as experts, telling readers that this computer program is impervious to hackers, that Agent Orange had no adverse effects on American troops, or that recovering alcoholics can go back to controlled drinking. Or that because this article is in a professional journal, its findings are 99 percent correct. If you remember how some of your classmates produced term papers, you will begin to shudder about newsroom "experts" in specialty fields. Foreign affairs expertise, especially contained in wire stories, is yet another field that few copy editors question. Only when this author was working on a newspaper in the Mideast did she discover that many foreign correspondents lived like the British Raj and paid those they called "local flunkies" to do all the legwork of covering stories. Those locals, in turn, were not stupid. They usually provided what they perceived the correspondents wanted to file or what Americans wanted to believe about this leader or that event. Is it any wonder that the readers have little idea of what is going on in parts of the world where English is *not* spoken or where the only newspapers cater to those in power? The point being made here is that when you are processing stories written by "experts," you need a healthy skepticism about the content. Put as many attributions to the claims as you would a labor and management dispute or football coach boasting about the team's prospects for the coming season.

You can practice your skepticism about research methods on a Pew Research Center study released in March 1999. It revealed that half of the 552 news professionals interviewed admitted that the newspaper business's main problems were "sensationalism, a lack of objectivity and inaccurate reporting."[3] But who did the researchers interview: newspaper staff members? publishers? Were respondents working for a weekly paper, a small daily, a major national publication? What questions were asked? Was this a telephone interview at the dinner hour or was it confined to e-mail or a mailed survey? When was the study done, during vacation months? During a news lull or after a major event? Who funded the project? How reliable is that research organization? Syndicated columnist Charley Reese instantly extrapolated the results as if only readers/viewers had been interviewed and, on that basis, warned present and future journalists:

> What's bad for the future of the industry is that people don't care much what we opinion writers say, but they are enraged by bad reporting. They absolutely hate going to a public meeting and not being able to recognize it from the next day's news account. They despise watching something on C-SPAN and then seeing how news reporters distort it. A slanted news story is like a lie—the whole paper is tainted, for if readers can see error or deception in one story where they happen to know the truth, then it is a safe assumption that a similar pattern may be present in all stories.[4]

The foregoing anecdote should shake your belief that anything printed is holy writ, and authors write with the kind of authority no copy editor should ever question. Edit copy with all this in mind.

Joseph Pulitzer: "What a newspaper needs . . . is . . . accuracy, accuracy, accuracy!"

The man in whose name Columbia University annually awards the printed word's top prizes, publisher Joseph Pulitzer, once summed up his recipe for making millions off his best-selling newspapers:

> What a newspaper needs in its news, in its headlines, and on its editorial page is terseness, humor, descriptive power, satire, originality, good literary style, clever condensation and accuracy, accuracy, accuracy![5]

Loud and lively though headlines were in his *New York World* back in the 1880s—shocking only the puritanical—its copy editors were as scrupulously accurate as the stories they trumpeted.[6] Carry on Pulitzer's tradition by making sure that headlines, copy, and captions are accurate. When red flags go up, even if a story is written by a careful reporter or moved by a highly respected wire service like *The New York Times*, trust your instincts and knowledge. Once again: "When in Doubt, Leave It Out." Or insist on changes.

Your gullibility or newsroom awe will decrease with each piece of copy you process, much like a beginning teacher who gets increasingly exacting after discovering many top students are either cunning plagiarists or incredible dupes. Idols fall while a healthy skepticism about *all* writing rises. If that copydesk philosophy seems disturbingly negative, if you don't believe that mistrust of copy is a *must,* you will adopt that attitude when a story eventually turns out to be inaccurate and letters and a lawsuit turn up. Experience is not only the *best* teacher on the copydesk, it is usually the *only* teacher.

Every copy editor has war stories about "catches" (of errors) that required either killing a story or caption or making major alterations. Pulitzer Prizes have had to be returned because copy editors were flummoxed or fearful of challenging newsroom stars. Yet many copy editors have stood their ground and refused to be intimidated by "experts." Outraged reporters may stop speaking to you for a time if you do ask questions about doubtful aspects of a story, but be assured they usually are inwardly relieved that *your* "catch" may prevent a mistake from appearing in the paper. Don't expect effusive displays of appreciation—or thanks. Your only reward will lie in having prevented those errors.

The same vigilance should be shown on all "outside" copy from the wire services, syndicates, online authors, and local historians. Beginners often assume that because stories come via the wire service "ticker" or off the Internet, the fax machine or over the counter, they are flawless. Technological magic somehow makes stories inviolable. Don't believe it.

Do believe desk gossip about untrustworthy stories and sources. Your colleagues are not being jealous or cynical. They're trying to keep you from the land mines they have stepped on.

From the inception of the wire services before the Civil War, correspondents' copy has involved errors. That's why "CORRECTION" bulletins exist today. In that war, both the early Associated Press and the Confederate Press Association could not afford competent, draft-exempt reporters, even if they were able to get around military censorship or attempt scooping star correspondents like A. D. Richardson or Felix de Fontaine.[7] It's still a given considering that correspondents gather and file news under extraordinarily hectic or dangerous conditions.

In the main, copy editors can make any number of minor corrections to AP copy, and they often merge it with other stories in "roundup" treatment. But a major "catch" that makes a material change needs to traverse the chain of command from you and then your slot to the bureau chief. So before you scroll through outside copy under the presumption that it's without blemish, give it at least one more careful read on the keyboard before writing a headline.

Syndicated columns are different. Slots differ on changing errors of *fact* (not viewpoints or thrusts) from these famous writers. When one of the "stars" identified the Czech town of Lidice as a concentration camp, a copy editor on an eastern daily announced to the slot that she was making a change. Lidice, she pointed out, was the village plowed under like Carthage (men shot, women and children sent to concentration camps) as Nazi revenge for the nearby assassination of SS Obergruppenführer Reinhard ("the Hangman") Heydrich. Unimpressed with this World War II trivia, the slot snarled, "Don't change anything! Let *him* hang! His readers will teach that overpaid right-winger something about accuracy!" Presumably, some did.

Time, Inc. Publications:
Role Models for Exemplary Accuracy

Perhaps the best-researched and most accurate publications in the United States—hard-news or features—are from Time, Inc.'s empire of magazines (TIME, PEOPLE, SPORTS ILLUSTRATED, LIFE, FORTUNE, MONEY, and others). The Lidice error would have been instantly detected, the writer notified, and the copy changed. Subjective though Time, Inc. presentations might be, if a story states that, say, Amritsar was founded in 1577 and is near the Ravi and Beas Rivers in India, every word of that statement has been *minutely* verified by the company's legendary checking process. In the days when LIFE's circulation was at 25 million, the magazine's attorney used to terrify rookies into even greater measures of verification by warning that an injunction over a *single* error, one unrelated to libel, would prevent the post offices and distributors from delivering the magazine to newsstands and subscribers.

No daily has the luxury of weeklong deadlines, the pick of the best journalistic crop, or a morgue rivaling the archival staff and inventory of the New York Public Library. But the eagle-eyed staffers of that magazine empire and their counterparts on the copydesks of thousands of newspapers do have the opportunity to obey Pulitzer's charge and to engage in the hot pursuit of errors and the delight in rooting them out. A rim of "fussy" copy editors *does* force Pulitzer standards on reporters and contributors to redouble efforts in checking "facts."

It's also comforting to remember that not since Aristotle walked the earth has one person known everything. Even a Carr Van Anda relied on references. The smallest newspaper has reference tools ranging from an atlas to a dog-eared dictionary. If the rallying cry at Time, Inc. for unparalleled accuracy has always been "I need to look it up," a copy editor on any newspaper certainly can adopt that philosophy with even minimal resources at hand.

Pride and laziness need to be thrust aside and the discipline of reaching for the dictionary must become ingrained. Thumb through the AP stylebook to determine whether it's *effect* or *affect*. Check the atlas for the location of Timbuktu (a.k.a. Tombouctou). Dip into the desk's reference toolbox and get familiar with the *World Almanac*, the state "blue book," and the *U.S. Statistical Reports*. Photocopy the desk's telephone list of most-called-experts on local history, crime, business development, taxation, zoning, waterways, and "moles" at the courthouse. Morgues usually have a set of encyclopedias as well as the newspaper's back copies and file cabinets overflowing with clippings on people, places, and notable events.

Computer linkage with the Internet's riches puts a global library at your fingertips once you know the Boolean operators AND, OR, and NOT, even for data entered yesterday. Be warned, however, that because even crackpots and seven-year-olds can input data, many online sources and documents are highly unreliable. The best source for encyclopedic matters is still the *Encyclopaedia Britannica,* now online.[8] If your state and county government records are accessible, learn how to locate data to verify "facts" that look fishy, even in a reporting team's 25-part series that took six months to research and at prohibitive expense.

Accuracy involving mathematics is the bane of any liberal arts major who's ever had to retake College Algebra 101.

Every newspaper has its corps of readers with sharp pencils who gleefully pounce on flawed calculations just like a Pecksniffian algebra teacher. Use your calculator to check the math in local and outside copy, especially before writing a headline involving numbers. Copy editors who have been badly burned on "number" stories usually have no compunction about doing computations. The major mistakes in headline numbers, by the way, usually are made in transferring digits from the story and in erring on the number of zeros and misreading billions as millions.

Ultimately, the best way to compile an outstanding record for accuracy is a sense of humility in "hard-editing" every story and caption and in writing every headline. Fatigue, lassitude, fear, and revulsion all play a role in making errors, but the biggest offender seems to be smugness. Yet the fresh air any story brings to this most isolated and airless corner of the newsroom—the copydesk—should keep you green and growing. So learn to enjoy hunting down the suspicious "fact" like Sherlock Holmes. Double-check that dubious source and question numbers that "look funny." There's great satisfaction in "rescue" work on text or catching a goof in a caption or headline before it goes to press.

Lawsuits:
College Publications Are Eligible Too

To get students concerned about libel probably would require a million-dollar lawsuit brought against the campus newspaper or broadcasting station. Few have ever been sued for libel, slander, or invasion of privacy or even errors in picture captions—so far. Never believe it can't happen, however. In today's litigious climate, attorneys take a case *at no charge* for a third of the settlement—in or out of court. Most college newspaper staffs have no idea that they are without a high school paper's protective mantle, and that their bank accounts (or the institution's "deep pockets") present more inviting targets to the aggrieved and their lawyers than those of the town newspaper— which probably carries from $300,000 to $1 million in libel insurance.[9] Because federal law mandates that campus police now keep records open to campus newspapers and because most libel suits on outside papers stem from blotter items, it is increasingly possible that students might wind up as defendants in such litigation.

The editor, the adviser, and the media board of one university daily once held its collective breath for a potential suit when a student copy editor blithely played jury and judge with the headline "Rapist Arrested" on a campus police story. She seemed unaware that in arrests, the charges often are dropped the next day, but reputations and businesses can be ruined forever. Luckily for them, the suspect apparently did not know his rights, and a hungry lawyer didn't see the story.

The day is not far off when someone—student or professor, custodian or off-campus "civilian"—will take offense at editorials, pictures or captions, stories, or letters to the editor that smack of smart-aleck malice or are written with "reckless disregard for the truth." If what is happening in the "outside" world is any indication, the plaintiffs will not be mollified by a "correction" or back down because of threats from university officials. They will exact sweet revenge either in cash or in the satisfaction of seeing the callow and the careless staff snivel and shake in court.

When that scenario finally plays out, even a contentious editor's chair and the usual sardonic clique of editors, staff reporters, and photographers probably will begin attending the media law class with some regularity. For the first time, many might hang on every scrap of information provided by textbook and professor. If you did not give that class your undivided attention, take time to review the AP stylebook's section on libel, slander, and invasion of privacy in copy and illustrations. You might well save your newspaper from a million-dollar lawsuit.

Even When Papers Win, the Lawsuit Is a Lose-Lose Situation

Most American newspapers, especially the weeklies, do not have the financial resources of Time, Inc. or its brilliant legal staff, nor could most publishers pay its staggering premiums for libel insurance. A weekly's publisher in the late 1990s might spend $1,000 per year for $1,000,000 of coverage.[10] Yet whether it is a TIME researcher's unwitting lapse about a film star or a newspaper copy editor's unthinking gaffe on a cop-beat story, the pain and strain of a lawsuit, even one that never gets into a courtroom, are the same. So it was for the New York weekly that had a $2.1 million judgment overturned in 1995, but faced bankruptcy in the nearly three years it took to win that appeal. So it was, too, for the employees of a California weekly who were jobless after a $16 million judgment against the paper.[11]

Even if a legal action has no merit, copy editors still bear the heaviest emotional and professional burdens of proving a newspaper's innocence. Copy editors do fret about a story, a headline, or a caption that comes into question. Reputations for being the newsroom's role models of accuracy are shattered even if a decade of "misses" can be counted on one hand. Evidence must be amassed, testimony must be prepared, and unspoken suspicions that they *were* asleep at the switch must be endured from angry coworkers and even friends and family. The paper's financial ability to survive a loss has been and is certain to be questioned by advertisers, subscribers, and even the staff itself.[12]

Further, a paper's reputation for reliability also slips under a cloud while the plaintiff's unproved claim seems to be believed. It's also true that although libel insurance premiums can be deducted as a business expense,[13] any kind of action will result in a claim that can and often does raise premium rates.

"Serial Killer Arrested," "Marijuana Cases," and Other Libelous Headlines

Former publisher David K. Fraser of Louisiana's Hammond *Daily Star* is among those pointing up the truism that most libel suits stem from police-blotter items of three and four lines. When his paper omitted the critical word "Jr." on the name of a son picked up in a drug raid, his father, a radio station owner, was among those named in the standing headline of "Marijuana Cases."[14] The vengeful "Sr." waited for nearly 365 days to sue for libel, charging that his business had been damaged and he had been subjected to contempt. Not even a correction the next day saved the *Star* from months of aggravation and a nuisance claim of $2,500 in damages.[15]

If the paper permits the use of arrest items instead of waiting for suspects to be charged, a multimillion-dollar libel suit is not only possible but probable. That's because those arrested are often never charged. Dropped charges never travel at the speed of the original story, nor do they get equal treatment in headline size or page play. And if names are printed, especially in relating grisly crimes, reputations and businesses often are ruined.

For example, a hunt was on some years ago for the Pacific Northwest's Green River serial killer. A Portland businessman was arrested but quickly released. The printing of the arrest wrecked his life and business. The same thing happened to a suspect in the 1996 Olympic bombing in Atlanta, an incident that caused two deaths and a hundred injuries. The suspect, Richard Jewell, won millions in damages from the media. British newspapers avoid such risks by not naming even those charged with crimes until the verdicts are in. Yet in this country, where suspects are presumed innocent until proved guilty, the hue and cry for a name and photograph of those arrested continues to prove costly.

By contrast, some aggressive and wealthy publishers, such as those producing supermarket tabloids, welcome lawsuits because taking on someone able to sue—especially celebrities—only sells more papers. Too, falling stars either get to revive careers or at least some financial fallout. As a class, most publishers echo the view of a former president of the American Society of Newspaper Editors who confessed that in his 30 years as an editor and a publisher he lived "on a daily basis with the fear of the big libel suit."[16]

War Stories of "Near Misses" and "Direct Hits" May Be the Best Libel Teachers

Perhaps the best training for avoiding libel is provided by the rare copy editor willing to admit to "near misses" or the direct hits caused by a moment's carelessness or the failure to follow suspicions that "something is not quite right" about this copy or headline. Newcomers hearing such harrowing tales usually remember them, clearly understanding that if someone right across the aisle was involved in a libel suit, lightning might strike again. Unfortunately, most copy editors say nothing because of pride or fear that such a revelation might damage their careers.

Yet some *do* see the importance of recounting libel experiences to stave off a lawsuit. One former corporate publications director uses her "lapse" to shake up peers and journalism students, warning them not to trust even distinguished or seemingly reliable sources. She believed the "facts" about a Japanese agent provided by a historian for a billion-dollar corporation's anniversary book who trusted "old-timer" stories. The historian shrugged off the error as if it had been a misspelling instead of an error that could have cost the company millions if the agent had been alive. She talked to the man's survivors before the book came to their attention and set things right with an article in the next issue of the company magazine—their version of the story as well as photographs from the family albums. The moral of the anecdote is to be wary of stories putting ordinary people in disrepute.

The Increase of Multimillion-Dollar Lawsuits and the Uniform Correction Law

Today, neither contrition nor retractions prevent lawsuits, especially when both papers and plaintiffs refuse to back down "on principle." Malice and reckless disregard for accuracy *do* happen, especially these days when cost cutting has meant that copy editors must also take on duties of page makeup. Add to this the juries who reflect the public's increasing hostility toward newspapers.

Not even a change of venue is likely to favor the press. Or contrition or corrections. Of the 31 states that have retraction laws, plaintiffs in half of them can win damages for "out-of-pocket costs and loss of reputation" even if they cannot prove malice.[17]

It seems clear that were John Peter Zenger on trial for libel today instead of in 1735,[18] under the protections listed in the AP stylebook, many juries would not hesitate to find him guilty. As the twentieth century came to a close, many juries obviously saw nothing amiss in chipping away the First Amendment rights guaranteed by the Constitution more than 200 years ago.

The litany of awards in this last decade may not be as effective a preventive tool against lawsuits as hearing a fellow copy editor's "near miss" story, but it should erase your illusion that "it can't happen to me." That's what the news staff thought on *The Wall Street Journal* until it lost a $22.7 million suit (the original sum was $223 million). So did employees on papers in four states (Arkansas, Georgia, Indiana, Missouri) in 1996 alone. A few sobering statistics from the 1990s are shown below for the edification of those about to process copy and captions and write headlines:[19]

Paper	Libel Award
The Dallas Morning News	$58,000,000
The Philadelphia Inquirer	$34,000,000
Harte-Hanks Co.	$29,000,000
Capital Cities	$18,000,000
The (Cleveland) *Plain Dealer*	$13,500,000
The Ottumwa (Iowa) *Courier*	$ 2,380,000

The profession has been fighting a rearguard action since it became clear that courts also were sweeping aside the American press's traditional defenses of "truth" and "privilege" and the right to comment on the deeds of public officials and private citizens who thrust themselves into the public limelight. Publishers' newest weapon, predicated on adverse rulings, has been the Uniform Correction or Clarification of Defamation Act. Drafted in 1994 by the profession as a bill for all state legislatures, its intent was to get "the story right by fixing the problem rather than punishing a paper for having published a defamation." The Uniform Act specifies that:

> . . . a request to correct has to be made within 90 days of the original publication in question and the correction must be published within 45 days after the request. And the Act requires a person seeking a correction to disclose any information material to the alleged defamation. If these requirements are not met, then the plaintiff is limited only to out-of-pocket costs even if the correction is not published. A defendant also would be able to limit damages with a later correction any time before trial, but is required to pay the plaintiff's legal fees up to the time of the correction.[20]

Few count on this law to diminish damages or to mollify those out to punish newspapers. As of 1998, only North Dakota's publishers could convince their legislators to pass the law.[21] Even the publishers' prime lobbyist for this statute is pessimistic about its passage in other states because of trial lawyers' opposition to limiting punitive damages and because legislators usually have far more pressing priorities during the annual sessions. North Dakota has a small population with few problems, and moving the bill was fairly easy to do, he said.[22] But even if all 50 states, the District of Columbia, and our other territories were to pass the Uniform Act, the courts would still have to test its constitutionality.

A Sampler of Practical Protective Systems for Copy Editors

The only protective shields that have survived seem to be the copy editors who maintain eternal vigilance against potential lawsuits. They have been aided recently by professional journals—particularly state press association newsletters—alerting newsrooms about litigation threats, cases, and advice on how to avoid suits. The Louisiana Press Association's monthly *Bulletin* carries a much-read

"Legal Corner" containing cases, opinions from the attorney general, and actions of the LPA's alert legal wing. Trend stories are not pleasant. Early in 1998, the Kansas newsletter gloomily noted that retractions now were useful only to "mitigate or reduce damages."

The *Columbia Journalism Review* still holds out hope that copy editors like you might turn the tide. One article listed the nine "misconceptions" of libel law. It was apparent that the AP stylebook might be the "bible" concerning libel, but plaintiffs and courts were fast making it obsolete. So if copy editors are to be the last guardians of a free press, it's vital that they take steps to avoid falling into traps involving prime "misconceptions" about the crumbling legal protections for the press. The basic steps to follow are:

1. Don't pass libelous statements made by others—hard news, opinion pieces, or letters to the editor.
2. If public records are being quoted, the "lifts" must be accurate and fair—truly a *public* record—and actually filed.
3. Public officials and public figures are not "fair game" for criticism even though they must prove "actual malice."
4. Headlines as well as ads and art can trigger libel suits.
5. Because a "disproportionate number of libel plaintiffs are lawyers," never consider them to be "great sources and writer-friendly."
6. Convicts certainly *do* sue over headlines and stories, thanks to law libraries and plenty of "time on their hands."
7. People outside your area—state or nation—can and do sue and may force the paper's defendants to their "home court," even if it's a foreign country.
8. It's not the monumental pieces that cause libel suits. Those get scrutinized by the newspaper's lawyer. It's the "innocent slip or the negligent omission"—and then not printing a prompt correction—that can bring about a suit.
9. Truth is, indeed, still privileged, but if it's the only defense in a libel suit, providing proof for truth is "time-consuming, painful and expensive."[23]

Less formal systems work too. Some copy editors stay out of trouble by envisioning a loved one as the suspect or as the politician being pilloried in the copy they process. Others mull whether the "stopper" story has moral or ethical worth, or whether the questionable sentences or paragraphs could be softened or killed under the precept of "When in Doubt, Leave It Out." Still, other newsroom officials prefer the blunt and simple warning signs that essentially ask the following questions.

Has the writer of this story held up any *private* citizen to be

1. an object of pity?
2. an object of hatred?
3. an object of ridicule?
4. an object of contempt?

Will that story cause any *private* citizen to be

1. shunned or avoided?
2. put out of business?
3. identifiable to others?

If you pass a libelous story, you will be fired immediately and Guild membership will not protect you on this paper.

Some final warnings are essential on crime news: It's assumed by now that you have added new words to the forbidden list in Chapter 5. You now know that people detained by police are "suspects" and not "murderers," "rapists," "arsonists," and so on. You also know the dangers of variations of the word "alleged" and know better than to confuse "jailed" with "being held."

Add to all the foregoing the desk's traditional safety measure of never permitting the expression "found not guilty" in headlines or stories because of the potential for omission of the word "not." The supercautious use either "found innocent" or "was acquitted." They also refrain from headlines about suspects "confessing to murder" because they "confess to the police."

For copy editors—even the newest—to be forewarned about accuracy and how to stay out of the courtroom all depends on being forewarned and forearmed in an era of constant challenges to press freedoms once guaranteed under the Constitution's First Amendment.[24]

In short, as has been suggested repeatedly in this book, when in doubt, you'd better leave it out.

23 | Job Hazards: Dealing with Too Many Earthquakes, Monicas, and Shootings

Even if journalism training simulates traumatic situations to prepare future journalists for such trauma, it is a given that none will be presented for those who will become copy editors. The rationale has been that they're not out facing the action. Yet copy editing ordinarily is a high-stress job of monumental proportions, not in just using editorial skills but also in the daily ingestion of the content appearing either on the computer monitor or in hard copy. Add to that the pagination role some copy editors must assume. To date, only one journalism program in America has started "trauma" training, something found helpful for the 80 percent of its graduates who were exposed to traumatic events. Most were reporters on assignment, however, not copy editors processing the shocking details in copy or pictures.[1] Besides, copy editors traditionally view themselves as indestructible emotionally, crusty sorts making sport of anyone seeing counselors or, worse, buying self-help books about stress. That sort of thing is for sissies. But is it?

One relevant copydesk story almost never mentioned in journalism history or copy-editing classes has to do with the accumulative toll from years of processing tragic news on the copydesk. When the excursion ship *General Slocum* burned and sank in New York City's East River on June 15, 1904, killing 1,030 churchgoers,[2] veteran reporters may have wept while gathering the details, but at least one copy editor on New York dailies bolted for the rest room to vomit. That was just the initial and physical reactions to a gruesome story that, on at least one paper, was visible from the newsroom window. But no one dared admit difficulties in concentrating on other stories or the private hours spent mulling the event. Some might have used alcohol to forget about the story, but anyone who wept said nothing about this healthy outlet. The view was that "it's just *another* story," when in fact it was not just *another* story.[3]

Nor does any current journalism history textbook recount what is perhaps the most famous example of newsroom breakdown indirectly related to the *Slocum*'s sinking.

The example illustrates how unrelenting pressures over time can trigger not only deep clinical depression and insanity, but even murder by editors. Joseph Pulitzer's brilliant and sadistic editor, Charles E. Chapin of the New York *Evening World*, was considered to be one of the greatest city editors of all time in the early 1900s. Interestingly, he replaced another city editor who had gone insane over job stress on the eve of the Spanish-American War in 1898.[4]

Chapin's reaction to the *General Slocum* disaster that afternoon, described by an eyewitness, was this:

> He would run up and down, peering over shoulders to read the nauseating details of the tragedy as they were typed out. Then, standing erect, he would shout, 'Women and children jumping overboard with clothing afire! Water full of charred bodies!' And between these jackal outcries he would strut exultantly up and down, humming a simmering, happy, tuneless tune.[5]

The only difference between him and Carr Van Anda at the *Times* in orchestrating a major event of coverage and copy editing was that Van Anda did not sing, strut, or crow about the deluge of related stories that would sell thousands of papers. Chapin's breakdown took 20 more years of "great stories." His tyrannical rule culminated with the long-planned, cold-blooded execution of his wife in 1918 as they lay in bed. It ended with his raising exotic flowers for the rest of his days at Sing Sing prison.[6]

Today, members of the armed services, police officers, firefighters, and even schoolchildren who are traumatized by violence generally are provided with counseling services as well as rest and relaxation. Many reporters who have covered horrendous events are awarded "sabbaticals," but no such "administrative leave" has been provided for those on the desk, nor, to be fair, have any copy editors demanded such treatment. Many would see Chapin as the ideal tough-as-nails copy editor. But these days an equal number don't. Like reporters, copy editors "cover" such stories in processing copy about them, writing the headlines, the pullout quotes, and often the captions for horrifying pictures. Some rejected photos can never be erased from the mind's eye. In addition, a reporter may cover only one or two traumatic stories per shift, but copy editors often cover *several*.

Though far removed physically from these shattering events, the copy editor's mind registers *every* shock paraded before it. Most copy editors are not insensitive automatons or sociopaths. They could not write the heads they do if they did not feel deeply about the events and the people whom they encounter in stories and pictures week in and week out. Some days offer nothing but cataclysmic stories that sometimes break simultaneously.

For instance, on the same historic day that the House of Representatives was voting to impeach President Clinton and the Iraqi bombings had been resumed, copy editors around the nation absorbed those events on overhead television sets, radios, and the wire copy before them while editing regional and local stories. A "General Slocum" (stress overload) was at hand. The onset of great fatigue always signals a crash and burn. Pay attention to it. Post-traumatic effects can't be tossed aside by eating a candy bar from the canteen or by stepping into the street for air or by drinking or drugging. Those are Band-Aids for gaping, work-related wounds.

The path to long-term damage manifests itself first in sleeplessness, in thinking about stories and the ordinary high-speed stress of any day on the copy desk. That's followed by physical and psycho-somatic ailments, perhaps treated with the socially approved anti-dotes of alcohol or medications. The usual result is eventual slippage in judgment and in the ability to process *any* stories. If the police of-ficer and soldiers now feel no shame in showing their feelings—about highway fatalities and psychopaths mowing down teachers, students, or churchgoers—then you as a copy editor must learn to put the occupational tradition of unflappability behind you and seek help for what truly *is* post-traumatic stress.

Most newspapers' health insurance carries some kind of counsel-ing coverage. Employee assistance plans also offer trauma counsel-ing anonymously and on sliding-fee scales. Unfortunately, too many copy editors are like Chapin and scoff at ever resorting to any kind of counseling, viewing it as a blot on their legendarily tough hides. But *underneath* those hides, every piece of copy and caption processed has registered, as any insurance actuary can attest. It's also good to remember that novelist Ernest Hemingway ("Mr. Macho"), who literally rode the four horsemen of the Apocalypse in his life-time, did idealize fortitude under fire. But he also ended his long un-treated depression, about his ability to continue writing, with a bul-let to the head.

A copy-editing career depends on sharp minds and quick judg-ment about bad-news stories the year-round. If you want to do well on the desk, you will use those employee benefits—or, if pride stands in your way, by seeking outside counseling paid out of pocket. Otherwise the "overwhelms" will begin to take their toll. To con-tinue to process stories of mayhem, California bombings, hurricane and flood cleanups, and drive-by shootings—along with genocidal revolts abroad and gunfire in churches and schools—requires the commonsense approach of seeking some kind of counseling. Ignore it at your peril.

NOTES

Chapter 1. Headlines: The Prime Seller of Newspapers
and the Copy Editors Who Write Them

1. Edwin Emery and Michael Emery, *The Press and America: An Interpretive History of the Mass Media*, 5th ed. (Englewood Cliffs, N. J.: Prentice-Hall, 1984), 1.

2. After the advent of Edison's incandescent bulb, many copy editors wore transparent green eyeshades to cut glare from overhead lighting so they could focus for long hours on putting stubby "copy pencils" to what is now called "hard copy." Today's copy editors suffer even greater eyestrain from the computer monitor. Many use computer eye drops or special clip-on lenses. The upright position of monitors has also created neck strain and a growing clientele for chiropractors and massage therapists.

3. Conference for Journalists, Oregon State University, April 25, 1990.

4. Before computers were introduced into newsrooms and copy editors were shunted into cubicles, they sat around the "rim" of a large horseshoe-shaped "desk." The chief copy editor sat *inside* the "U"—called the "slot"—to log and pass stories to the staff for editing and headlines and to monitor finished work. From there, copy/headlines were dispatched to the composing room either by a "copy boy" or, after 1900, by pneumatic tube. The terms "slot" and "rim" still survive.

5. Leon Stein, *The Triangle Fire*, New York: Carroll & Graf/Quicksilver Publishers, 1985, 215.

6. A "deck" is a subordinate headline.

7. *The New York Times,* June 16–22, 1904.

8. An "en" is the width of the letter N. Likewise, an "em" is the width of an M.

9. ©1969, 1989, *The Washington Post*. Reprinted with permission.

10. Fillers, also called "time copy" or, at *The Wall Street Journal*, "ever-greens," are one-paragraph news items or trivia facts used to fill out the bottom of columns.

11. *The LPA Job Bank* (Louisiana Press Association), December 1998.

12. Starting pay scales on union papers tend to bring copy editors 22 percent more money than starting reporters at many papers, but on some, salaries are the same for "writers, reporters, copyreaders, photographers, artists and layout persons, picture desk workers" (1998 contract, Newspaper Guild of the Twin Cities), 6.

Chapter 2. Headlines: The Door to Copy Editing Mastery

1. Emery and Emery, 5th, *Press and America*, 331.

2. "Non sequitur" is Latin for "it does not follow" and means that the front end of the sentence—like "Earning a BS degree in chemistry," is unrelated to the sentence's end: "she became chief operating officer at Unisys." It's quite different, when the reporter writes: "Earning a BS degree in chemistry, she was hired as an organic chemist at Nichols Agricultural Products, Inc." Non sequiturs usually occur when a story involves a biographical rundown—obituaries, weddings, business profiles—and a reporter trying to cram as much data into a sentence as possible.

3. Keller and Johnson v. Aymond, Avoyelles Publishing Co., Marksville, La.

4. The verdict about "teens/teenagers" was handed down by participants at the 1998 Youth Editors Association of America meeting (Missouri Press Association *Bulletin & Presstime*, October 1998).

Chapter 3. "Counting" the Headline

1. Frank Luther Mott, *American Journalism* (New York: Macmillan Co., 1941), 44.

2. *New York Journal*, May 2, 1898.

3. Anthony R. Fellow and Thomas N. Clanin, *Copy Editors' Handbook for Newspapers* (Englewood, Colo.: Morton Publishing Company, 1998), 121.

4. Ed Alderman, interview, December 19, 1998.

5. The words "upper case" and "lower case"—often marked "uc," "lc," or "ulc"— are printing terms from the days of metal type. A font case contained big drawers of type sorted into compartments by alphabetical user. The capital letters were in the "upper" part of the "case," the regular or small letters in the "lower" section.

6. The record holder for System 1 took 11 seconds; for System 2, took 4 seconds.

7. The count is: Line No. 1, 16; No. 2, 17.5; No. 3, 17.

Chapter 4. Specialty Headlines

1. *The Memphis Daily Appeal*, August 10, 1858.

Chapter 5. The Master Lists of Forbidden Words in Headlines

1. Lake Charles (LA.) *American Press*, December 21, 1998.

2. "Haz-mat," is short for "hazardous materials," and was launched in April 1999 by the Lake Charles *American Press* because the increasing incidents of such goods being moved through that part of Louisiana. That there was even space for a pronoun in this spacious head indicates no nickname was necessary (ibid., April 16, 1999).

3. Born in 1840, "OK" started out as the Democrat's "Old Kinderhook Club," named for the New York hometown of Martin Van Buren who was running for re-election (Allen Walker Read, "The Evidence on O.K.," *Saturday Review of Literature*, July 19, 1941, 3–4, 10–11). The term then came to stand for "oll korrect" that appeared as endorsements on official documents (*Webster's New International Dictionary of the English Language*, 2d, [Springfield, Mass.: G. & C. Merriam, Company, Publishers, 1950], 1694).

4. Roy H. Copperud and Roy Paul Nelson, *Editing the News*, Dubuque, Iowa: Wm. C. Brown Company Publishers, 1983), 60.

5. Charles Dickens, *Martin Chuzzlewit* (London: Macmillan & Co., Ltd., 1954), 246–47.

6. *The Associated Press Stylebook and Libel Manual*, Ed. Norm Goldstein, 29th ed. (New York: The Associated Press, 1994), 10, 5.

Chapter 6. Setting Up a Work Regimen and Determining the First Word (the Subject)—and the Second (the Verb)

1. Plutarch, *Lives*, 2, quoted in *The Oxford Dictionary of Quotations*, 2d (London: Oxford University Press, 1955), 120: 13.

2. Copperud and Nelson, *Editing the News*, 38–39.

3. William Shakespeare, *The Tempest*, Act 2, Sc. 1, line 12.

4. Copperud and Nelson, *Editing the News*, 120.

5. Ibid., 32.

Chapter 7. Headline Punctuation, Abbreviations, and the Use of Numbers and Symbols

1. Lake Charles (La.) *American Press*.

2. *The Washington Post Desk-Book on Style*, Ed. Thomas W. Lippman, 2d ed. (New York: McGraw-Hill Publishing Company, 1989), 42.

3. *AP Stylebook*, 29th ed., 3.

4. It may have been Hammarskjold's serious demeanor and writings, but few slots passed "*Dag*."

5. In an editorial titled "The Gorilla Hobnobbing with the Elephant," *The Memphis Daily Appeal* publisher McClanahan's perception was that Lincoln's granting time to a black delegation attempting to establish an African-American colony in

Liberia was a cynical political sham by the President that would come to nothing (ibid., August 25, 1862).

6. Former Vice President Al Gore knew his name would lend itself to being both a noun and verb.

7. Ralph Waldo Emerson, "Self-Reliance," *Essays*, ii.

Chapter 8. Line breaks, Decks, Jumps—and 2d-Day Headlines

1. Vic Albro, interviews, 1949–52.

2. Howard B. Taylor, and Jacob Scher, *Copy Reading and News Editing* (New York: Prentice-Hall, Inc., 1951), 161.

3. Floyd K. Baskette, Jack Z. Sissors, and Brian S. Brooks, *The Art of Editing*, 6th ed. (Boston: Allyn and Bacon, 1997), 166.

4. Subheads have been steadily vanishing from many newspapers in the trend to trim long articles or to stud them with pull-out quotes or infographics. But the texts of major speeches and long Sunday pieces still require them.

Chapter 9. The Art of Writing Feature Headlines

1. The author was Ed Alderman, then a fourteen-year veteran copy editor of the Lake Charles (La.) *American Press*.

2. *Modern Maturity*, January-February 1999, 58.

3. John B. Bremner, *Words on Words: A Dictionary for Writers and Others Who Care About Words* (New York: Columbia University Press, 1980), 184.

4. Copperud and Nelson, *Editing the News*, 46.

5. Bremner, *Words on Words*, 184.

6. On the occasion of this poet's death, one famous headline at the Minneapolis *Star Tribune* was: "It's time to stash/Ogden Nash" (Trudi Hahn, interview, April 10, 1999).

7. Taylor and Scher, *Copy Reading*, 190.

8. Copperud and Nelson, *Editing the News*, 47.

9. Bremner, *Words on Words*, 184.

10. Fellow and Clanin, *Copy Editors' Handbook*, 126.

11. Lake Charles (La.) *American Press*.

12. Taylor and Scher, *Copy Reading*, 191.

Chapter 10. Different Papers, Different Head Styles

1. James J. Kilpatrick, *The Writer's Art* (Kansas City: Andrews, McMeel & Parker, Inc., 1984), 36.

2. Ibid., 35.

3. *Webster's Ninth New Collegiate Dictionary* (Springfield, Mass.: Merriam-Webster Inc., Publishers, 1991), 164–65.

4. Lake Charles *American Press*, December 23, 1998-January 8, 1999.

5. Joseph Pierson, the cable editor for the *Tribune*, noted that when they dropped foreign news for a few days, they got only three complaints. But when they dropped the comic strip "Little Orphan Annie" for a day, 50,000 complaints followed (Curtis McDougal, *Newsroom Principles and Policies* [New York: Macmillan, 1947], 109–110).

6. *AP Stylebook*, 29th, 53.

Chapter 11. An Overall Look at Copy Editing Today

1. Buck Ryan, "Editing Takes on a New Look," *Quill*, 81 (March 1993), 19.

2. Author's Observation (AO)

3. Ryan, "Editing Takes on a New Look," 21–24.

4. Hugh Morgan, "Orchestrating News Coverage: Maestro Directs Newsroom Musicians in Journalistic Symphony," *Quill*, 81 (March 1993), 27.

5. Kathy Hinson, interview, May 24, 1999.

6. Morgan, "Orchestrating News Coverage," 24.

7. As one writing coach noted: "The only time [reporters] read a story is on the computer screen under the crunch of deadline and that leaves little time for pondering, for searching out annoying trends, misused words, [and for] questions." (*Louisiana Press Association Bulletin*, February 1997).

8. Hinson, interview.

9. Ron F. Smith and Loraine M. O'Connell, *Editing Today* (Ames, Iowa: Iowa State University Press, 1996), 92.

10. Alderman, interview.

Chapter 12. The Editing Routine

1. Hard copy is paired with computerized output on many newspapers and most alternative weeklies, almost all magazines, professional journals and corporate publications as well as book publishing. The usual routine is for the writer to produce a piece on the computer and submit the work in *both* hard copy and on computer diskettes or compact disc. An editor or peer reviewer then marks the manuscript with the traditional symbols shown on the inside cover of this textbook and may add advice or applause in the page margins. The writer then inputs corrections from the "markup," again on both diskette and hard copy . In book publishing, an author could go through a half-dozen cycles of hard copy/diskette before the work is approved. The diskette copy eliminates the publisher's need for typists and compositors. The publisher's production staff uses the diskette data, reformatting it to

page size, font and point size. Professors undergo the same regimen with academic journals or in presenting papers, except they must submit several hard copies, along with the diskette, at the start.

2. Arthur Plotnik, *The Elements of Editing: A Modern Guide for Editors and Journalists* (New York: Collier Books, Macmillan Publishing Co., 1982), 52.

3. *Wisconsin Newspaper Association Bulletin*, June 1996, quoted by the *Louisiana Press Association Bulletin*, April 1997, 6.

4. The word "minuscule" has been misspelled so many times as "miniscule," that the newest Webster's surrendered and lists "miniscule" as a "variant." Ask your editor what version is preferred.

5. The coding is for *The Oregonian*, and the headlines are typed across from the head order portion of the code. The code is translated as follows:

Line 1: "hs*t*" is the copy editor's initials

Line 2: "hedr" means "head regular"—here a font called Minion semibold. The order is for a 4 column, 36-point, 1-line headline.

Line 3: "decks,11.03." "Deck*s*" means a standard deck. The "11.03" is the pica width of one column. Ergo, this deck is 1 column, 3 lines. of what is half the size of the main head set in a prescribed font.

Line 4: names the reporter.

Line 5: [/staff]. "Staff" produces the standard staff identifier for second line of the byline ("*The Oregonian*").

6. Sonny Marks, interview, May 5, 1999.

7. *Macintosh PowerBook User's Manual* (Cupertino, Calif.: Apple Computer, Inc., 1998), 86.

8. Bausch & Lomb's Computer Eye Drops contain glycerin and benzalkonium chloride, but the wet washcloth works just as well.

9. *Macintosh PowerBook Users Manual*, 86.

10. Today, green eyeshades are difficult to obtain except at novelty stores.

Chapter 13. Editing for Organization

1. The organizational method involves the author's variation of an outline system used to teach composition structure. It has been quickly grasped even by slow students and has been used successfully by thousands of students around the nation's high schools and universities since 1970 when it was first detailed in the author's composition textbook (*How to Write Themes and Term Papers*, 3d, Barrons, 1989).

2. *The New York Times*, March 26, 1911.

3. Ibid. Paragraph 2 about the building's fireproofing was re-emphasized in Paragraph 5.

4. AO as a former staff member of the Beirut *Daily Star*.

Chapter 14. Editing the Lead

1. Charles S. Holmes, *The Clocks of Columbus: The Literary Career of James Thurber* (New York: Atheneum, 1972), 84.

2. Ibid.

3. Ibid.

4. Thurber learned his craft from 1920–24 as a reporter for the Columbus (Ohio) *Dispatch* under the sneers of the legendary city editor Norman ("Gus") Kuehner, a rude, crude, old-time newsman who chewed up interns and detested wry-humored intellectuals like Thurber. Even as a cub, Thurber was no slouch in covering fast-breaking news, but his elegant, meticulous style did not suit Kuehner's perception of a straight-forward story (Robert Emmet Long, *James Thurber* [New York: Continuum, 1988], 224–25). Years later, Thurber recalled how he valued Kuehner's instructions for a hard-news story, criteria still valid today: "'Write a flowery introduction in the first paragraph . . . In the second paragraph, tell who, when, where, what, and how. Then in as few paragraphs as possible, relate the most important details. Write an equally flourishing conclusion. Spend the next five minutes finding the sharpest pair of shears in the office, and cut off the first and last paragraphs. You'll have a helluva good news story.' [Kuehner] had a noisy antipathy to 'literary' writing, or anything that smacked of style, even in feature stories, and his criticism when he encountered such a monstrosity sounded like the roll of thunder. '*This* story is in *bloom!*' he howled at the author of a flamboyant article, and on another occasion he bawled at a reporter, 'You did this damn story with *feeling,*' giving the word all the force of an obscenity. He liked short paragraphs, hated long sentences, and never used a semicolon in his life" (James G. Thurber, *The Thurber Album: A New Collection of Pieces About People* [New York: Simon and Schuster, 1952], 226).

5. With the trend to paid obituaries, families have changed that classic style of abbreviated facts into wordy sentiment.

6. Copperud and Nelson, *Editing the News*, 72.

7. Lake Charles (La.) *American Press, June 2, 1999.*

8. The Lafayette (La.) *Daily Advertiser*, June 2, 1999.

9. Jean Folkerts and Dwight L. Teeter, Jr., *Voices of a Nation: A History of Media in the United States*, 2d ed. (New York: Macmillan, 1994), 481–82.

10. Ibid., 1st, 1989, 549.

11. The Baton Rouge (La.) *Advocate*, June 2, 1999.

12. Lake Charles (La.) *American Press*, June 3, 1999

13. Ibid.

Chapter 15. Editing the Close and Quotes

1. Lake Charles (La.) *American Press,* June 4, 1999.

2. Baton Rouge *Advocate*, June 2, 1999.

3. Lake Charles (La.) *American Press*, June 4, 1999.

4. AP, quoted by the Lake Charles (La.) *American Press*, June 4, 1999.

5. Baton Rouge *Advocate*, June 2, 1999.

6. *USA Today*, June 3, 1999.

7. AP, quoted by the Lake Charles (La.) *American Press*, June 7, 1999.

8. Ibid., June 8, 1999.

9. Ibid.

10. Anatole France, *Golden Tales of Anatole France*, no trans. listed, (New York: Dodd, Mead & Company, 1926), 1–25.

11. AP, quoted by Lake Charles (La.) *American Press*, June 4, 1999.

12. Barbara G. Ellis, *Content Analysis of the Associated Press Copy for Quotes as Contained in the Lake Charles American Press*, June 10, 1999.

13. AP, quoted by the Lake Charles *American Press*, September 16, 1996.

14. Ibid.

15. Ibid., June 2, 1999.

16. Ellis study.

17. AO, 1961–73.

18. Masson v. *New Yorker* Magazine, Inc., et al., *U.S. Reports*, 501 (October 1990), June 20, 1991 (Washington, D.C.: U.S. Government Printing Office, 1995), 496–528. The "new fiction" is part of the "new journalism" of the 1960s (Folkerts and Teeter, *Voices of a Nation*, 2d, 481–82).

19. Masson v. *New Yorker*, 521.

20. Brian S. Brooks, George Kennedy, Daryl R. Moen, Don Ranly, *News Reporting and Writing* (New York: St. Martin's Press, 1996), 111–12.

21. Masson v. *New Yorker*, 496. Two justices (Byron R. White and Antonin Scalia) dissented, but only because they apparently felt the majority had missed the core issue and had not come down harder against Malcolm's "knowing falsehood" (526) by straying into determination of whether the phony quotes changed the substance of a source's remarks. They wrote: "This ignores the fact that under *New York Times* [NYT v. Sullivan], reporting a known falsehood—here the knowingly false attribution—is sufficient proof of malice. The falsehood, apparently, must be substantial; the reporter may lie a little, but not too much" (527).

22. Most of Forrest's battle reports, communiqués, orders, and speeches were polished by a press aide, Matt C. Gallaway, a publisher of *The Memphis Avalanche* (O.F. Vedder, *History of the City of Memphis and Shelby County Tennessee* Vol. II [Syracuse, N. Y.: D. Mason & Co., Publishers, 1888], 134).

23. *Montgomery Daily Mail*, November 26, 1864, quoted by J. Cutler Andrews, *The South Reports the Civil War.* (Princeton, N. J.: Princeton University Press, 1970), 474. The the publisher was union sympathizer Henry Watterson, famed post-war

editor of the Louisville *Courier-Journal*. His correspondent was Captain Theodoric Carter who wrote under the pen name of "MINT JULEP."

24. The Ellis study of quote contents showed that in wire or syndicated hard news and features, only 12 percent of the lineage was devoted to quotes; in overall sports copy, the statistic was 16 percent overall, and rose to 19 percent for features or advances (Ellis study).

25. AP, quoted by the Lake Charles (La.) *American Press*, June 8, 1999.

26. Copperud and Nelson, *Editing the News*, 89.

27. *The Memphis Daily Appeal*, March 30, 1862.

Chapter 16. Adds and Trims

1. Setting stories for later use on a "bank" galley tray so outraged *Daily Star* compositors that type for an editorial prepared for the impending death of French singer Edith Piaf nearly ran in several pages (sports, business, etc.) and finally had to be hidden at the author's apartment until the singer's demise.

2. Measurements generally are based on extracting an inch of typeset copy from three different portions of a story set in one column width and averaging the number of lines. The same is done for stories set in the various bastard widths.

3. Hahn, interview.

4. This story was filed by a correspondent named "B" (William Barr), *The Memphis Daily Appeal*, June 27, 1863.

5. *Louisiana Press Association Bulletin*, June 1999.

6. Kilpatrick, *Writer's Art*, 88.

7. *AP Stylebook*, 29th ed., 219.

Chapter 17. Editing Stories Involving Numbers

1. Columnist Garrett Ray points out that despite several math-for-newspaper-staffer workshops staged by the Colorado Press Association, few participants attended. He put much of the blame on journalist's lifelong fear of math ("A Teeny Little Math Class for Reporters Terrified of Numbers," *Publishers' Auxiliary*, November 18, 1996, A–7).

2. Ibid.

3. The source was a survey by the Institute for Policy Studies and United for a Fair Economy, reported by the Los Angeles Times-Washington Post Service, quoted by *The Oregonian*, August 30, 1999.

4. The Consumer Price Index (a.k.a., "cost-of-living adjustment," CPI) is a service of the Bureau of Labor Statistics. Items measured include common household expenses such as food, housing, utility bills, clothing, transportation, health care,

and even cell-phones rates. Governmental entities and many private sectors use the CPI to make cost-of-living adjustments in salaries and pensions.

5. John Steele Gordon, "Dubious Statisticians Have Your Number," *USA Today*, June 21, 1999.

6. Ibid.

7. Of the eight subjects, none were newborns; two were youngsters raised in foster homes. Despite such a minuscule pool of subjects and a broad range of variables—one mother was 44 years old—the researchers still dared to extrapolate that drinking during pregnancy was directly related to teratogenic defects in children. This pioneer study at the University of Washington medical school study evidently was considered so important that editors of *The Lancet* made it the leading article in this prestigious medical journal (Kenneth L. Jones, David W. Smith, Christy N. Ulleland, and Ann Pytkowicz Streissguth, "Patterns of Malformation in Offspring of Chronic Alcoholic Mothers," *The Lancet*, 1, (June 9, 1973), 1267. The second and third studies by the same research group involved only 11 and 23 children, respectively (Kenneth L. Jones, David W. Smith, Ann Pytkowicz Streissguth, and Ntinos C. Myvianthopoulos, "Outcome in Offspring of Chronic Alcoholic Women," *The Lancet*, 1, (June 1, 1974), 1076–78.

8. Mailings of 100,000 or more require significant funding sources just for bulk-mailing costs. Other expenses involve the sums paid to questionnaire designers, the printers, the clerical staff inputting data, and the statisticians who compile the results. Such expenditures suggest that most vested interests have a large stake in findings supporting their views or theories, an admission made in 2001 by one of the major medical journals.

9. The study was done at Harvard University, sponsored by the National Heart, Lung and Blood Institute, and published in the prestigious *New England Journal of Medicine* (August 26, 1999). The article was reprinted by *The Oregonian* (August 26, 1999) from the *Los Angeles Times-Washington Post* Service.

10. One of the most famous "indexes," but hardly the most definitive among other indexes today, is the Dow Jones industrial average (a.k.a. as "the Dow"). Dow Jones was founded in 1882 by Charles H. Dow and Edward D. Jones, co-publishers of the daily set of financial-news sheets ("flimsies") for New York City financial houses that became today's *The Wall Street Journal* ("Dow, Charles Henry," Micropaedia 3, *Encyclopaedia Britannica* [Chicago: Encyclopaedia Britannica, 1979], 645–46). The Dow Jones index started on May 20, 1896 and involved twelve companies that were a mix of industries, utilities, and transportation companies. Today, the "Dow" industrial measures only thirty companies, including "blue chippers," but outside of its specialty indexes—Dow Transport, Dow Utilities, Dow 65—it no longer measures trades in transportation and utilities and includes no high-technology companies (Mick Culham, interview, August 26, 1999).

11. Analysts in the overheated selling climate of the stock market in the late 1990s often pay far more attention to the Standard & Poor index (S&P) of 500 companies. Other indexes include Nasdaq (National Association of Security Dealers' Automated Quotes), 1,500 companies; Russell, 2000 small companies; Wilshire, 5,000; plus Lipper's two mutual-fund indexes.

12. *The Oregonian*, August 25, 1999.

13. Philip Meyer, *The New Precision Journalism* (Bloomington, Ind.: Indiana University Press, 1991), 24.

14. Ibid.

15. Ibid. 26–27.

16. *AP Stylebook*, 29th, 24.

17. Mitchell ("Mitch"J) G. Dewey, interview, August 26, 1999.

18. Ibid.

19. Ibid.

Chapter 18. Attributions, Identifications and 2d References

1. *The Clackamas County News* (Estacada, Ore.) printed a letter from a school-board candidate passing himself off as a neighbor and praising the candidate's qualities (March 3, 1999). When he won, his rival sued on grounds that the letter violated the state law about making a "false statement of material fact." The letter claimed the candidate was a good listener, "very easy to talk and work with" on area problems and "responds promptly to our concerns." A circuit judge refused to unseat the new board member because of his nom de plume tactic (*The Oregonian*, August 10, 1999).

2. Emery and Emery, 5th, *Press and America*, 426.

3. AP, quoted by *The Oregonian*, September 1, 1999.

4. Copperud and Nelson, *Editing the News*, 17.

5. Perhaps the purists' cruelest thrust of all is using the bracketed Latin word "sic"—something quoted verbatim—directly after a quotation by those whose writing or speaking skills are perceived as falling far short of exacting standards. The use of the bracketed "*sic*" has been largely confined to books and academic journals, areas of writing with few time constraints and many peer reviewers. But the practice is slowly emerging in some newspapers and has prompted comments by one copy editor about how "sic" some newspapers are getting.

Chapter 19. Catching Errors in Grammar and Usage (That/Which, Who/Whom, Parallelism, Subjunctive Mood, and Other Pitfalls)

1. John Ivan Simon, "Why English Is Good for You," *Paradigms Lost: Reflections on Literacy and Its Decline* (New York: Clarkson N. Potter, Inc., Publishers, 1980),

210. Simon believes that: "The person who does not respect words and their proper relationships cannot have much respect for ideas—very possibly cannot have ideas at all" (*Ibid.*, 204). For the conscientious, he added: "Even if no one else notices the niceties, the precision, the impeccable sense of grammar and syntax you deploy in your utterances, you yourself should be aware of them and take pride in them as in pieces of work well done" (*Ibid.*, 208).

2. The system was part of the highly successful "Spellers Anonymous" program created by the author.

3. Copperud and Nelson, *Editing the News*, 123–24.

4. *AP Stylebook*, 29th, 23.

5. Copperud and Nelson, *Editing the News*, 123; *Webster's Ninth Collegiate Dictionary*, 692.

6. *Webster's New International Dictionary*, 2d, 1701.

7. Copperud and Nelson, *Editing the News*, 128–29.

8. "Exile, Babylonian," Micropaedia, Vol. 4, *Encyclopaedia Britannica*, 1979, 5; Psalms: 137, 4.

9. In English classes, standard grammar usage offers the same explanation in different terms: "If the dependent clause is *essential* for sentence clarity, it's called *'restrictive.'* If the clause is *not* essential, however, it's called *'nonrestrictive.'*"

10. Remember that a clause has a subject and verb although it may not be a complete sentence. The *main* clause contains the "meat" of a sentence; the *dependent* clause *"depends"* on the main clause for its existence.

11. Purists declare that when a mix of single and plural nouns create a compound subject, the noun *nearest* the verb is the determining factor. Yet in such an arrangement the verb is almost always plural because either the writer or copy editor generally rearranges the nouns so that the plural form is nearest the verb. Few are brazen enough to place a plural verb next to a singular noun, like: "Palestinian leaders and President Bush *is* still not in agreement about permitting Arab refugees to resettle the West Bank of the Jordan river."

12. Baskette, et al., *Art of Editing*, 6th, 409.

13. *The Oregonian*, September 9, 1999.

14. William Strunk, Jr., and E. B. White, *The Elements of Style*, (New York: The Macmillan Company, 1959), 46.

15. Copperud and Nelson, *Editing the News*, 132.

16. Lyrics reproduced by permission of Jerry Bock Enterprises and Mayerling Productions Ltd. © 1964; renewed 1992 from *Fiddler on the Roof*.

Chapter 20. Transitions and Forbidden Words in Text

1. AP, quoted by *The Oregonian*, September 12, 1999.

2. Ibid.

3. Jay Clarke, Knight Ridder News Service, quoted by *The Oregonian*, September 12, 1999.

4. Carolyn Spencer Brown, *Los Angeles Times-Washington Post* Service, quoted by *The Oregonian*, Sept. 12, 1999.

5. Larry Bingham, Knight Ridder News Service, quoted by *The Oregonian*, September 12, 1999.

6. *The Oregonian*, September 12, 1999.

7. Although Kilpatrick first gained national attention as a conservative political columnist, his shift to word usage earned him thousands more readers, chiefly among writers, copy editors, and English teachers. His columns were clipped, photocopied for students and filed in hundreds of copydesk drawers.

8. Kilpatrick, *Writer's Art*, 69.

9. Ibid., 67.

10. The sources include: Baskette, et al. *Art of Editing*, 6th ed., 102–103; Richard Bayan, *Words That Sell* (Chicago: Contemporary Books, Inc., 1984), 82; Copperud and Nelson, *Editing the News*, 59–63; Ellis, *How to Write Themes and Term Papers*, 3d, 68–71; Fellow and Clanin, *Copy Editors' Handbook*, 58–61; Karen Judd, *Copyediting: A Practical Guide*, 2d ed. (Menlo Park, Calif.: Crisp Publications, Inc., 1988), 134–35; Lauren Kessler and Duncan McDonald, *When Words Collide: A Journalist's Guide to Grammar and Style*, 4th ed. (Belmont, Calif.: Wadsworth Publishing Company, 1996), 155; Ray Laakaniemi, *The Weekly Writer's Handbook* (Bowling Green, Ohio: Brittany Books, 1993), 40; Kilpatrick, *Writer's Art.*, 67; Smith and O'Connell, *Editing Today*, 73–75; James Glen Stovall, Charles C. Self, Edward Mullins, *On-Line Editing* (Northport, Ala.: Vision Press, 1994), 9; Taylor and Scher, *Copy Reading*, 55–56; William Strunk, Jr. and E. B. White, *The Elements of Style* (New York: Macmillan Co., 1959), 17–19, 33–51; Digby B. Whitman *The Road to Readability: Basics of Writing and Editing* (Chicago: Ragan Books, 1993), 52–56, 60–65.

Chapter 21. Writing and Editing Captions

1. The word "caption" has been used since 1670 to denote material with a document (*Webster's Ninth Collegiate Dictionary*, 205). "Cutline," a term first used in 1943, grew out of the era when illustrations were made by acid that "cut" into the engraving plates (ibid., 318). The *National Geographic* staff calls captions "legends," an outgrowth of its century-old roots of exploration and cartography. Its editors adopted the printing term for brief descriptions under illustrations (*Webster's New International Dictionary*, 2d, 1412). The Associated Press uses the term "*caption*," as do thousands of publications.

2. Tim Harrower, Newspaper Designers' Workshop, Lafayette, La., November 20, 1997.

3. When *The Charlotte* (N. C.) *Observer*, closed a Sunday sports section with three captionless pictures for the first of three editions, James Bennett, assistant night sports editor, declared that he got no complaints. The *Observer* sports department averages one or two missing captions every three months in its first edition, something he believes is an accepted practice today for many newspapers' first editions. He notes that the 10-person copydesk staff in the sports department is so pressed for time that captions either haven't been written by deadlines, or captions haven't made the page before it's sent to the platemakers. "The important thing is to get the page out, to get the presses rolling," he says. A few thousand copies will be produced before a press break when the replated page correcting errors and omissions is slipped onto the press cylinders. Replating takes time and money, is a fraction of the costs and reader complaints if the paper misses home-delivery schedules (Interview, Sept. 16, 1999). No AP picture captions should run "bare," however, because they are transmitted electronically with the illustration and require only a paginator's "click" to release the caption into filling the space.

4. *The* Seattle *Post-Intelligencer*, September 14, 1999.

5. Susan Walsh photo, AP, printed in *The Oregonian*, September 24, 1999.

6. *The Oregonian*, September 24, 1999.

7. *AP Stylebook*, 29th, 293.

8. Ibid.

9. Robert A. Daugherty, interview, September 20, 1999.

10. Frank Luther Mott, journalism's venerable historian, notes that pictures had been transmitted *before* telegraphy existed, but it took the invention of the photoelectric cell to make it useful to publishers (Mott, *American Journalism*, 682).

11. *AP Stylebook*, 1998, 307.

12. Aside from the AP's capitalized cardinal rule of "NEVER WRITE A CAPTION WITHOUT SEEING THE PICTURE," its ten other classic requirements about caption content are: (1) Is it complete? (2) Does it identify, fully and clearly? (3) Does it tell when? (4) Does it tell where? (5) Does it tell what's in the picture? (6) Does it have the names spelled correctly, with the proper name on the right person? (7) Is it specific? (8) Is it easy to read? (9) Have as many adjectives as possible been removed? (10) Does it suggest another picture? (*AP Stylebook*, 29th, 294). The AP's Daugherty noted that photographers "don't put the effort into a caption that they do in their work." Bob Myers, one of AP's photo editors, added: "We have to do a lot of guesswork off the story for those captions. Newspapers omit basic things like the city, the date of the photo" (Daugherty, interview). If part of the text is being copied for a caption, that explains why papers fail to comply with AP requirements.

13. *AP Stylebook*, 1998, 307, 309–10.

14. AO.

15. *The Atlanta Journal-Constitution*, September 5, 1999.

16. Kathy Johnson photo, AP, appearing in *The Oregonian*, September 19, 1999.

17. Stephan Savoia photo, AP, appearing in *The Oregonian*, September 19, 1999.

18. Daugherty, interview.

19. A content analysis of a cross-section of fourteen dailies by the author showed the "cut-and-paste" practice on staff photographs was ongoing at such papers as *The Atlanta Journal-Constitution* (five instances, September 5, 1999); The Charlotte (N.C.) *Observer* (two, September 12, 1999); *The Chicago Tribune* (four, September 12, 1999); the Cleveland *Plain Dealer* (one, September 12, 1999); *The Detroit News and Free Press* (seven, September 12, 1999); *Miami Herald* (two, September 12, 1999); *The Philadelphia Inquirer* (two, September 5, 1999); the St. Louis *Post-Dispatch* (one, September 12, 1999); *USA Today* (one, September 14, 1999).

20. Daugherty, interview.

21. Ibid.

22. Patty Reksten, interview, September 17, 1999.

23. *The St. Petersburg Times* was founded in 1884; Edwin and Michael Emery, *Press and America:* 5th, 666–67.

24. Sonya Doctorian, interview, September 22, 1999.

25. Ibid.

26. *The St. Petersburg Times*. Photographer Dirk Shadd's journalistic eyes *and* ears led to the meaty notes enabling him to write the original caption which was then up touched up by copy editor Sarah Lomasz.

27. *AP Stylebook*, 29th, 293.

28. Digital photos shot on final deadlines still have to be proofed in the pagination process.

29. Seattle *Post-Intelligencer*, September 14, 1999.

30. *The St. Petersburg Times*, September 22, 1999.

31. Cleveland (Ohio) *Plain Dealer*, September 12, 1999.

32. Seattle *Post-Intelligencer*, September 14, 1999.

33. The Minneapolis *Star Tribune*, June 24, 1999.

34. *The Oregonian*, September 19, 1999.

35. *Miami Herald*, September 12, 1999.

36. *Detroit News and Free Press*, September 12, 1999.

37. Some newspapers use group forms and insist photographers get permission slips signed by *all* subjects. If the paper plans to use the photo for promotional literature or ads, the subject usually is paid a nominal fee and informed of such use. The form won't list the job title or street number, but it will provide documentation on spelling of names and is a good lead for any subsequent search for identifications.

38. *The Philadelphia Inquirer*, September 5, 1999.

39. *The New York Times*, September 14, 1999.

40. Daugherty, interview.

41. The plaintiff was prominent in Florida society and even held press conferences about the divorce action. But the U. S. Supreme Court still ruled against TIME

magazine because by Palm Beach social standards, Mrs. Firestone had no "special prominence" and "did not thrust herself to the forefront of any particular public controversy in order to influence resolution of the issuers involved in it" (*AP Stylebook*, 1998, 289).

Chapter 22. Two Safeguards for Headlines and Copy: Pursuing Accuracy and Avoiding Lawsuits

1. Folkerts and Teeter, 2d, 481–83, 493.

2. Back cover blurb of the paperback edition of Tom Wolfe's *The Kandy-Kolored Tangerine-Flake Streamline Baby*, 9th ed. (New York: Pocket Books, 1972), quoted in Folkerts and Teeter, 2d, 480.

3. Lake Charles (La.) *American Press*, March 31, 1999.

4. Ibid., April 10, 1999.

5. Alleyne Ireland, *Joseph Pulitzer: Reminiscences of a Secretary* (New York: M. Kennerley, 1914), 116.

6. Thousands might snap up copies bearing a banner blaring, say, "Love-Nest Shooting Claims Mayor," under the assumption that New York's mayor had been fatally dispatched by a jealous husband. When the story revealed a small-town Iowa mayor had blundered into an Alabama hideaway, critics might have charged that such big play should be reserved for major stories, but they could never say the headline was *inaccurate*. *The New York World*'s superb and accurate news coverage and features written by star reporters like Nellie Bly, made Pulitzer's flagship paper the most profitable American daily published up to 1886 (Mott, *American Journalism*, 441–43).

7. Barbara G. Ellis, *Mr. McClanahan, Mrs. Dill, and The Moving Appeal* (Macon, Ga.: Mercer University Press, 2002); *The Memphis Daily Appeal*, January 2, 7, 19, 1862; ibid., January 17, 1863; Quintus C. Wilson, "Confederate Press Association: A Pioneer News Agency," *Journalism Quarterly*, 26 (June 1949), 160–66; Mott, *American Journalism*, 338.

8. *The Encyclopaedia Britannica* is still considered a "red-check" source by the staff of publications from TIME, Inc. (*TIME, LIFE, PEOPLE*, SPORTS ILLUSTRATED, MONEY, etc.) for facts of yesteryear. A red-check source gets its name from being one of the most authoritative sources used for verification at that company. Other words in a story get "black checks," but are no less accurate.

9. Karen S. Johnston, interview, December 28, 1998.

10. Jerry Wise, interview, December 28, 1998. Wise is the publisher of two Louisiana community newspapers (*The Cameron Pilot, The DeQuincy News*). He pays near $1,000 per year and has $450,000 of coverage—with a $10,000 deductible—because he has had five or more years of claim-free history. Wise attributes his forty years of publishing without a single libel suit to "special cautiousness" (ibid., January

15, 1999). In late 1998, a publisher of a half-dozen community newspapers, if a member of the National Newspaper Association, would have paid its discounted rate of from $500 to $3,000 in premiums for $300,000 to $500,000 in coverage, respectively (Johnston).

11. Edward Seaton, editor-in-chief, *The Manhattan* (Kan.) *Mercury*, quoted by "The Legal Corner," the Louisiana Press Association *Bulletin*, February 1998, 1.

12. Ibid.

13. Wise, interview.

14. The Hammond (La.) *Daily Star*, January 23, 1992.

15. Ibid., January 24, 1992; David K. Fraser, interview, March 23, 1993, December 23, 1998.

16. Louisiana Press Association *Bulletin*, February 1998, 1.

17. Ibid.

18. Emery and Emery, *Press and America*, 5th, 54–58.

19. Louisiana Press Association *Bulletin*, February 1998, 1.

20. Ibid. The mainspring for the Uniform Act was the National Conference of Commissioners on Uniform State Laws. The NCCUSL has had the support of the American Society of Newspaper Editors, state newspaper associations, and the National Newspaper Association, which represents weeklies and small dailies. The act has since been endorsed by the American Bar Association's House of Delegates, but not trial lawyers. Up to early 1999, the law had been submitted to only seven legislatures and the District of Columbia. NCCUSL legislative director John McCabe was dubious about the law's quick passage even in those states (John McCabe, interview, Dec. 28, 1998).

21. Louisiana Press Association *Bulletin*, February 1998, 1.

22. McCabe, interview.

23. *The Columbia Journalism Review*, quoted by "The Legal Corner," Louisiana Press Association *Bulletin*, October 1997, 1.

24. In force as of December 15, 1791, and called the "Bill of Rights," the text of the First Amendment says: "Congress shall make no law respecting an establishment of religion, or prohibiting the free exercise thereof; or abridging the freedom of speech, or of the press; or the right of the people peaceably to assemble, and to petition the Government for a redress of grievances" (U. S. Constitution). It should be noted that while these guarantees are given, those who exercise them need to expect, within seconds, physical or emotional threats to these freedoms.

Chapter 23. Job Hazards: Dealing With Too Many Earthquakes, Monicas, and Shootings

1. The training has been provided at the University of Washington's journalism school (Jan Maxson, "Training Journalism Students to Deal With Trauma," paper

delivered at the 1999 Annual Convention of the Association for Education in Journalism and Mass Communication, New Orleans, La., August 5, 1999).

2. The World Almanac and Book of Facts 1998, Mahwah, N.J.: World Almanac Books, 1997), 264.

3. Allen Churchill, Park Row (New York: Rinehart & Company, Inc., 1958), 235.

4. Ibid., 249–66.

5. Ibid., 259, 249.

6. Ibid., 302–11.

Glossary.

1. Baskette, et al., 6th, *Art of Editing*, 440.

GLOSSARY OF
COPYDESK TERMS

5W's The five classic elements of a hard-news story's lead: the who, what, when, where, why, and sometimes the how.

Articles The words "the," "a," and "an."

Bank In the days of "hot type," this was a case of galley trays containing stories that could appear at any "time" (e.g., obituaries for the famous, features) that could be put in pages instantly.

Banner A big headline stretched across the top of a page, usually on Page-1 or a break page 1 like the Metro or Sports sections. Alternate words have been "streamer," "line," and "ribbon."

Basket A computer term sometimes used instead of "queue" (literally a lineup), which designates a department for a story.

Body Copy (a.k.a. text and straight matter) Text without headlines.

Bold or Boldface A special type style for a word(s) that is blacker (heavier in "weight") than regular font. Bold treatment is used to gain the reader's attention from regular type.

Bounce When a headline is either too long for the specified column width or more than two units short, the slot will hand it back for redrafting.

Bow Designed for easy reading, a "bow" involves a three-line headline having middle lines that are either longer or shorter than their first and third mates.

Broadsheet A newspaper size, today measuring about 13″ × 23″ or 13.5″ × 22.5.″

Caps-Carry (a.k.a. a wild photo) A caption that carries the entire burden of an illustration's description and explanation. Some designers box illustration and caption and run an overline headline just above the art.

Caret A copy-editing symbol (^) that is placed under the line for inserted words, paragraphs, or punctuation.

Catch The discovery of a mistake in facts, a potentially libelous story, or errors in grammar, mechanics, or spelling. It's also called a "save."

Coach   An experienced reporter or editor contracted by a publisher to teach reporters how to improve their writing.

Condensed   This is a typography term involving the classic five weights, or strokes, provided with each font, for example, regular, bold, and italic. For "condensed," the font designer deliberately tightens the width of the character, whereas a font is widened in the "extended" weight. The opposite style is called "extended." *See* Extended.

Conjunctions   These are words like *and, or, nor, yet, but, for,* and so on.

Copy (a.k.a. text and straight matter)   Any written material to be published.

Copydesk   The work area of copy editors. Also called "the desk" and "the rim."

Count   The unit used in headline writing that specifies the space required by each letter, punctuation mark, and number.

CQ   This military abbreviation for "call to quarters" was adapted by hams in the early days of shortwave radio to announce that they could begin talking to each other. It gravitated to journalism when the wire services used the letters to indicate that an unusual spelling of a name was correct.

Cutoff Test   When copy editors must trim hard-news stories for space, they cut from the bottom and move steadily upward toward the lead. The story is presumed to have been written in an organizational structure of the inverted pyramid, whereby the first paragraph contains the 5W's of "who, what, when, where, and why." The remaining paragraphs contain information of declining importance.

Deck (a.k.a. RO, or read-out)   This is a subordinate head that follows a newspaper's main headline, usually a banner.

Delayed Lead (a.k.a. extended lead)   Instead of setting out the 5W's in the first paragraph of a story in what is called an "immediate" lead, a delayed lead provides either a paragraph or two on interpreting the content's impact or an anecdote to attract readers into the story.

Desk   A nickname for a copydesk, the work area of copy editors.

Downstyle   Not capitalizing common nouns after they follow a proper noun, like Tennessee river or St. Patrick's hospital. Its origination was to save costs and time when compositors either had to reach into a type drawer for capital letters or, after 1888 when Ottmar Mergenthaler's Linotype machine ended hand composition, the compositor had to turn to the keyboard at the right to trigger capital letters.

Dutch Wrap (a.k.a. raw wrap)   A story that has no headline running above it.

Extended   This is a typography term involving the classic five weights, or strokes, provided with each font, such as regular, bold, and italic. In "extended" type, the font designer deliberately widens the width of the character, whereas a font is pulled together in the "condensed" weight. *See* Condensed.

Extended Lead (a.k.a. delayed lead) Instead of setting out the 5W's in the first paragraph of a story in what is called an "immediate" lead, a delayed lead provides either a paragraph or two on interpreting the content's impact or an anecdote to entice the reader into the story.

Fingernails An old-fashioned term for parentheses.

Flipped A photograph that has been printed backward.

Fold The midsection of a newspaper in broadsheet size that is creased to cut storage room in a newsstand or carrier's bags.

Font Though the term's historical definition is a basin, in a print shop it alludes to the particular design of the type. In the early days of movable metal type, most shops had only one design—a shelving arrangement convenient to compositors. When a printer could afford more than one font, he would store them in a drawer of a cabinet ("case") sturdy enough to hold the weight of several alphabets of that particular font and its styles of regular, bold, italic, condensed, and extended, plus numbers and accent signs. Fonts take the names of their designers or descriptive terms, like Caslon, Bookman, Goudy, New Century Schoolbook.

Graf An abbreviation of "paragraph."

Hammer A special form of kicker headline that contains a first line (48+ points) that is at least twice the weight and point size of the main headline below. *See* Kicker.

Hard Copy This is a either manuscript printed out from computer material or an original manuscript unset by a computer.

Head (a.k.a. hed) A nickname for a headline.

Head Chart A chart for one type font that provides a copy editor with the unit counts for letters, numbers, and punctuation when they are set in different point sizes and weights (bold, italic, condensed, extended) for the various columns that will contain a story.

Head Order/Hed Order The printing specification instructions given by a slot to the copy editors for a headline's column and point size, number of lines, and sometimes the font name or weight (boldface, condensed, extended).

Header An Associated Press term that involves noncaption material for an illustration suited for locating it after it's filed in the archives. It includes the date, time, location of the shot, names of people, places, objects, and some description.

Headline The title of a story that usually runs directly above the text.

Headlinese Short-count verbs like "flays," "solons," and "eyes" that copy editors resorted to in head orders with tight counts. They did not take on a pejorative meaning until media critics and language purists pronounced them so. Some began rhyming "headlinese" with "journal-slease."

Hed A nickname for a headline.

Hellbox   A wooden box used in the days of "hot type" in which overset was tossed for remelting into lead bars used by the Linotype machines to set type.

Hot Type   So called because the type was formed by heating lead bars ("pigs") that forced the molten lead through a "throat" of a Linotype machine to a line of type matrixes triggered into place by a keyboard operator.

Image   Another term for illustration or photograph.

Immediate Lead   The first paragraph of a hard-news story providing the content with the 5W's.

Infinitive   This is a verb form that sometimes performs as a noun and follows the word "to" as in "to go," "to sleep," "to speak," and so on.

Infographic   Graphs, maps, charts, schematics, and other kinds of explanatory illustrations.

Journal-slease   *See* Headlinese.

Jump   A story that is continued on another page. Its head is called a "jump" head and usually involves a tagline word from the original story so that readers can easily locate the continuation of the story on another page.

Justified   Lines of type set so that they fit against the column rulers.

Kicker   A short, lead-in headline, often in caps and italics, that sits atop a main headline. Generally, half the size of the main head, the kicker is designed to attract readers into the story.

LC   An abbreviation for "lowercase" that involves using the alphabet's small letters. It originated in the days when fonts were kept in a type "case," or cabinet. The capital letters were in the top drawers of the case. The small letters were in the lower part of that case because they were used far more often than the capital letters.

Compositors in Johannes Gutenberg's time (c. 1490) did not have a "case," according to woodcut illustrations of sixteenth-century print shops. They lacked the array of font "weights," such as "bold" and the like. Their "case" was one "drawer" tipped for easy reach and rapid motion, with caps in one place and lowercase letters in another. Letters that get the greatest use, like *E* in the English language, still had the biggest compartment, one centrally located for the compositor's convenience.

Lead (a.k.a. lede)   The first paragraph of a story. Another definition of "lead" has to do with metal. Prior to the offset process, lead was the principal ingredient in the type set by the Linotype machine. It hung in "pigs" that were heated to a molten state in the Linotype's "pot."

Lede   *See* Lead.

Legman   A reporter gathering facts out in the field on deadline who telephones the information to someone designated in the newsroom—usually a copy editor—to shape the data into a story in time for the next edition or extra edition. To obtain instant connection to the newsroom, the legman would telephone the copydesk for "rewrite" and a copy editor would take the facts and write the story. On many papers, the legman and the copy editor share a byline.

Line Break   The literal end of each line of a headline.

Lowercase   *See* LC.

Maestro System   A newsroom management dynamic that, like an orchestra, has an overall leader. The entire newsroom staff communicates across traditional stratified areas to provide input on story ideas, focus, production, treatment, and the like.

Newshole   The space for text in a newspaper page.

Non Sequitur   This is a Latin term for "it does not follow." It means that the front end of a sentence, like "Earning a B.S. degree in chemistry," has absolutely nothing to do with its tail end: "she became chief operating officer at Unisys."

Notes Mode   In many computer systems, the slot's instructions for editing and a headline will come from a code located at the top left-hand corner of the screen.

Nut Graf (a.k.a. nut graph)   This is the paragraph that contains the gist of the story's content. It could be the 5W lead with all the facts. In the "new" or "literary" journalism, a nut graf still contains the article's gist, but it is placed directly after these openers have teased readers into the piece.

Overset   Unused type from a story.

Pagination   Computer software that enables users to design and then create newspaper pages.

Paginator   A person responsible for turning page designs into pages that will be made into printing plates. Like a shop foreman in the days of metal type, this individual pours illustrations, type, and rules into each page of the newspaper. But instead of performing this task on a printer's stone with chases for type, she or he does it on a computer screen.

Pic   A nickname for a single picture. The plural form is "pix."

Pica   A printing measurement for width that is 1/12 of an inch, so that one inch involves 12 picas. The term, from medieval Latin, dates back almost to Gutenberg's invention of movable metal type and involved the press lockup forms (chases) for prayer books and missals.

Pix   The plural of "pic" for pictures. The singular form is "pic."

Plugger   A note to readers explaining that, say, sports scores had not come in as the paper was "put to bed" (put on the press).

Point   Because of metal type's European ancestry, the letters' vertical size is not measured in the form of inches but is a modification of the French measurement system. A "point" is close to 1/72 of an inch. Another printer's measurement—for width—is the "pica," and there are 12 picas to the inch. A 72-point headline is close to one inch in height. The point system was adopted in 1886 by the U.S.

Type Founders' Association to establish a uniform measurement system when producing fonts for printers.

Pullout Quote (a.k.a. dropout quote)   A key quote from a story that has been lifted and set in 14- to 18-point type with rules or boxes. It is used to break up the grayness of text, as well as to attract readers into the story.

Put to Bed   A printer's term indicating that the type has been moved to the press's "bed" and is ready for the run.

Queue   Literally, it means a "waiting line," which, in computer diction, could mean either the copy editor's name or a story's departmental designation. The term is sometimes used instead of "basket."

Raw Wrap (a.k.a. Dutch wrap)   A story that has no headline running above it.

Rewrite Men   A newsroom-based staff member, usually from the copydesk, who took information telephoned from the field by reporters (legmen) and then shaped it into a story. On many papers, the legman and copy editor share a byline.

Rim   Another term for the copydesk.

River   A text phenomenon in which wide spacing within a line is repeated in subsequent lines so that it actually resembles a "river" of poor spacing.

RO (a.k.a. deck)   This is a "read-out" or subordinate head that follows a newspaper's main headline, usually a banner.

Sans Serif   A font that has been stripped of all ornamentation. *See* Serif.

Save (a.k.a. catch)   The discovery of a factual mistake, a potentially libelous story, or errors in grammar, mechanics, or spelling.

Second-Day Head   This kind of headline freshens up yesterday's story with fresh facts contained in the lead.

Serif   Ornamentation that embellishes the end of a letter stroke. A touch by a font designer adds this extra surface to a letter to provide great readability.

Short   A headline that is shorter than the two counts permitted in a maximum fit. The term is also used to signify a short news story, a brief.

Sidesaddle   A multiline headline that is flushed against the left or right side of a story or illustration. It is used to avoid raw wraps occurring when an advertisement is not quite a full page and leaves two inches of newshole space to fill. The head rides beside the story.

Slot   The individual who supervises a shift of copy editors.

Space Holder   Type or numbers like "0000" used to hold space for information that is forthcoming. On pagination programs like Quark, the space holder is found in the sample's document feature under the file name "ASCII text" and pours out Latin (e.g., "Si meliora dies, ut vina, poemata reddit").

Split   In headline writing, this term identifies an error in words used at the line breaks, leaving either a preposition, conjunction, or adjective at the end of a line. In wire service diction, a split denotes a break in transmission of news on the teletype so that the regional or state desk may insert its stories.

Stacking Headlines of the same point size that are used atop each story on one page.

Stepline A form of headline writing that requires the copy editor to indent subsequent lines.

Stet The Latin abbreviation for *stet processus* ("let it stand") for reviving deleted words or paragraphs.

Style A newspaper's preferred treatment of everything from acceptable pictures and comic strips to acceptable news stories and typographic dress. On a copydesk it's shown in preferences on abbreviations and acronyms, forbidden words, punctuation, spelling, capitalization. Add to that the treatment of crime news, prominent citizenry, the powerless, and local business and industry.

Stylebook A newspaper's reference book or pamphlet listing its preferences in spelling and language usage.

Subhead A small headline, usually set in bold and in the same point size as the text. Its function is to break up lengthy expanses of text and it usually points up a factor in the subsequent paragraph.

Tabloid A newspaper size that is about half the size of a broadsheet, ranging from 11.5″ × 16″ to 11.5″ × 13.″

Take One page in hard copy of a story or manuscript.

Take a Sit A composing room idiom that gravitated to the copydesk. It means doing a work stint for a printing shop or newspaper.

Team A term now used to designate groups of newsroom staffers—reporters, copy editors, photographers—who cross work boundaries so that cooperative viewpoints on operations, stories, and so on are shared.

Text Stories. Also called "body copy" and, by printers, "straight matter."

Time Copy Stories that have a timeless quality and are retained to fill space as needed. *The Wall Street Journal* calls them "evergreens." Other terms are "plug copy" and "grape."[1] Time copy provided work for compositors during slow periods while ensuring that on "no-news" days, those stories could fill empty space in the newshole. *See* Bank.

Tracking This word-processing program feature permits copy editors and paginators to "tighten" paragraphs so that more words can be squeezed into a line of type.

UC An abbreviation for "uppercase" that involves using the alphabet's capital letters. It originated in the days when fonts were kept in a type "case" or cabinet. The capital letters were in the top drawers of the "case," and the small letters were in the lower part of that case.

Uppercase *See* UC.

Upstyle   Putting capital letters on common nouns, generally used by newspapers that prefer exactitude and formality in printed matter. *See* Downstyle.

Voice   A determination in a sentence of whether a subject is doing the acting or is the recipient of the action. If the subject is the "actor," the voice is considered to be "active." If the subject is the "receiver," the voice is said to be "passive."

Wicket   A special form of kicker headline containing a first line that is at least twice the weight and point size of the main headline below. However, like a kicker, the wicket is short and, though set in a different font than the main head, lacks the embellishments of a kicker's italics, caps, and an underline. *See* Kicker.

Widow   A line of only one or two words in the last line of a paragraph or caption.

Wild Pic (a.k.a. caps-carry)   A caption that carries the entire burden of an illustration's description and explanation.

BIBLIOGRAPHY

Books and Periodicals

American Newspaper Guild. 1998 Contract. Newspaper Guild of the Twin Cities, Minneapolis.

Andrews, J. Cutler. *The South Reports the Civil War.* Princeton, N.J.: Princeton University Press, 1970.

Arnold, Edmund C. *Editing the Organizational Publication.* Chicago: Lawrence Ragan, 1982.

———. *The Associated Press Stylebook and Libel Manual.* Edited by Norm Goldstein. 29th ed. New York: The Associated Press, 1994.

———. *The Associated Press Stylebook and Libel Manual.* Edited by Norm Goldstein. Reading, Mass.: Perseus, 1998.

———. *Media Writer's Handbook: A Guide to Common Writing and Editing Problems.* Madison, Wis.: Brown & Benchmark, 1996.

Baskette, Floyd K., Jack Z. Sissors, and Brian S. Brooks. *The Art of Editing.* 4th ed. New York: Macmillan, 1986. 6th ed., 1997.

Berg, A. Scott. *Max Perkins: Editor of Genius.* New York: Dutton, 1978.

Bernstein, Theodore M. *The Careful Writer: A Modern Guide to English Usage.* New York: Atheneum, 1973.

Bremner, John B. *Words on Words: A Dictionary for Writers and Others Who Care About Words.* New York: Columbia University Press, 1980.

Brooks, Brian S., George Kennedy, Daryl R. Moen, and Don Ranly. *News Reporting and Writing.* 5th ed. New York: St. Martin's, 1996.

Churchill, Allen. *Park Row.* New York: Rinehart, 1958.

Copperud, Roy H., and Roy Paul Nelson. *Editing the News.* Dubuque: Wm. C. Brown, 1983.

"Dow, Charles Henry," Micropaedia, 3, *Encyclopaedia Britannica*, Chicago: Encyclopaedia Britannica, 1979].

Ellis, Barbara G. *Content Analysis of the Associated Press Copy for Quotes as Contained in the Lake Charles American Press.* June 10, 1999.

————. *How to Write Themes and Term Papers.* New York: Barrons, 3d ed., 1983.

————. *Mr. McClanahan, Mrs. Dill, and The Moving Appeal.* Macon, Ga.: Mercer University Press, 2002.

Emerson, Ralph Waldo. "Self-Reliance," *Essays.*

Emery, Edwin, and Michael Emery. *The Press and America: An Interpretative History of the Mass Media.* 5th ed. Englewood Cliffs, N.J.: Prentice-Hall, 1984.

Fellow, Anthony R., and Thomas N. Clanin. *Copy Editors' Handbook for Newspapers.* Englewood, Colo.: Morton, 1998.

Folkerts, Jean, and Dwight L. Teeter Jr. *Voices of a Nation: A History of Media in the United States.* 1st ed. New York: Macmillan, 1989. 2d ed., 1994.

France, Anatole. *Golden Tales of Anatole France.* New York: Dodd, Mead, 1926.

Garst, Robert E., and Theodore M. Bernstein. *Headlines and Deadlines.* 4th ed. New York: Columbia University Press, 1982.

Holmes, Charles S. *The Clocks of Columbus: The Literary Career of James Thurber.* New York: Atheneum, 1972.

Ireland, Alleyne. *Joseph Pulitzer: Reminiscences of a Secretary.* New York: M. Kennerley, 1914.

Jones, Kenneth L., David W. Smith, Ann Pytkowicz Streissguth, and Ntinos C. Myvianthopoulos. "Outcome in Offspring of Chronic Alcoholic Women." *The Lancet,* June 1, 1974, 1076–1078.

Jones, Kenneth L., David W. Smith, Christy N. Ulleland, and Ann Pytkowicz Streissguth. "Patterns of Malformation in Offspring of Chronic Alcoholic Mothers." *The Lancet,* June 9, 1973, 1267–1271.

Judd, Karen. *Copyediting: A Practical Guide.* 2d ed. Menlo Park, Calif.: Crisp, 1990.

Kessler, Lauren, and Duncan McDonald. *When Words Collide: A Journalist's Guide to Grammar and Style.* 2d ed. Belmont, Calif.: Wadsworth, 1988.

Kilpatrick, James J. *The New York Times Style Book for Writers and Editors.* Edited by Lewis Jordan. 3d ed. New York: McGraw-Hill, 1962.

————. *The Writer's Art.* Kansas City: Andrews, McMeel & Parker, 1984.

Laakaniemi, Ray. *The Weekly Writer's Handbook.* Bowling Green, Ohio: Brittany, 1993.

Long, Robert Emmet, *James Thurber.* New York: Continuum, 1988.

Maxson, Jan. "Training Journalism Students to Deal With Trauma." Paper delivered at the 1999 annual convention of the Association for Education in Journalism and Mass Communication, New Orleans, August 5, 1999.

McDougall, Curtis M. *Newsroom Problems and Policies.* New York: Macmillan, 1947.

Meyer, Philip. *The New Precision Journalism.* Bloomington: Indiana University Press, 1991.

Mott, Frank Luther. *American Journalism.* New York: Macmillan, 1941.

Perrin, Porter G. *Writer's Guide and Index to English*. Edited by Karl W. Dykema and Wilma R. Ebbitt. 4th ed. Chicago: Scott, Foresman, 1965.

Plotnik, Arthur. *The Elements of Editing: A Modern Guide for Editors and Journalists*. New York: Collier Books/Macmillan, 1982.

Read, Allen Walker. "The Evidence on 'O.K.'" *Saturday Review of Literature*, July 19, 1941.

Simon, John Ivan. *Paradigms Lost: Reflections on Literacy and Its Decline*. New York: Clarkson N. Potter, 1980.

Strunk, William, Jr., and E. B. White. *The Elements of Style*. New York: Macmillan, 1959.

Taylor, Howard B., and Jacob Scher. *Copy Reading and News Editing*. New York: Prentice-Hall, 1951.

Thurber, James. *The Thurber Album: A New Collection of Pieces About People*. New York: Simon & Schuster, 1952.

Tollefson, Stephen K. *Grammar Grams*. New York: Harper & Row, 1989.

——. *The Washington Post Deskbook on Style*. Edited by Thomas W. Lippman. 2d ed. New York: McGraw-Hill, 1989.

Vedder, O. F. *History of the City of Memphis and Shelby County Tennessee*. Vol. 2. Syracuse, N.Y.: D. Mason, 1888.

——. *Webster's New International Dictionary of the English Language*. 2d ed. Springfield, Mass.: G. & C. Merriam, Company, Publishers, 1950.

——. *Webster's Ninth New Collegiate Dictionary* (Springfield, Mass.: Merriam-Webster, Inc., Publishers, 1991.

Whitman, Digby. *The Road to Readability: Basics of Writing and Editing*. Chicago: Ragan, 1993.

Wilson, Quintus C., "Confederate Press Association: A Pioneer News Agency," *Journalism Quarterly*, 26, June 1949, 160–167.

Newspapers, News Services, Newspaper Associations

American Press, Lake Charles, La.
Associated Press
Atlanta Journal-Constitution
Baton Rouge Advocate
Charlotte Observer, Charlotte, N.C.
Chicago Tribune
Detroit News and Free Press
Knight Ridder News Service
LA Times-Washington Post Service
Louisiana Press Association
The Memphis Daily Appeal
Miami Herald

Minneapolis Star Tribune
The New York Times
New York Times News Service
The Oregonian, Portland, Ore.
Philadelphia Inquirer
Plain Dealer, Cleveland, Ohio
Post-Dispatch, St. Louis
Seattle *Post-Intelligencer*
St. Petersburg Times, Florida
Tampa Times
Tampa Tribune
Times-Picayune, New Orleans, La.
USA Today

Talks and Interviews

Albro, Victor. Shop foreman, Forest Grove (Ore.) *News-Times*.
Alderman, Ed. Production editor, Mosby, Inc., St. Louis, Mo.
Bennett, James M. Assistant night sports editor, *Charlotte* (N.C.) *Observer.*
Cesarz, Kevin R. Sports design editor, *Star Tribune*, Minneapolis.
Culham, W. M. ("Mick"). Account executive, A. G. Edwards & Sons, Inc., Portland, Ore.
Dewey, Mitchell G. Oddsmaker, Multnomah Kennel Club, Portland, Ore.
Doctorian, Sonya. Former assistant managing editor/photography, *St. Petersburg* (Fla.) *Times.*
Daugherty, Robert A. Director of state photo desk, the Associated Press, Washington, D.C.
Downer, Brett. Executive editor, Lake Charles (La.) *American Press*.
Fraser, David K. Former publisher, Hammond (La.) *Daily Star*.
Hahn, Trudi. Copy editor, *Star Tribune*, Minneapolis.
Harrower, Tim. Presenter, Newspaper Designers' Workshop, November 20, 1997, Lafayette, La.
Hinson, Kathy. Assistant copy desk chief, *The Oregonian*.
Johnston, Karen S. Libel underwriter, Walterry Insurance Brokers, Clinton, Md.
Marks, Sonny. Reporter, Lake Charles (La.) *American Press*.
Myers, Robert. Photo editor, state photo desk, the Associated Press, Washington, D.C.
Nardi, Linda. Chief of research, LIFE magazine, New York.
Reksten, Patty. Director of photography, *The Oregonian*.
Stasiowski, Jim. Writing consultant, Baltimore, Md.
Wise, Jerry. Publisher, *Cameron* (La.) *Pilot* and *DeQuincy* (La.) *News*.

INDEX

Headline Counts

Letter, Number, etc.	Upper Case (UC)	Lower Case (LC)
M, W	2	1 1/2
I	1	
F, L J	1	1/2
T	1 1/2	1/2
Others	1 1/2	1
Spaces	1/2 or 1	
Punctuation	1/2	
Number 1	1/2	
Others	1	
Symbols ($, %, &, etc.)	1	